Back to the Barrens:
On the Wing with da Vinci & Friends

by George Erickson

hancock
house

ISBN-10 0-88839-642-2
ISBN-13 978-0-88839-642-6
Copyright © 2007 George Erickson

Cataloguing in Publication Data

Erickson, George, 1932-
    Back to the barrens : on the wing with da Vinci & friends / George
Erickson.

Includes bibliographical references.
ISBN 978-0-88839-642-6

    1. Erickson, George, 1932- --Travel--Canada, Northern. 2. Canada,
Northern--Description and travel. 3. Bush flying--Canada, Northern.
4. Air travel--Canada, Northern. I. Title.

FC3956.E73 2007   917.1904'4   C2007-903719-4

Editor: Theresa Laviolette
Production: Mia Hancock
Cover Design: Ingrid Luters
Cover Photograph: George Erickson
Author photograph: George Erickson

Published simultaneously in Canada and the United States by

HANCOCK HOUSE PUBLISHERS LTD.
19313 Zero Avenue, Surrey, B.C. Canada V3S 9R9
(604) 538-1114 Fax (604) 538-2262

HANCOCK HOUSE PUBLISHERS
1431 Harrison Avenue, Blaine, WA U.S.A. 98230-5005
(604) 538-1114 Fax (604) 538-2262

Website: www.hancockhouse.com
Email: sales@hancockhouse.com

Contents

Back to the Barrens is dedicated

To Leonardo da Vinci, who wrote,
"There shall be wings!
If the accomplishment be not for me, 'tis
for some other. The spirit shall not die, and
man...shall have wings.... When once you
have tasted flight, you will forever walk
the earth with your eyes turned skyward,
for there you have been, and there you will
long to return."

Notes

Like its predecessor, *True North: Exploring the Great Wilderness by Bush Plane,* Back to the Barrens is based upon experiences gathered during the author's many flights through the far North.

Natives that we once called "Eskimos" now prefer the word "Inuit," their word for "the people."

Unless otherwise noted, all costs are in US dollars.

In keeping with our illogical system of weights and measures, temperatures are listed in Fahrenheit, volumes in gallons and weights in pounds.

Readers with Internet access will benefit by following the route of the *Tundra Cub II* via satellite images on www.googleearth.com.

The symbol TN within the text indicates a subject covered in detail in *True North: Exploring the Great Wilderness by Bush Plane.*

Other books by George Erickson

True North: Exploring the Great Wilderness by Bush Plane
Time Traveling with Science and the Saints

A personal note to the reader

In 1996, when I began to write *True North: Exploring the Great Wilderness by Bush Plane,* I didn't expect that more than one publisher would want my work, but the fact that they did was the first of many surprises.

When *True North* was published, it quickly climbed onto the Canadian Booksellers' Coast to Coast Bestseller List, and was subsequently published in the U.S. by Globe Pequot/Lyons Press

Reviews, letters, e-mails and phone calls came pouring in, all of them positive, including an endorsement by multimillion-copy author Clive Cussler. Some readers requested up to twenty signed copies to use as gifts before they'd even finished the book! One wrote, "I am the nut who keeps ordering copies of *True North*…I have read it at least three times and I take a copy with me when I travel." Another three-timer e-mailed, "After flying in corporate aviation for twenty-five years I had become burned out, but *True North* rekindled the flame THANKS!" Others wrote, "I just finished *True North* and I'm sorry I'm done," and "Want to know what your book means to me? I'm starting again at chapter I." A United Airline 747 captain wrote, "I met you at Oshkosh. You were right I should have bought ten books!" And one reviewer summed it up, writing, "Diamonds, Darwin, Death and Deceit—*True North* has them all."

My slide presentations based on *True North* have taken me to cities large and small, including Los Angeles, Minneapolis, Chicago, Winnipeg, Toronto and Houston, and repeatedly to the annual Experimental Aircraft Association convention at Oshkosh, Wisconsin, where I added a forum presentation titled "Bush Flying for Beginners." Prompted by friends, I produced a CD of 167 unique color photos that follow *True North* from cover to cover. The CD is available only from me at 4678 Cedar Island Drive, Eveleth, MN 55734 for $10 US including postage. *True North: Exploring the Great Wilderness by Bush Plane* is available from the usual sources, but for signed copies that include a special map, mail $15 U.S., postage included, to the above address. All profits are donated to educational charities.

A second book, Time Traveling with Science and the Saints, soon followed and was published by Prometheus Books.

Since I began to write *True North,* I've returned to the North many times, often alone, seeking new sights and stories to tell. Now, at the urging of my readers, I sit down to compose the sequel on a computer that dwarfs the tiny capabilities of the IBM PC Jr., on which I began *True North.*

Like Robert Service, Jack London and Rudyard Kipling, the giants who will forever captivate readers with tales told across a flickering campfire, I invite readers to set their cares aside, climb into the Tundra Cub II and again seek out the land where the northern lights shimmer, trees disappear and the rivers run deep and cold.

We'll camp on a fog-bound Hudson Bay island, alert for polar bears. Heading west, we'll follow musk oxen, stroll through caribou herds and laugh at arctic hares that run on their hind legs like men. Near the Arctic Circle, we'll enter a land where the sun, like a moody teenager, sometimes refuses to go to bed, then six months later declines to rise.

As we wander from campsite to campsite like a bee from blossom to blossom, we'll dust off treasured memories that reach back forty years.

Preface

You cannot sail new oceans if you won't let go of the shore.
                                                                 —ANON

My office sits high in the sky. Like the upper floors of the Sears Tower or Kuala Lumpur's Petronas Towers, or even Taiwan's lofty Taipei Tower, which tops them all, my office sways with the wind. Despite their luxury, their soft music and their breathtaking views, the towers and the people who work in comfort within them are fixed to the ground, while my noisy, narrow cubicle can respond to my whims, climbing even higher to attain a broader perspective and a panoramic view.

Today, I'm making a test flight to be sure things work as they should. My Piper PA-11 seaplane, the *Tundra Cub II,* is almost identical to the original *Tundra Cub* that has faithfully carried me across northern Quebec, Nunavut, the Yukon and Northwest Territories and into Alaska.

The Cub should be perfect. It's fresh from the shop and an annual inspection, but experience has shown that this is a time when things can go wrong—a screwdriver forgotten on top of an engine, its plastic handle melted into the engine's heat-radiating fins, a brake part wrongly replaced on a Lake amphibian, making it impossible to taxi, and on another occasion, a fuel flow sensor secured to the wrong fitting. All of these have happened to me. None caused a serious problem, but they prove the wisdom of the Cold War precaution: Trust, but verify.

I'm flying at 9,000 feet. Far below, in a deep, three-mile-long trench carved by Minnesota's most recent glacier, a clear, spring-fed body of water called Ely Lake smiles up at me. The lake's southern shore cradles a seaplane base within a sheltering bay. Directly across from the base, my pine-shaded home overlooks a sandy beach where I keep the *Tundra Cub II*.

Day after day, an assortment of Piper, Stinson, Cessna and de Havilland aircraft slip down from the sky while others roar away from the base. When winter arrives, silence briefly returns as ice begins to form. A week or two later, fishermen arrive on snowmobiles. In December, ice-fishing houses appear, towed into place by cars and trucks, adding a new hazard for aircraft that have switched to skis.

Three miles to the north is the town of Virginia, the place of my birth. There, a community college and dozens of homes and businesses spread across the former site of the Virginia and Rainy Lake Lumber Mill. Once the largest white pine mill in the world, the "Rainy" set records in the 1920s, sawing a whopping million board feet of lumber per day.

A few miles beyond Virginia, the long, east-west spine of the Laurentian Divide separates much of northern Minnesota into three watersheds. The westernmost feeds the Mississippi and, therefore, the Gulf of Mexico.

Some of the showers that fall on the Divide's southerly slopes wash taconite dust from behemothlike trucks, loaders and excavators—great, lumbering creature-machines so huge that they seem to have come from a *Star*

Wars film. Their purpose: to consume great bites of rock-hard, charcoal gray taconite iron ore.

Others are trapped in a ninety-mile-long, east-west scattering of deep, red-walled pits—the exhausted remains of the hematite mines that gave the Mesabi (Sleeping Giant) Iron Range its name, but most of the rain will find the St. Louis River, there to meander through ninety miles of bog, forest and marginal farms to Lake Superior, where it begins a multicentury journey through the Great Lakes and the St. Lawrence Seaway to reach the Atlantic Ocean.

Showers that fall on the Laurentian's northern slopes will follow a different path, forming streams so rich with iron and bog tannins that they wear a root beer-like hue. Some will feed Lake Vermilion, the Ojibwa's "Lake of the Sunset Glow." Flowing past my cabin, where in the 1930s we purchased blueberries for ten cents per quart from Ojibwa families in birch bark canoes, they'll seek Rainy Lake, Lake of the Woods and big Lake Winnipeg before cascading down the Nelson River to a salty Hudson Bay.

This is northern Minnesota, the Land of Ten Thousand Lakes, a country laced with rivers and streams that the Ojibwa were paddling long before the Egyptians devised the clepsydra, the water-clock that measured a much longer river—the endless river of time. Centuries passed, bringing voyageurs who propelled themselves inland with biceps and brawn, shouldering their loads over hills and through bogs to yet another river and yet another lake.

I feed in a touch of aileron to begin a gentle left turn, then throttle back and watch the world revolve. Twenty miles to the north lies Cook, the home of the Wien brothers, the bush pilot founders of Wien Air Alaska who began with airplanes much like my Cub and ended up owning jets that they couldn't have dreamed of while rafting the Little Fork River that periodically attempted to flood their boyhood home.

When the Cub turns northwest toward the home of Peter Leschak, a fire-fighting helicopter crew chief and the author of *Letters from Side Lake* and *Hellroaring: The Life and Times of a Fire Bum,* I remember Pete's encouraging words after reading the manuscript of *True North.* I recall his notes that said, "This is nice" or "this needs expanding." And I remember the words of his non-flying wife, who, after reading just one chapter, told Peter, "I'd read this book!"

As the compass pivots through 270 degrees, a budding cumulus cloud briefly obscures Hibbing, the birthplace of slugger Roger Maris, the city where the Greyhound Bus Line was born, the city with the world's largest open pit iron mine—a mine so large that it supplied a fourth of the iron required for World Wars I and II—and the city that gave music lovers a guitar-strumming folk/pop/rock star named Bob Dylan.

By the time I've turned just east of south, I'm down to 8,000 feet, but even from this height, fifty-mile-distant Lake Superior is just a sliver of water, backlit by the midmorning sun.

The Ojibwa called the lake *Gitchi Gummi,* meaning "big water." It's a very appropriate name. As the world's largest fresh water lake, Superior's depths, which extend 733 feet below sea level, contain one-tenth of the world's supply of fresh water. The other (much shallower) Great Lakes raise the total to 20 percent, a figure matched by Russia's smaller, but immensely deep, Lake Baikal.

Superior, which is large enough to have tides, holds much more than water, having swallowed hundreds of ships, the most famous being the 700-foot *Edmund Fitzgerald,* the ill-fated vessel immortalized by Gordon Lightfoot's sonorous *Gales of November,* which asks, "Does anyone know where the love of God goes when the waves turn the minutes to hours?" Loaded with 26,000 tons of taconite iron ore pellets, the *Fitzgerald* fell victim to high winds, snow squalls, thirty-foot waves and, perhaps, insecure hatches, sinking in 530 feet of cold, clear water. The captain and crew numbered twenty-nine souls, and not a one survived.

This greatest of lakes is fringed with history. Strewn along its northern shore are beds of stromatolites, the fossilized remains of algae-like organisms that began to breathe oxygen into our primitive, carbon dioxide-rich atmosphere some two billion years ago, eventually making life possible for oxygen-lovers like us who thrive today, but would have perished before the algae worked their magic.

Near Superior's confluence with Lake Michigan, a seventeenth-century French explorer named Jean Nicollet frightened the Winnebagos by appearing too godlike when he donned a radiant damask robe that he had planned to wear when he stepped ashore—in Japan! A few decades later, two more Frenchmen, Pierre-Esprit Radisson ("Radishes") and his brother-in-law Medart Chouart Sieur de Groseilliers ("Gooseberries"), began to explore the country to the north of Lake Superior, laying the ground work for a massive trade in furs, the "soft gold" of the North that would give birth to two giants of commerce: the Hudson Bay Company and its chief rival, the North West Company, the company that relied on 600 pound, thirty-six-foot *canots de maitre* on the Great Lakes, then switched to twenty-six-footers with half the weight for the inland lakes and rivers far to the north and west.

In 1902, near the north shore town of Ilgen City, five young entrepreneurs set out to make grindstones from an outcropping they thought was corundum. The "corundum," however, turned out to be a softer look-alike, and when the news leaked out, the company's stock dropped to "a couple of shares for a shot, and cheap whiskey at that." Discouraged, but undaunted, the five persevered, becoming so successful that by the 1990s, their Minnesota

Manufacturing and Mining Company (3M) was posting record sales of $15 billion per year with a long list of popular products like sandpaper, Scotch tape™, Scotch-brite™, synthetic dental filling materials and the ubiquitous Post-it™ notes.

Today, the "big water" port of Duluth is alive, not with the fur trade, but with taconite pellets from the Iron Range, with Midwest coal and grain, with ocean-going cargo and cruise ships bearing German tourists, and with a foresighted industry that has become the world's number one builder of single engine aircraft—an innovative firm called Cirrus Designs.

When I've turned full circle, I still have a mile to descend, so to hurry the process, I lose a few thousand feet by practicing power-off stalls. Tiring of stalls, I drop the left wing, push in right rudder and raise the nose a trifle. The Cub side-slips earthward, dumping buckets of height. A few minutes later, I'm standing on the float. When I open the cowling, I'm pleased to see that the engine is dry. There are no fuel or oil leaks, and nothing is out of place. Tomorrow, when the sun has baked away the predicted fog, I'll head north in an aircraft stuffed with camping gear, food, maps, three books (Stefansson's *My Life with the Eskimo,* Bill Bryson's *A Short History of Nearly Everything* and an entertaining old friend, *Herter's Professional Guide's Manual)* plus four new items —a noise-canceling headset, a GPS that I don't know how to use, a sieve from our kitchen and a war surplus "foxhole" shovel for my whimsical search for the new Mother Lode of the North—diamonds. Watch out, DeBeers!™

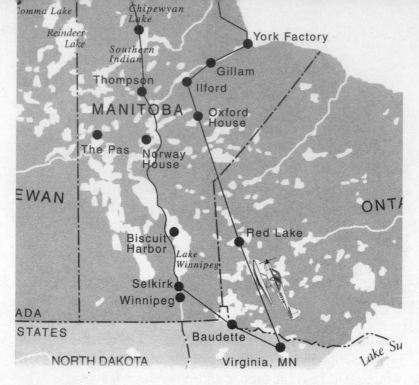

Chapter 1

Minnesota to Gillam, Manitoba

You only live once, but if you work it right, once is enough.
—BOXING CHAMPION JOE LEWIS

It's the second week of July. Sirius, the Dog Star has returned to its lover to rise and set with the sun. The Ojibwa month of the Strawberry Moon has slipped away, replaced by the Molting Moon, the Cree Moon of the Falling Feathers.

The spring peepers that romanced the nights away in a nearby bog have gone silent, their trilling replaced by an inquisitive owl that queries the night like a forlorn detective, asking over and over—who, who, who? On the forest floor, dainty pink hepatica, as if exhausted from their spring fling, have gone green. In their place, bunchberries bloom; sweet and juicy, red-lobed dewberries beckon, and ripening blueberries are turning cobalt blue.

Global warming, which thaws northern lakes a full week earlier than in the sixties, has delivered an early start. That's convenient for me, but it's trouble for polar bears that patrol the shrinking pack ice in their winter-long search for seals. Those who profit from global warming are still in denial, but summer adventure seekers with shallow draft boats are finally free to explore northern Canada's formerly ice-bound shores.

While the sun attacks the morning fog and I stow my gear in the Cub, I think back to the winter of 1966, the year that Sam Brown, the flight instructor at Brown's Seaplane Base plunked me into the left seat of a Cessna seaplane and said, "Let's go." An hour or two later, having neither wrecked nor sunk the Cessna, I had added a new rating to my pilot's license: "Single engine land and sea."

The following spring, I sold my beautiful, fast, quiet and comfortable Beechcraft Bonanza and bought a nicely restored twenty-year-old, slow and noisy Piper Family Cruiser, installed a new set of floats, then waited until late July to let the northern lakes shed their shackles of ice. Despite the wait, my father and I arrived a little too early, but we managed by using shoreline strips of open water.

I've wedged my life preserver into the overhead fuselage bracing. It's a practical place for it—out of the way and quickly accessible—but it's never quite secure. Constantly seeking freedom, it will slowly sag in response to engine vibrations until it gently touches my head, saying, "It's me again." Although I'll rearrange it time and again, it will always return. Faithful to its name, my preserver weighs against solitude, reminding me periodically that I am not alone.

I give my wife a hug and promise to be careful. I'm eager to leave, prodded perhaps by Kipling's "We must go, go, go away from here. On the other side of the mountain we're overdue…" I set the magnetos to "both" (aircraft engines have two independent ignition systems), step to the front of the float and give the prop a spin. On the third spin, the ninety-horsepower Continental barks to life.

As the engine warms, I scan my chart, smiling at the string of familiar landmarks that will lead me north. The oil temperature needle rises from its peg as I turn full circle to check for landing aircraft, then swing into the wind and pour on the power. My newly overhauled engine quickly pulls the Cub onto the step and within seconds we're airborne, heading north in a steady climb. Virginia falls behind and then the Laurentian Divide. A few minutes later, my right wingtip points toward a played-out underground iron mine at Soudan, where a new research project is studying the tiny, elusive particles that scientists call "neutrinos."

Two thousand feet below the surface, a 6,000-ton detector (a catcher's mitt, if you will) is fielding neutrinos pitched through 450 miles of the earth's rocky mantle by a particle accelerator at Chicago's Fermilab. There, the accelerator's mighty arm hurls protons at a carbon target to create neutrinos, some of which race toward Soudan at the speed of light. Undeterred by solid rock, the smaller-than-atom neutrinos zip beneath Lake Superior so quickly that they reach Soudan just 2.5 milliseconds after their birth. There, they are analyzed to see if the little chameleons have changed from one type to another while en route. That answer, along with other experiments, might help solve two problems: Where is the missing mass of the universe that physicists believe exists, and, will a better understanding of particle physics lead to a new, cheap and almost unlimited source of energy?

Years ago, when novelist John Updike turned his mind to neutrinos, he summed them up this way:

Neutrinos, they are very small,
They have no charge they have no mass
And do not interact at all.
The Earth is just a silly ball.
To them, through which they simply pass,
Like dustmaids down a drafty hall
Or photos through a sheet of glass.
They snub the most exquisite gas,
Ignore the most substantial wall,
Cold shoulder steel and sounding brass,
Insult the stallion in his stall,
And, scorning barriers of class,
Infiltrate you and me! Like tall
And painless guillotines they fall
Down through our heads into the grass.
At night they enter at Nepal
And pierce the lover and his lass
From Underneath the Bed – you call
It wonderful; I call it crass.

They'll be giving tours of the mine today. It's 80 degrees on the surface, but outside the heated lab it's chilly down there, thanks to our latest glacier. To overcome the lingering cold, we'd need to burrow straight down another two thousand feet. But to really warm up, we'd have to go deeper still. In South Africa's Western Deeps gold mine, which is two miles deep, cool air must be pumped down the shafts to counter temperatures of 140 degrees. Not hot enough? Dig down another three miles and you'll hit 500 degrees.

I'd be jealous of the speedy neutrinos if the headwind was strong, but it's gentle today, and I soon pass the western border of Minnesota's Boundary Waters Canoe Area, an immense region of pristine lakes and forest reserved for canoeists, kayakers, backpackers, skiers and dogsledders, but not for motorcycles, ATVs, power boats or seaplanes. The only oxygen-burning, carbon compound-consuming engines allowed are living creatures like you and me.

Canada, the great sprawling bounty that the British won in the French and Indian Wars, fills my view from wingtip to wingtip. The Brits should have been thrilled, but with the war won and the prize in hand, their resolve began to diminish. Some even suggested trading Canada back to the French for a tiny Caribbean island that we now call Guadalupe.

As the Cub descends toward the seasonal Canadian Customs office, I think back through forty years of border crossings here at Sand Point Lake. Here a misinformed Customs Agent made me return my rifle to a friend at nearby Crane Lake because he was certain it was illegal to bring it into Canada. (He was wrong, but what could I do?)

Here, I labored through the difficult job of hand-propping my Lake amphibian back to life when its starter failed, only to have to dive for the cockpit to shut it down when a bystander headed straight for the whirling prop.

On these docks, I watched a pilot load the bodies of two teenagers into an airplane for their final flight home. Neither could swim, and neither wore a life preserver but, filled with the exuberance of youth, they decided to canoe-surf huge waves raised by a powerful storm that would flatten thousands of trees. They capsized. Foam-filled chambers kept the canoe afloat, and they clung to it, hoping to drift to shore, but it was early spring and the water was close to freezing. They began to shiver. Within minutes, they lost control of their muscles and drowned.

Contrary to cynics who call Canada "a region just north of summer," it's a beautiful 80-degree day, and I'm close to sweating as I begin to secure the Cub. Distracted by a weary-looking de Havilland Beaver rumbling away from the pier and a friendly golden retriever that wants to help with the knots, I don't notice the customs agent arrive, so when I stand up to greet him, I'm surprised to see that he's a she, and an attractive one at that. It's her first summer here, and she loves it.

"Not much night life, though," she says with a wistful tilt of her head. "Crane Lake (a tiny, U.S. settlement just three miles away) is all there is, but it's a fair exchange. I've already applied to come back next year."

The retriever is hers. One of my sons has a goldie, too, so after a few minutes of dog-lover tales, we get down to business. The questions are still the same:

"Where will you be going?"

"Nunavut and the Northwest Territories."

"And how long will you stay?"

"About two weeks."

"Are you carrying any alcohol?"

"No."

"Tobacco?"

"No."

"Firearms?"

"No." (I've always brought a rifle, but because a permit is now required and I've never needed one, I've left it behind—no red tape and five pounds less to carry.)

She asks me to open a float compartment, which surprises me because that's never happened before. I ask, "Which one?"

She points.

I open the compartment, which holds nothing but air and a few drops of water.

"Another?" I ask.

"No," she says, returning my passport. "That's it. Nice talking with you. Enjoy your stay in Canada."

As the Cub idles away from the pier, the bows of my

floats cut through the dark water, creating curling wakes that bring childhood memories of crossing Lake Vermilion in the fourteen-foot dory that my grandfather built from strips of hand-planed ash. While our two-horsepower Evinrude roared away, I'd trail a twig in the water at different angles and depths, captivated by the changes in drag and the tiny wake it produced.

A few years later, a three-horsepower ELTO twin replaced the single, and as it propelled us to and from our island cabin I wondered what ELTO meant, later to learn that it stood for Evinrude Light Twin Outboard, the new model that a Norwegian immigrant named Ole Evinrude developed in 1928, years after inventing the first outboard motor, which eased his way across Wisconsin's Lake Okauchee to get ice cream for his girlfriend Bess, whom he later married. Now, more than sixty years later, moving water still calls to me, whether ocean, lake or stream. Dissolved in rambling thought, I can watch its ripples and waves for hours, but flat water, perhaps because of its deathlike pallor, always leaves me cold.

The Tundra Cub II parallels the international boundary for twenty miles, and then leaves the border behind at Rainy Lake, the site of the last of Minnesota's marginal gold discoveries. There, in 1894, the town of Rainy Lake City leaped into being when George Davis found a vein of gold-bearing quartz that became the Bushy Head mine. Three hotels, a boarding house, stores, tents and seventeen saloons appeared almost overnight. One roofless saloon even stayed open during the first month of winter until their roofing arrived. The boom soon collapsed. None of the buildings survive, but the entrance to the Bushy Head mine still stands open, as if waiting for one more optimist to make a run for the gold.

A few miles to the west, the Rainy River begins a downstream run to the border town of Baudette and a walleye factory called Lac du Bois—the Voyageurs' Lake of the Woods. Although it's midsummer, the river still brims from heavy rains, creating a broad, blue, eighty-mile runway all the way to Baudette.

I'm not the first to admire the Rainy, the voyageurs' "Riviere de la Reine"—the Queen River. Alexander Mackenzie, the Northwest Company's premier administrator/explorer, loved the Rainy, calling it, "one of the finest rivers in the northwest...Its banks are covered with a rich soil...with the open groves of oak with the maple, the pine and the cedar."

The Rainy flows across the Canadian Shield, the immense, rocky lens of ancient stone that covers much of Canada and parts of the northern U.S. Here, in the thin layer of topsoil that took thousands of years to form, the boreal forest thrives, each species within its own niche. Black spruce loves the acidic bogs. A few steps back from the bog, the slightly dryer ground nurtures a progression of alder, tamarack, cedars and balsam. As the terrain rises, tall stands of red maple, aspen and birch take over, only to be replaced by dominant white, red and jack pines. It's undeniably beautiful, but for me, it's like eating steak every day. Give me two weeks out on the tundra, or in the Yukon's Ogilvie Mountains, and the boreal forest will shine again.

Those who live where glaciers have never intruded might find it hard to believe that this lake-strewn, river-webbed land was created by masses of ice that have overwhelmed almost a third of the globe. Author Janine Benyus explained it this way, "The northland is one of the most recently uncovered places in the world. Less than 10,000 years ago, when civilization was well under way in the Middle East, parts of the north woods were still under an icecap that stood two miles high…The enormous weight of the ice caused the lower layer to bulge outward, bulldozing mountains and gouging the earth as it moved."

We now know that the last ice age lowered ocean levels some 3,000 feet, uniting Alaska with Siberia, England with France, and almost closed off the Strait of Gibraltar. And though the glaciers extended well into Minnesota and Wisconsin, paradoxically, much of Alaska and Siberia remained ice-free.

Centuries later, when the glaciers began to thaw, great rivers flowed across the land, leaving behind the heaps of rock, gravel, sand and clay that form the lake-strewn landscape that draws thousands of tourists today.

Red Lake, the Ontario community that derives its name from the lake's russet waters, lies 180 miles to the north. We attribute the lake's hue to an assortment of minerals, but an Ojibwa legend claims that during the ancient times, two hunters spotted a large moose standing in the shallows of a beautiful lake. Believing that the animal contained a Matchee Manitou, an evil spirit, they tried to kill it, but the wounded moose escaped by diving into the lake. When its blood tinted the water red, the hunters named the lake Misque Sakigon or "Color of Blood Lake," and that's how Red Lake received its pre-white-man name.

I've flown this route so often that I can recite the waypoints and recall their contours and sights: linear Red Gut Bay with its pendant-shaped log booms, then island-studded Manitou Lake, where one spring I fished all day for lake trout, but caught just one while my companions boated their limits. (When I grumbled about my lack of success, my friends reminded me of the fellow who also caught a single fish during his stay at an expensive resort. When he complained, "That's $2,000 per fish," his guide replied, "Be glad that you didn't catch two!")

A logging road leads north to Eagle Lake and the trans-Canada Highway, followed by the seaplane base at Vermilion Bay where I once sought shelter while a nest of roiling thunderstorms stalled overhead for hours. Beyond Vermilion Bay lies Wabigoon Lake, which is packed with muskellunge. Packwash Lake ends at Snake Falls, where the Chukuni River begins its run to Red Lake, the town where an eighty-year search for wealth continues in the gold-rich 2.7 billion-year-old greenstones of world-class mines like Placer Dome and Goldcorp, Canada's largest gold producer.

How large, you ask? Goldcorp alone is expected to yield 740,000 troy ounces of gold per year from shafts that will extend 7,000 feet below the surface, and as I pay my fuel bill—gas is expensive up here—I'm reminded that for every miner who works below, hundreds more make a living by mining the wallets of tourists like me.

Knowing that water could do most of the mining, prospectors first searched the grit and gravel of streams for "color" by swirling the water-earth mix in a pan or rushing it through a sluice box to carry off the waste and concentrate the gold. Thus, the first gold seekers were "placer" miners who panned for gold in streams and rivers. Why "placer"? Because the Spanish word carries the meaning of "pleasure," and panning for gold is undeniably more pleasant than blasting out a living in a dark and dangerous underground mine.

The tables at the Waterfront Restaurant are full, so I take a stool at the counter beside a lean fellow with a scruffy, gray beard and enormously dirty glasses. Leonard is a sixty-something mining engineer who, as it turns out, loves to talk.

"So," I ask, "how many gold mines are there?" while wondering if there's a polite way to ask why he doesn't clean his glasses, which really bother me. How, I wonder, can he see through those things?

"Well," says Leonard, "there are three major mines plus a bunch of smaller producers, but they're not just here at Red Lake. They're in the Red Lake area—at places like Balmertown, Cochenour, McKenzie Island, Madsen and Starratt Olsen. Production began in the twenties but there's still a heap of gold. Last I heard, reserves around here stood at something like 23 million ounces. At $600 Canadian per ounce, that's—let's see— almost 14 billion dollars!"

When our conversation drifts farther north, I mention Jack London, the budding author who left the Yukon without finding more than pocket change gold, and ask if here, as in the Yukon, most of the gold seekers left empty handed or fell back on conventional work.

"I suppose so," he says, "but I wasn't here until the sixties, so I really don't know, but if you haven't already heard it, I'll tell you a story about one fellow who finally struck it rich despite all sorts of setbacks."

"Love to hear it," I say.

Leonard slowly removes his bespeckled spectacles, folds in the temples and dips them into his drinking water. He then polishes them with his napkin, which produces a huge improvement, leaving behind only a few spots that look like welding torch splatter.

"His name was Marius Madsen, and if that sounds familiar, that Madsen Mine and the town of Madsen take his name. If anyone ever lived an interesting life," he says, with a lift of his eyebrows, "it was this guy.

"In 1920, when he'd just turned nineteen, this kid became the youngest member of an expedition into the Arctic for some Danish company. When they were hundreds of miles north of the Circle, their ship got crushed by pack ice and began to sink, so the crew hauled whatever they could to a hut on a nearby island. They didn't have a radio—no way to tell the world of their troubles—so they figured that a year would pass before anyone tried to find them.

"They lived on whatever they could shoot and some twenty-year-old canned goods they found in the shacks, feeding it first to their cat, which they used as their 'taster.'

"When rescue finally came, Marius decided to remain in Greenland at one of the company's posts. Two years later, Marius and two companions found themselves drifting away from shore on pack ice that had suddenly broken free. They had two choices: either stay on the ice and hope to be found before it fell apart or attempt to swim the widening gap between the ice and the mainland. They decided to swim.

"After barely making it through 200 feet of freezing water, they were still four miles from their camp. Their clothing froze, and frozen clothing gets stiff as a board, eh? By the time they reached the shack, all three were too weak to move. The way Marius tells it, two days passed before he managed to crawl out of his sleeping bag to start a fire.

"When they bathed their frostbitten feet, their toenails fell off in the water, which they emptied outside. Then they discovered that they couldn't tolerate their wool socks rubbing their raw toes, so they went looking for their toenails, which had frozen in lumps of ice, so they thawed them out, and after deciding which nails fit whom, held them in place with bandages.

"By the time Marius arrived in Canada, his toenails had grown back, so he set out for the interior, making the final 100-mile trip north from the railroad to Red Lake by dogsled in 1926, and right away staked a claim.

"That claim turned out to be one of the best. The gold it produced let Marius retire in Jamaica. And you know, whenever I think of that guy, I wonder about the twists and turns in our lives. For some, they bring despair, but for others, riches. For this guy, every decision he made moved him closer to his big payoff. He survived an arctic shipwreck and then a deadly swim. He arrived at Red Lake at just the right time. He drove his stakes in just the right place, and now he's remembered by a mine and a town that bears his name. Lots of others died or went bust. Makes you wonder, eh?"

The waitress arrives, leans on the counter and writes up our bills.

"Leonard," I say, "that's a great story. Could I have your phone number, so I can call you when I get home?"

"Oh, hell," he says, "I can't remember it—don't call myself, you know. Just write your address on a piece of paper and I'll send it to you."

When Leonard rises to pay his bill, I notice that he cannot straighten one knee.

As he limps out the door, the waitress asks, "Have nice chat with Lennie?"

"Yes," I reply, "I did."

"I heard him tell you about Madsen," she says, "and that story's true, but don't count on getting that phone number. Lennie doesn't have a phone, and he's not a mining engineer. He prospected for years and then went broke, so he worked in the mines, and that's where he got banged up. What he does have, however, is a lot of friends, and that's worth something, too."

Red Lake is famous for gold, but it's also the Norseman Capital of the World, the Norseman being not a Scandinavian, but a huge aerial workhorse that can be switched from wheels to skis to floats as the seasons change. They're the oldest aircraft in regular commercial use in Canada, but most of the remaining forty-three Noorduyn Norsemen are out of license. In fact, the greatest concentration of airworthy Norsemen is in Red Lake, where five still serve the needs of the North. Every year at Red Lake, the remaining Norseman aircraft come together late in July for Norseman days. The town is abuzz with sea-planes. There's a fly-by and a parade with children riding in modified gas drums with stubby wings and tails. There are also rumors of beer!

At a nearby park, where a float-equipped Norseman has been mounted atop a graceful pylon, I begin to appreciate its size. The fuel capacity, at 245 gallons, is huge for an older single-engine airplane Add a twenty-three-gallon oil tank and it becomes apparent that the Norseman was meant to stay aloft for hours. That said, she's a load-lifter, not a racehorse, which explains why critics call the Norseman an "eighty-five" airplane—takes off at 85 knots, flies at 85 and lands at 85. Truth is, with a 600-horsepower Pratt & Whitney engine, she'll do better than 100 knots (115 mph) on floats.

I sit in the shade of the Norseman, thinking of the early days of the fur trade. In the 1700s, six weeks of hard paddling separated Hudson Bay from Great Slave Lake, a distance that the Tundra Cub can span in one long day I marvel at how far aviation has come since the Gold Rush days of 1926 when Jack Elliott and Harold Farrington, each with a single passenger, made the first commercial flights to Red Lake, where they landed in three feet of snow. When taking off in deep snow proved impossible, they hired Natives to pack down a half-mile-long runway. The delay forced an after-dark landing back at the railroad, but they landed safely, thanks to a runway hastily outlined with dozens of flaming, fuel-soaked rags.

In the twenties, a few enterprising Canadians began flying "liquid gold" from Canada to Minnesota during the Prohibition-created drought. One pilot filled his floats with bottles to hide them from the feds and headed off to the states, but the lake where he landed was so rough that all of his bottles shattered, leaving a crowd of thirsty men staring down into the floats. However, a hose was found, and the celebrants were soon having a great time sitting on the edge of the dock, sharing the hose until good sense finally made them quit, or they tumbled into the lake.

By the thirties, bush planes were dominating travel to the gold fields, just as they would eventually replace the "cat trains" that hauled huge cargo sleds through forests and across frozen lakes with bulldozers, the "Iron Huskies" of the North. By 1936, aircraft were landing at fifteen-minute intervals at Red Lake, Gold Pines and Hudson, making them the busiest airports in the world.

Green Airways is busy today, so to give them some space at their crowded docks I fill just the emptiest tank, check the oil and fire up the Cub. The wind has dropped, and with one tank full and the other down just a little, I should have plenty of fuel for the four-hour flight to Ilford.

As I taxi out, I flip on my portable radio, wait for a break in the transmissions and give Red Lake a call.

"Red Lake radio, Piper 4855 Mike is ready for takeoff at Howie Bay. Please activate my flight plan."

"Piper 4855 Mike, your flight plan is activated. Wind is north at 4 knots. Pressure is 29.94. Call when clear of the zone. Good day."

I love my new ANR (active noise reduction) headset! Unlike conventional sets that only insulate one's ears, my ANR headset also reduces background clutter by generating sound waves that cancel out much of the unwanted noise. Powered by two AA batteries, it's so comfortable and effective that during long flights I sometimes become like the princess who was troubled by a pea beneath her mattress. Annoyed by the remaining sound, I begin to think

I've forgotten to turn the headset on or that the batteries have died, but when I turn it off to see if it's working, I'm astounded by the crush of sound. With my new headset, I no longer need to strain to understand the tower or ask for repeats. Now it's just like using a phone.

Thirty minutes later, Pikangikum slips behind. "Pik," like Sandy Lake and Cat Lake, is one of many settlements that are home to the Swampy Cree and the northern Ojibwa whose ancestors labored to supply furs to the Northwest Company and the Hudson's Bay Company. In that rivalry, the HBC had an advantage over the French because the French traded expensive brandy for furs, but the economy-minded Bay used cheaper gin, which, when tinted with iodine, looked like brandy and produced the same results.

Some Ojibwa believed that a beaver dove to the bottom of an all encompassing sea to bring up the first bit of land from which the continents were formed, but these Ojibwa call themselves the *Anishinabek,* the "Spontaneously Created People"—a satisfyingly primal name. I admire its simple theology: No miracles. No passion to proselytize. No excuse to mount a Crusade or declare a Jihad. No threats of hell for those who fail to toe the theological line, and no fancy creation story needed. They're simply here!

It's 300 miles to Ilford, so to entertain myself I dig out my new GPS and try to learn a few tricks. With the stick between my knees and my feet on the pedals plus an occasional glance ahead, I begin to read the manual, which was apparently written for people who have already owned a GPS, but not for greenhorns who dislike buttons with multiple uses that vary from time to time. As the Cub drones on and my frustration increases, the last of the roads fall behind, replaced by jack pine forests, rivers and lakes. When I finally give up, the brown waters of Varveclay Lake lie well off to the right, thanks to my drifting off course while trying to learn a new way to navigate.

The Cub briefly parallels a long, meandering stream. On its flanks, hundreds of round, cream-white dots of various sizes peer up at me. I wonder what they are, but when a pond and a beaver dam appear, I realize that the dots are the tops of aspen stumps left behind by beavers that compulsively dam streams to create ponds in which they build their mud and stick homes, their winter refuges.

It was long thought that the sight of running water stimulated beavers, but Bill Calvin in *The River That Flows Uphill* argued that it's the sound that drives them. According to Calvin, one researcher "put a loudspeaker on a riverbank and played a tape of a bubbling brook. The beavers plastered the speaker, not the river, with mud and sticks." When the tape was turned off, the beavers stopped, apparently satisfied with their efforts.

Island Lake, a huge lake so strewn with inlets and islands that it would take a lifetime to learn its secrets, slowly passes below. When the ice is at least thirty inches thick, forty-ton semis ride its frozen face, hauling freight from lake to lake across the frozen muskeg. If they're empty, the trucks boot right along, but when they're fully loaded, drivers slow to ten miles per hour. Drive a loaded semi too fast, and the sagging ice creates a subsurface wave in front of the rig, breaking the ice from below as the wave approaches the shore.

I've entered Manitoba, the Cree's "land where the spirit lives," but despite being aloft for two and a half hours, I'm only halfway to Ilford. That's just 72 mph! A glance at the lakes reveals the reason: The wind is up. Way up, in fact, as the white caps plainly reveal. To reassure myself that I have plenty of gas, I glance at the gauges and get an even bigger surprise. The left tank is two-thirds empty, and so is the right! At first I think I'd forgotten to put the gas cap on, and the fuel's been sucked out of that tank, but that can't be the reason, because I've done that before, and I've been VERY careful since.

After a minute of head scratching, I realize what has happened. In my rush to get out of the way at Red Lake, I inadvertently filled the wrong tank, the one I'd barely used. Fortunately, Oxford House lies right on my course, and after fighting the headwind for hours, I finally circle the settlement to attract attention, and then land close to the Northern Store.

The clear waters of Oxford Lake reveal shallows that ground the Cub while it's a hundred feet from shore. Removing my boots and socks, I retrieve two collapsible gasoline jugs from the baggage compartment, roll up my pants and step into the frigid water. There's nothing to tie to, so I pull the Cub toward shore until it's firmly grounded. With bags and boots in hand, I wade ashore, where I'm met by a smiling Cree in a 4 x 4 Explorer, who offers a ride to the mayfly-dotted Northern Store. (If they're mayflies, why are they here in July? Because mayflies were named by folks in the southerly states where they hatch in May. Minnesota mayflies appear in June, but up here they arrive in July.)

Bill is the local constable, so he knows the ropes. He tells me I have to pay before I fill the bags, which I gladly do. I'd like to stay for a visit, but it's getting late, and if I'm to reach Ilford by dark, I need to get moving. Unfortunately, the bags' small spigots slow the flow, so to save time, I decide that one bag will do, toss the second into the back seat and take off.

An hour later, as the gas gauge readings descend, I chastise myself for not dumping both bags into the wings. Worse yet, there are few lakes from here to Ilford, so I land at the next, dump in the second bag while the wind shoves me back toward a swampy shore, and then return to the air. Finally, after fighting headwinds for five hours, Ilford crawls into view as the sun angles slowly down toward the black spruce horizon.

As I circle the town to alert someone to pick me up at Moosenose Lake, I get yet another surprise—the rustic Gold Trail Hotel™ where I've spent so many pleasant nights is gone, replaced by a charred hole in the ground.

Were I extra cautious, I'd stop for the night, put up my tent, buy more gas in the morning and leave, but it's just forty-two miles to Gillam. The gas gauges look pretty good, and when I turn toward Gillam, the wind, which is dying, will come from the side. Decision made, I head for Gillam, following the railroad that leads beyond Gillam to Churchill and the western shore of Hudson Bay.

My groundspeed climbs to 87 mph. I fly on the one-eighth-full tank, holding the emptier tank in reserve. If the engine falters, I'll switch tanks and land on the first lake that's close to the tracks. If worse comes to worse, and both gauges are lying, I'll land on the tracks when the engine dies, then flag down the Muskeg Express before it mangles the Cub. The Cub, being light, could easily be dragged from the tracks by the crew or passengers, who would have an interesting story to tell.

Forty-two miles at 87 mph should take twenty-nine minutes, and as the twilight fades, I treasure the softening light. A railroad milepost called Nonsuch finally passes, and as the Nelson River creeps into view, I remember that the *Nonsuch* was the first ship to return to England (in 1668) with an eye-popping load of New World furs. Commanded by Captain Zachariah Gillam, the *Nonsuch* was a fifty-footer (we have semis longer than that) with a gross weight of 43 tons. Worse yet, the *Nonsuch* was slow and hard to maneuver—definitely not a vessel that I'd want to take to sea.

When Gillam appears, I still have plenty of fuel, but now I've a different concern: Will there be enough light? Ten minutes later, the wind drops to zero, street lights appear, and in the last of the twilight, the Cub whispers down from the purpling sky, skims the tips of the lakeshore pines and skids across the mirror-smooth waters of Gillam's Landing Lake.

The weather-beaten shack that serves as the seaplane base office of Gillam Air isn't locked. (In fairness, their main airport office is first rate.) Fortunately, the phone works, and after fueling the Cub (and learning that I had fifty miles of fuel remaining despite my worrying), I'm soon talking with the G & G taxi driver, who delivers bad news: There's a funeral tomorrow for a well-known Cree, so the Gillam Motor Inn and the Aurora Gardens Motel are full. Worse yet, when I call the DOT to close my flight plan and ask why they didn't answer my radio calls, they tell me I wasn't heard. I can't believe that there's really no room in the inn for a weary traveler, so, I grab my radio and slide into the cab.

The clerk at the Gillam Inn is sympathetic, but confirms that they're really full. She lets me use her phone to call the Aurora Gardens Motel, and then takes pity on me when I get the same response.

"Listen," she says, "try Doug's Lodge."

"Where's that," I ask.

"It's 'round in back of the Inn—just an old house with a bunch of rooms that Doug sometimes rents. I'll give you the number, but you'd better let the phone ring, 'cause he's probably already in bed."

On the eighth ring, Doug MacRae, a retired contractor, grumbles hello and reluctantly takes me in. A large sign on his fence warns "Beware of Dog," but tail-wagging "Goofy," a yellow lab, presents no threat. At sixty-five pounds, he's just a big lover.

Doug's "lodge" is a one-story house surrounded by heaps of junk and a four-foot fence, but its three tiny bedrooms are neat and clean, so I'm pleased to stay. And at $30 a night, it's a bargain. As I crawl into bed, I wonder what has happened to my transmitter, and how can I get it repaired?

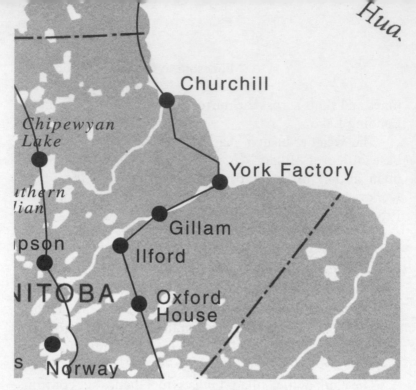

Chapter 2:

Gillam to Churchill, Manitoba

> *It's when things are going just right that you'd better be suspicious. There you are, fat as can be. The whole world is yours, and you're the answer to the Wright brothers' prayers. You say to yourself, nothing can go wrong... all my trespasses are forgiven. Best you not believe it.*
>
> — ERNEST K.GANN

Were it up to me, I'd sleep till noon, but Doug is banging around at 7:00, so I join him for breakfast, then check on my radio. When I open the push-to-talk switch, I find a broken solder connection, but the break is so inaccessible that an ordinary soldering gun won't do. A phone call or two later, Patrick, the friendly operator of Gillam Air, puts me in touch with a budding aviator named Jason Crozier, who works for Manitoba Hydro and who, by coincidence, is a fan of *True North,* which he purchased in Toronto.

In a reprise of the old saw "everyone knows someone," Doug knew Patrick, who suggested I contact Jason, who phones his friend Marcel, who is a communications specialist for Manitoba Hydro. Marcel, however, is gone for the day, and by the time we track him down, he's sitting in his driveway enjoying a beer with his wife. Though it's Friday evening, Marcel agrees to leave his wife and beer to return to work to solder my broken connection. In ten seconds, it's fixed. And that's exactly the sort of helpful attitude that I've repeatedly found in the North.

I'm pleased that my transmitter's repaired, but the long wait for Marcel has used up the day, which means another night at Doug's lodge. There, accompanied by dangerous Goofy, who is licking my hand, I notice that Doug's kitchen and living room walls are plastered with attractive "pin-ups" in various degrees of undress. When I start to laugh, Doug asks, "What's so funny?"

Pointing to the posters, I tell him, "I can't believe I didn't notice your pin-ups last night. Man, I must have been tired!"

I ask Doug if he's seen the replica of the *Nonsuch* in the Winnipeg Museum or if he knows how his town got its name, he says "no" to the first and guesses that Gillam got its name from a bush pilot named Gillam.

Harold "Thrill-em, Chill-em, Never kill-em" Gillam, as he came to be known, built a reputation of being able to fly in weather that others avoided. True, he crashed six airplanes during his first six months, but then something changed, and according to his fellow pilots he became a "wizard with wings." Some folks thought he was crazy, but others praised his skill. "The best pilot in the world," they'd say and refuse to fly with anyone else.

Throughout the thirties he flew the mail run along Alaska's Kuskwin River, a route that other pilots deplored, having been turned back too often by weather. But after Gillam took over the run, settlers in the twenty villages he served began to set their watches by the sound of his arriving Pilgrim, and not by just the hour, but by the minute. Year after year, Gillam flew from Fairbanks to Bethel and back, never failing to arrive on time, and always with the modest air of someone who was simply doing his job. And then, as so often happens, his good fortune suddenly changed.

As reported by Kim Heacox in *Bush Pilots of Alaska,* when Gillam was flying five passengers north from Seattle in a twin-engine Lockheed Electra in 1943, "he hit a bad storm and dense fog. Confused by a map that didn't show the latest navigational aids along the Ketchikan range, he circled Annette Island and tried to orient himself. But ice formed on the wings. An engine went out, and a downdraft plummeted the plane four thousand feet Gillam got on the radio. 'I'm in trouble....' He gained control and barely missed one mountain, but not another as the plane plowed into a forested slope." Gillam and his passengers survived the crash, but before rescue arrived one passenger died, as did the man they called Thrill-em, Chill-em, Never kill-em Gillam.

Patrick, the owner of Gillam Air who ferries tourists to and from York Factory in a variety of aircraft, epitomizes modern bush pilots who have replaced their more reckless "kin" that relied on luck in the face of worsening odds, pushing on instead of landing and radioing for fuel. Afraid of being embarrassed, they rolled the dice with death. Folks thought they were big shots if they got through. Before long, even the pilots began to believe it. But the odds were against these men, and eventually, all but the luckiest fell from the skies.

John McFee, who traveled Alaska while writing

Coming Into the Country, wrote about one daredevil who ran out of gas while out on the ice on a polar bear hunt: "He chopped off his fuel tanks with an axe and used the tanks as boats. He and the hunters paddled out. He was then regarded as a hero. He was regarded as Eddie Rickenbacker and Smilin' Jack. But he was guilty of outrageous technical behavior. He was the fool who got them into the situation in the first place."

I'm pleased with my stop at Gillam because now my radio's fixed. This year, Gillam's been good to me. I've met new friends and toured the dam while awaiting Marcel's return. In a way, it evens my score with the town because thirty years ago, Gillam kicked me square in the wallet.

I'd just taken off from Gillam's gravel runway in a Lake amphibian, heading north to Churchill, when the exhaust gas temperature shot into the red. Throttling back to minimum flight power, I made a quick 180, grabbed the mike and called Gillam.

"Gillam radio, this is Lake One Zero Seven Niner Lima—six miles north—returning to the airstrip with a hot engine and reduced power. I'll be landing downwind. Please advise traffic."

"Seven Niner Lima, this is Gillam radio. We copy. Traffic is a Twin Beech ten miles southwest. Beechcraft Four Five Romeo, do you copy?"

"Beech Four Five Romeo is affirmative. We'll delay until the Lake is down."

As I landed and taxied in, the Lake's engine continued to run, and the exhaust gas temperature quickly fell, but when I added more than half-throttle the Lycoming engine lost power, bucking and backfiring.

The aviation mechanic was out of town, so I was on my own. Armed with only the vaguest idea of where my troubles lay, I cleaned fuel injectors, checked for spark and tried an endless array of adjustments, working well past sunset in fading light. Everything failed.

Fatigued, nearly brain dead and ravishingly hungry, I staggered into Gillam's hugely busy Aurora restaurant, waited fifteen minutes for a table, then another five for a waitress while I read and reread the menu.

Max, the harried waitress, blew aside a strand of hair as she asked for my order. Her smile was genuine, but her weary posture said, "If I live through this shift I'm going to soak my feet for a week!"

"Rib eye steak done medium with a Thousand Island salad, onion rings and hash browns," I replied, trying to be efficient.

"Sorry," she said, "rib eyes are gone. We only have sirloin and we're out of Thousand Island."

"Okay, make it sirloin. How about ranch dressing?

"Just French and Italian."

"Okay, let's go French."

"Do you want your steak black and blue?" she asked.

Almost laughing as I envisioned someone pummeling a steak, I asked what she meant by black and blue.

"That's Cajun style with a blue cheese topping. It's a dollar more."

"No thanks, I'll pass."

I wanted to tell her that spices don't like me, that I don't care for smelly cheese, and that for me, the three essential food groups are sugar, butter and salt with maybe chocolate for a vitamin, but I didn't want to waste her time.

Morning found me climbing onto the Lake's wing once again to try yet another adjustment, only to have the engine resume bucking and snorting. Depressed and frustrated, I retreated to the shade of the operations building for a cola.

Then I had an idea. I had tried a number of adjustments, but only one at a time. Perhaps trying them in various combinations might do the trick. Returning to the plane, I began anew.

The Lake, like its famous ancestor, the Republic Seabee, is a "pusher" aircraft with an engine set above the fuselage and the propeller mounted behind the engine. Unlike the rounded top of the Seabee cowling, the top of the Lake's engine cowling is flat, making it a fine place to set (and forget) tools, which is what eventually happened.

I climbed into the cockpit and turned the key. When the engine fired, a tremendous jolt shook the plane and something flew away from the spinning prop. I quickly shut down the engine, climbed out and discovered what I already feared. I had forgotten a socket wrench with an eight-inch extension on top of the cowling.

When the engine started, the wrench slid into the whirling prop. The first blade lost a chunk of its leading edge when it ripped the handle from the extension and hurled it off to the side. The extension apparently bounced back from the fuselage into the second blade, which bent it sixty degrees, slammed it through the fuselage and through the metal top of the baggage compartment. I never found the socket, but I found the wrench a hundred feet away below a dent in a hangar door.

Realizing that my problem had jumped from toolbox to wallet, I left a message to have the prop replaced, the fuselage repaired and the fuel metering system sent to Winnipeg for repair, then took an airliner home.

Three weeks and several thousand dollars later I returned to Gillam to find a new prop, a nicely repaired fuselage and an aircraft that ran like a charm, despite a fuel flow meter that read "zero." With no way to consult the mechanic, who was gone again, I concluded, correctly, as it turned out, that the fuel flow probe had been attached to the wrong fitting during reassembly. Still, convinced that the engine held no more surprises, I turned south and headed home.

Gillam's Kettle dam is just one of several that span the Nelson River, creating reservoirs from which Manitoba Hydro spins out megawatts of electricity to customers along the U.S./Canada border. Large as it is, the Manitoba Hydro project is dwarfed by Hydro Quebec's plans for the eastern side of the Bay. There, dams with reservoirs as large as France will inundate entire ecosystems and alter the weather as well. Why would they alter the weather? Because the reservoirs will store huge amounts of heat and increase the region's humidity.

In the hierarchy of nature's heat reservoirs, air comes last, heating and cooling quickly. Next comes earth, but the most efficient is water. It takes 3,000 times as much heat to warm a given volume of water as it does to similarly warm the same volume of air. Now envision how much water will evaporate from an impoundment as large as France, and it's likely that the country downwind will see an increase of rain and snow.

One of the world's largest caribou herds, the George River herd, which was estimated at 370,000 animals during the eighties, dwells in and around the region to be submerged. In 1984, unusually high water levels in Quebec's Caniapiscau River swept almost 10,000 migrating caribou to their deaths when they attempted to cross the rain-swollen river. Quebec Natives, deprived of a portion of their food supply, alleged that Hydro Quebec, when pressed by heavy rains, had diverted massive amounts of water into the Caniapiscau watershed. One imaginative official theorized that the caribou themselves were at fault, having been attracted to waterfalls, which he said sound like a herd on the run, but a subsequent investigation revealed that

Hydro Quebec had, in fact, discharged 2,000 cubic yards a second into the Caniapiscau—doubling its normal flow.

With the dam behind, I glide downward into the river valley. White, haystack-like waves rear up toward the Cub as I race downstream. It's exhilarating, but it's not very safe. Were my engine to quit, I'd face an immediate landing in extremely rough water, so after a few minutes of fun, I climb high enough to be able to reach a calmer stretch of the river if my engine throws a fit.

It's 140 miles to York Factory, once the North American headquarters of the longest continuously running business in the world, the Hudson's Bay Company. I follow the Nelson most of the way, then angle east over forty miles of saturated forest and bog to pick up the Hayes River and York Factory. (The word "Factory" in many Hudson's Bay Company place names seems to imply a product, but it really means that the head man, the "factor," lived there.)

Twice a day the Hudson Bay tide runs dutifully up the Hayes, and twice a day falls back. When I arrive, the tide is out, leaving just one sufficiently deep channel on which to land. Fortunately, the Cub draws very little water, so after flying beyond a ringed seal that's also using the channel and ignoring the fellow who's trying to wave me off, I cut the power, drop below the river bank, land and taxi up to the floating pier. There, I learn that the "waver," is one of the guides.

"Hi there," says Blaine. As we shake hands, he adds, "I thought you were about to have a happening." Seeing my puzzled expression, he says, "When the tide is out, pilots in bigger planes, and even in Cubs like yours, sometimes scrape bottom—or worse. I didn't realize you knew where to land, so," pointing at the camera that hung around his neck, "I brought this along in case you had a happening."

It's hard to believe that the rectangular, three-story warehouse is all that remains of a community that once spread across this site, which was really the York Factory

III—the first two posts having been built downstream on ground so low that the erosive Hayes nibbled the earth from beneath them and took them out to sea. By the 1860s, York Factory III included more than fifty buildings. Within its palisades it housed an Anglican church, a school, a hospital and a doctor's house plus a bakery, library, blacksmith shop and cooperage for making barrels. Beyond its walls lay a powder magazine and a graveyard, but of all these structures, only the warehouse and the cemetery remain.

In 1869, the Hudson's Bay Company relinquished all charter rights in Canada for £300,000, but it retained 5 percent of its tillable land and all of the land occupied by its forts, including 500 very valuable acres beneath Winnipeg's Fort Garry. Duncan MacRae, Doug MacRae's great, great grandfather, helped build the fort just before witnessing Canada's closest thing to a civil war—the Metis Uprising, a conflict between mixed race settlers and trappers and the Hudson's Bay Company.

The last York boat left York Factory in 1874, done in by the railroad that finally connected Winnipeg to Port Arthur/Fort William (now Thunder Bay) and Toronto. After 1931, the HBC stopped sending its annual supply ship to the post, and in 1953, after almost 270 years of service to the Company, York Factory was abandoned. It was then deeded to Canada in 1968 a few years after the Bay sold its assets to the International Financial Association for £1.5 million— a fair profit above the £10,000 required when Radisson and Groseilliers persuaded Prince Rupert to begin the great "adventure" in and around Hudson Bay.

I'm hoping to find Betty Settee, the Cree guide whom I've met here before, but she's nowhere in sight.

"Blaine," I ask, "Do Betty and Jim still work here?"

"No," he replies. "I think they got tired of being so isolated. Last I heard, they moved to Shamattawa."

"They'll like it better there," I say. "No polar bears to bug them, and when it gets cold, maybe they can drive the winter roads to Thompson or Red Lake."

A raised boardwalk leads to the warehouse, and as we step inside, Gillam Air's twin-engine Islander passes overhead, heading for the Factory's gravel runway on an island just downstream.

"Gotta go," says Blaine. "I have to bring tourists over from the island, but feel free to show yourself around. You've had the tour before anyway."

Inside the warehouse, I walk silently over wooden floors polished smooth by moccasins, mukluks and sliding bales of fur. In this building, bales of mink, marten, beaver, fox and wolf pelts—and pelts from almost any fur-bearing animal—were stored, for in Europe, furs were "all the rage." In England, beaver hats had become so valuable that they were willed by fathers to their oldest son, and in the original story, Cinderella was rewarded with slippers made not from glass, but from squirrel hide.

Here, every fall from the late 1600s into the twentieth century, British ships sailed up the Hayes to anchor at Five Fathom Hole, then quickly emptied their holds of rifles, knives, hatchets, pots, pans, sugar, flour and white man's clothing and blankets. To avoid being trapped by the early Hudson Strait ice, they just as quickly stuffed their holds with fur and sailed for England, where in Garroway's Coffee House, the bales would be auctioned off "by candle"—the bale going to the last buyer to yell out a bid before a pin fell from the soft rim of a burning candle. Why Garroway's? Because there, a new beverage called "tea," whose leaves were worth more than gold, had been introduced in 1651 by the British East India Company. The phenomenal success of tea and coffee, the house's roominess and the fact that Garroway's was "the place to be" made it the logical choice.

When Radisson and Groseilliers first explored the wilds to the north of Lake Superior, there was no Hudson's Bay Company. In fact, the mercurial Radisson was lucky to be alive. Unlike his partner, who had a mundane upbringing, Radisson, when age fifteen, had been captured and adopted by the Mohawks near Lake Champlain. Years later, Radisson and a captured Algonquin contrived to escape, but were quickly recaptured.

The Algonquin was murdered and Radisson was tied to a scaffold. The soles of his feet were seared with red-hot iron. His fingernails were extracted, and the tips of his fingers dipped in glowing coals. A hot sword was driven through one of his feet, but just as he was about to follow the Algonquin to the Happy Hunting Grounds, he was rescued by his Mohawk family. For two years he waited, and then escaped again. Toughened by six years with the Mohawks, Radisson headed west and joined up with Groseilliers.

A few years later, when Radisson and Groseilliers returned to Montreal with a load of prime northern furs, a surprise awaited them. Instead of being lauded for their work and the fur that revived the colony's struggling economy, Groseilliers was briefly imprisoned for trapping without a license, and the bulk of their fur was confiscated.

Disgusted, they turned their backs on Montreal and headed for Boston. Two years later they sailed for England, arriving in London in 1665 at the end of one calamity (the Puritan, Cromwell reign that murdered Charles I, closed theaters, forbade walking on Sunday except to church, and even destroyed Maypoles) and the height of another—a bubonic plague that would claim 100,000 lives. There, aided by influential friends, they met the multi-mistressed

King Charles II, who desperately needed trade to offset the expense of restoring English science, theater and the declining Royal Navy. An appointment with Prince Rupert followed, and Rupert, whose intellect was said to rival Isaac Newton's, was instantly intrigued.

On May 2, 1670, following several trial voyages that returned with profitable loads of fur, King Charles II granted Rupert and his fellow investors a charter that named them "true lords and proprietors" of all the sea and lands of Hudson Bay and all its drainage system. This was a 1.5 million square mile tract called Rupert's Land that included much of Labrador, most of Nunavut, Quebec, Ontario, Saskatchewan, Alberta and the Northwest Territories. That's 43 percent of present-day Canada, plus a sizeable chunk of Minnesota and North Dakota.

Thus, on five sheepskin parchments, was born the "Company of Adventurers Trading into Hudson Bay," known variously as the Hudson's Bay Company, the "Company" or just the "HBC," the latter being interpreted in later years as Here Before Christ as a tribute to the company's longevity. On the down side, disgruntled workers often called it the Hungry Belly Company—a jab at the often tight-fisted, out of touch London committeemen who would nevertheless finance silly projects like shipping 150 copies of *The Country Clergyman's Advice to Parishioners* to Natives who could not read.

Granted the absolute right to enforce the law and judge all cases "on the spot" and to raise an army and navy to defend its interests, the officials of the HBC were like unto kings. As Radisson wrote, "We were Caesars, being nobody to contradict us."

The first governor to reside on the Bay was a man named Charles Bayley, and Charles had an "interesting" past. Kidnapped and shipped to America as a teen, Bayley endured fourteen years of bondage in Virginia, where he became a Quaker. On returning to London, he joined other zealous Quakers and set off for Rome to convert the Pope to his faith.

Bayley was briefly confined to a madhouse, and then ejected from Italy. Back in England, he refused to swear an oath to King Charles, and was imprisoned for several years. The king finally pardoned Bayley when he agreed to mend his ways, which he did, becoming a truly effective administrator during the company's fledgling years on the Bay.

Radisson and Groseilliers, after years of service to the Bay, became frustrated with London's refusal to establish posts to the west of the bay, so they switched to the French. But a few years later, when the New France (Montreal) government confiscated their ship and seized a quarter of their furs, Groseilliers called it quits.

Not Radisson! He set off for London, where the "Gentlemen Adventurers," who had finally realized that inland posts were essential, swallowed their pride and took him back. A decade or so later, Radisson retired to London, where the thankless committeemen reduced his pension. He sued, and, after five years, won its return. Once a "Caesar of the north," Radisson was reduced to begging the HBC for a job as a warehouse-keeper. He was refused, died in 1710, and lies somewhere in England in an unmarked grave.

While Blaine shepherds his new flock of tourists through the warehouse, I search out Floyd, the second guide, to see if he (and his shotgun) will accompany me to the cemetery. We're just 600 miles from Lake Superior, but this is polar bear country. And because it's summer, they're all ashore!

The cemetery is in the same condition as its occupants.

Some of the headstones have toppled. Others, judging by the rectangular depression at the head of some of the mounds, have been carted off, but a few are still upright and legible, with some dating back to the 1700s. Still others are outlined with the tilting remains of deeply weathered picket fences.

"That mound over there," says Floyd, "is supposed to be the grave of a guy who took his own life. Don't know for sure if it is or isn't, but they say he left a long trail of clothes that ended at the river."

The north is famous for bugs, and as we wave away the black flies that dance before our eyes, I tell Floyd, "I'm beginning to understand why Factor Hargraves called York Factory "nine months of winter, varied by three of rain and mosquitoes."

"That's not so bad," says Floyd as he opens his loose-leaf notebook, which contains his notes for tourists. "It says here that a clerk named Ballantine, who wintered here, called York Factory 'A monstrous blot on a swampy spot with a partial view of a frozen sea.' And one of the factors, a guy named James Knight, wrote in 1717, 'Here now is such swarms of sand flies that wee can hardly see the sun through them and where they light is just as if a spark of fire fell and raises a little bump...that burns so that we cannot forebear rubbing of them...our hands and faces is nothing but scabs.'"

The boardwalk from the dock to the warehouse extends all the way to the cemetery. As we return, Floyd suddenly stops and points to the boards. There, still damp, are several paw prints left by a polar bear. Big as dinner plates, they reveal that a bear must have lumbered down to the Hayes shortly after we'd passed.

"Jeez," says Floyd, "that really spooks me. I tell you, if they didn't let us carry shotguns, I wouldn't work here, that's for sure."

At the warehouse, Blaine releases his tourists to Floyd,

who heads back to the graveyard. I ask Blaine to name the most famous of the factors who served here.

"That's easy," says Blaine, "although this place is full of 'firsts.' In 1690 Henry Kelsey traveled inland from York Factory into Saskatchewan, and became the first European to see the plains bison and grizzly bears. Lots of sharp guys like Radisson, Groseilliers and David Thompson[TN] worked here, and, in my view, they served damn well, better, frankly, than their pay required, but no one comes close to James Knight.

"Most of the factors were appointed through privilege, but Knight worked his way through the ranks, serving first at Fort Charles—that's on the east side of James Bay—in 1676 after being hooked by an HBC ad that promised daily beer, fruitful gardens, hens, hogs and snug log cabins with big chimneys that they said would 'keep always Summer within, while nothing but Ice & snow are without doores.' (Blaine has a notebook, too.) As you've probably guessed, they lied.

"Gardening was pointless. The livestock froze. As for the 'snug cabin,' Knight called it 'a Little place not fitt to keep hoggs in.' But Knight hung in there, becoming chief factor at Fort Albany in—let's see—1682, then deputy governor in 1698.

"He loved it. In his diary he said that his increase in pay and furnishings included a 'suite of Curtaines, fine blanketts, a rugge, a bedstead and curtine rods, a carpett, 6 chaires, 2 spanish table matts' and the right to hire his brother Richard 'to waight upon him.' Then he became Governor Knight, serving at York Factory in a time of intense cold called the Little Ice Age, during which amputations of frozen fingers and toes were routine. Knight's journal records him ordering his blacksmith to make 'an amputateing chisoll' for one poor fellow's hands and feet. Makes a few mosquitoes sound pretty tame, eh?"

"So," I say, as we seek the shade of park office steps, "it sounds like the Company did pretty well when Knight was here."

"They did okay," says Blaine, "but they were really just getting started. After all, they'd only been in business for fifteen years."

"Well," I say, "something certainly changed. I've read that by the peak of the fur trade, beaver fur had become so valuable that they even sifted the sand from warehouse floors to retrieve every hair, and that the HBC shipped more than 3 million beaver pelts to England in a single twenty-five-year period. And that's just beaver pelts! Not fox, mink or marten or other fur bearers."

"That's right," says Blaine, "and Knight was largely responsible. Knight knew that if the HBC were to compete with the Voyageurs who were crowding up from the south, they'd have to trade with Natives to the west and north of Churchill, so in 1715 he sent out an expedition led by a guy named William Stewart and a Chipewyan woman called Thanadelthur who had been kidnapped by the Cree as a child.

"That Thanadelthur was a handful. She was so aggressive, even willing to use her fists to stand up to men, that the Cree called her Wetsi, which means Hearts on Fire. She could speak both Cree and Chipewyan, and because she had picked up English at the Factory, she became Stewart's interpreter.

"The choice was a good one. No—make that a great one. Unfortunately, the Chipewyans they located were afraid that the Cree would attack them. At first they refused, but Thanadelthur shamed them so thoroughly that they finally agreed to come if the Bay would build a post at Churchill. Stewart, who was stunned by her nerve, later wrote, 'Indeed she has a Divellish Spirit and I believe that if thare were but 50 of her Country Men of the same

Carriage and Resolution, they would drive all the (Cree) Indians out of there country.'

"Many of the Chipewyans, unlike the Cree, chose not to work for the HBC, preferring the freedom of their nomadic jaunts through taiga, which was fine for the men, but hell for the women who were exchanged like property and were little more than slaves. Unfortunately, some of the men who worked for the HBC didn't treat women much better. George Simpson, a competent HBC governor who had five children by four native 'wives' before marrying his eighteen-year-old cousin, demonstrated his cavalier attitude toward women when he wrote to a factor concerning a previous lover, '…if you can dispose of the lady it will be satisfactory as she is an unnecessary and expensive appendage….'

"When they returned, Thanadelthur plied Knight with tales of copper and other minerals, and promised to show him the way. She described a broad strait with tides that ebbed and flowed within her country, and told of "black pitch," which could have been the Athabasca Tar Sands that we mine for oil today. Other Chipewyans drew Knight a map showing how to reach the land of the Copper Indians near Great Slave Lake, and told him that beyond the copper hills lay a Great Western Sea with strange vessels, which Knight took to be Japanese ships trading at the western end of the Northwest Passage.

"Knight, as promised, built a trading post in 1717 near the mouth of the Churchill River, later replaced by Fort Prince of Wales, but when he was about to send out another expedition to summon the Chipewyans, a sickness fell upon the post, and Thanadelthur, whom Knight had become fond of, died."

Blaine flips to the last page of his notebook, which he hands to me. Within it lies an outlined paragraph in which Knight is mourning her loss: "I am so concerned for her

Death...that I am almost ready to break my heart...wee buried her abt 4 a'clock.... The finest Weather wee have had any Day this Season but the most Melancholys't by the Loss of her."

"That's really sad," I say.

"It is," says Blaine "But Knight, who was well into his seventies, still dreamed of leading an expedition to find the Northwest Passage and Thanadelthur's copper mines After receiving backing in London, he returned to Hudson Bay in 1719 in two ships, the *Albany* and the *Discovery,* and neither Knight nor his men were ever seen again."

It's hot by the time I return to the Cub. Budding cumulus clouds that formed above the mainland are drifting slowly out to sea. The tide is flooding up the Hayes, so with plenty of water beneath my floats, I take off upstream, then seek the security of height before crossing the spruce-covered peninsula between the Hayes and the Nelson River. Far below, the Parks Canada boat is plowing through the silty Hayes, ferrying the tourists back to the Islander.

The sun begins to redden as Port Nelson comes into view. When the visibility starts to drop, I remember a DeBeers helicopter crew at the Gillam Inn complaining about forest fires between Gillam and Churchill. At the time, I didn't think they'd create a problem because I'm nearing the Taiga, the Land of the Little Sticks, where the forest thins and there isn't much to burn, but as the minutes pass and the smoke thickens, it's obvious I was wrong.

Jumping the Nelson River, I follow the eighteen-trestle bridge that leads toward shore from a rusting dredge to the collapsing buildings of Port Nelson, the port that was meant to be the end of the rail line from which prairie wheat would leave for Europe. Port Nelson, however, proved much too shallow and difficult to dredge, so the project was abandoned and the railroad turned north to Churchill, the only deep-water port on Hudson Bay. In 1929, when dignitaries gathered at Churchill to drive home the traditional "gold" spike, only steel spikes could be found. Making do, a gleaming spike was soon produced and driven home—its iron core disguised with tin foil from a pipe tobacco can.

The pall of smoke requires a change of plans. I'd hoped to fly up the coast to photograph polar bears, but the dense smoke sweeping across my path lies so low to the ground that flying beneath it wouldn't be safe. Knowing that Churchill lies north of the fires and that it's enjoying the same high pressure that brings clear skies, I climb above the smoke and turn to the north-northwest on a course that will intercept the railroad to Churchill.

Forty minutes pass with nothing in sight but the seemingly endless smoke screen from smoldering tundra and pines. Then, somewhere near the smoke-obscured Owl River, which is one of the prime polar bear denning areas in the world, I remember the "adventure" of a Chipewyan named John Spence who had been trapping along the Owl in 1969.

Unlike the barren country to the north of Churchill, the Owl is far enough south to allow dense clumps of willows, black spruce and alder to spread outward from its banks. In one of those clumps, Spence was standing head down over one of his traps when a sledgehammer blow sent him flying. When he regained consciousness, blood was spurting from a huge wound in his upper arm, but the bear was gone. Spence's nearby companions provided emergency care that saved his life, but he lost his arm and all memory of the unseen attack.

The northern Greenland Inuit call polar bears Pisugtooq, "the wanderers," because they roam the ice as they search for seals, and though many bears remain near the tidal flats all summer, their inland range is also impressive: In 1978, one polar bear wandered three hundred miles from the Bay to Norway House, which is just 250 miles from Winnipeg. Polar bears, however, are not the only species of bear on the move. Biologist Mitch Taylor has seen barren ground grizzly bears on the ice hundreds of miles north of mainland Canada, including one that had killed a young polar bear.

The haze finally thins, revealing a land so cluttered with small, pothole lakes that I can only guess where I am. That guess, however, is confirmed when the railroad appears, complete with Via Rail's *Muskeg Express*. Heading south, its diesel engine is hauling a mixture of empty grain cars and adventure-filled passengers.

In 1967, when I first came to Churchill, it was still a frontier town. Maps of the region to the northwest of Churchill bore the huge understatement—"sparsely settled area." Even the authoritative book, *Science, History and Hudson Bay,* paid homage to Churchill's uniqueness, stating, "It is by no means similar to any other town in Canada." The U.S. airbase, a relic of World War II, had long been abandoned, and its neat rows of buildings, with their windows shattered, had become rusting scars on the tundra landscape. Natives were shooting and spearing beluga whales in an ill-fated attempt to make a killing in canned muktuk, the layer of fat just beneath the hide. Fortunately, the killing soon stopped, doomed by the discovery of mercury in the fat and a market that faded away. Today, the trusting belugas delight camera-toting tourists who enjoy their squeals, whistles, clicks and chirps that are piped aboard by hydrophones dangling from Sea North's launch, which is cruising the river below. As I circle the launch, several whales head straight for its side, then dive beneath it. Tourists rush from starboard to port as the belugas surface, and then dive again.

In the sixties, Parks Canada had no presence here. To cross the Churchill River to visit Fort Prince of Wales you needed a willing someone with time, a boat and a motor. If you were as lucky as my father and I were on our first trip north, you'd find a "someone" like Art Cripps, a young man so in love with the place that he boated us over and walked us through the fort without charge. On the path to the forty-two cannon fortress, you'd have paused beside a long heap of stones, a grave in a land where rock and permafrost discouraged burial, so stones were heaped on the bodies.

Despite these precautions, Natives knew that a bear or wolverine could roll aside the stones, and because the bodies would be scavenged, it became taboo to eat ravens, wolves and foxes for fear of consuming a dead relative. As I fly over the fort, I remember that just eight years later the stones were gone, carried off by vandals or souvenir hunters who just can't leave things alone.

My old friend, the freighter *Ithaca,* still lies aground about ten miles from town. Driven ashore by a potent storm, she seemed ready to put out to sea in the sixties despite her damaged hull, but in recent years, salvors (or perhaps scavengers) have sliced into her graffiti-strewn hull with cutting torches, leaving ragged openings wide enough to admit a two-ton truck.

On the way to the airport, I look for *Miss Piggy,* the C-46 that lost an engine while out over Hudson Bay and lumbered back to Churchill in "ground effect"—the cushion of air that helps support aircraft that fly very close to the surface. Unable to climb 100 feet to reach the runway, she still rests where she came to a heart-pounding stop amidst the coastal boulders. As I circle, I see that the same clowns who defaced the *Ithaca* have attacked one side of *Miss Piggy,* too.

I call Churchill radio, which has been keeping track of me during my sight-seeing tour, and ask them to send the fuel truck to Landing Lake.

"4855 Mike," replies Churchill, "The driver's gone for the day. Do you need a cab?"

"Yes, thank you. 55 Mike over."

The seaplane base is eight miles from town, so I've plenty of time to unload my gear and gas bags at the base's notoriously shabby "pier." Then, accompanied by a cloud of mosquitoes, I head up the road into a northerly wind that, combined with my brisk pace, soon leaves the bugs behind.

A round, banded stone catches my eye I pick it up, lick it to enhance its gray and russet striations and admire its silky surface. I roll it back and forth in my hand, deceiving myself that I'm adding a final polish to contours worn smooth by waves of time. My striped, mini-Jupiter is part of the great inverted bowl of ancient rock, the same pre-Cambrian Shield that I've flown over since leaving Minnesota. The Shield is much too old to contain fossil fuels, but it's laced with nickel, tin, copper, iron, silver, gold and platinum—and the newly discovered diamond "pipes" that are scattered across Canada from near Bathurst Inlet on the Arctic coast to "down south" at Attawapiskat—just east of James Bay—and near Oxford House, where I stopped for fuel.

When I'm a mile up the road, the cab—a four-wheel-drive pickup—arrives in a cloud of dust, executes a U-turn, and I'm soon rattling off toward Churchill.

Kevin, the driver, has been living in Churchill since 1996, and he plans to stay, which surprises me because many come up for the fun but after one winter can hardly wait to leave.

"I love it," he says, "and it's not just the bears or the whales. I'm glad that no road comes here. If one ever does, I'll move farther north—maybe Rankin Inlet or Baker Lake. The northern lights, they're fantastic, and the fishing's damn good. The people seem to get along better here than down south, and we've got homegrown motels and restaurants that are better than Holiday Inns and MacDonald's."

"Kevin," I say, "you'd have liked it even better forty years ago, though not everyone would have agreed. Back in the sixties, when Churchill began to call itself the 'Gateway to the North', which it was and still is, Farley Mowat was calling it the Asshole of the Arctic, which it wasn't, but only because a few other sites like Fort Chimo, the place they now call Kuujjuak, were worse. Even so, when I returned from my first trip up here, I told my wife that because of its frontier-like charm plus the bears and the whales, Churchill would someday be known to every travel agent in the U.S. and Canada, if not the world, and I was right! Mention Churchill to any decent travel agent today, and you'll have your choice of tours in seconds.

"One thing you wouldn't have liked, though, was that the Metis (part white and part native) were still living in a grubby area down near the river called 'the Flats.' Almost no one but 'Ernie' Senior, the editor of the *Taiga Times,* cared what happened to them. Because they were 'half-breeds,' they had no treaty rights. Worse yet, they were unwanted by both Indians and whites, and pretty much ignored by the government, so they had to survive here in the 'Home of the Wind Chill,' mind you, in makeshift hovels that would have glorified tar paper shacks.

"Back then, Camp 20, as it was called, was really just a holding facility for the Inuit that the feds had flown in from the bush, just as Camp 10 housed the Chipewyans. Camp 20 was supposed to train them for work, but of the ninety or so residents, the records show that during one year only two were 'employed,' one as a sweeper at the grain elevator and the other as a prostitute. During the sixties, *Science, History and Hudson Bay* said that preserving law and order in Churchill was 'a staggering challenge' and called Churchill 'probably the most difficult posting to which an RCMP constable can be assigned.' Fortunately, things got a lot better in the seventies when they provided decent housing for the Dene and Inuit and built the Town Centre, where kids can swim, play basketball and play in a polar bear built of spiked together 2 x 6s."

As we jolt through water-filled potholes and vibrate down the washboard road, I tell Kevin about a few of my other arrivals in Churchill.

"The first time was in 1967. My father and I had followed the railroad up from the Pas in my Beechcraft Bonanza. After landing in mid-afternoon, we wandered around this huge, almost empty airport for almost an hour before we finally found someone who told us to park the Beech—at no charge—inside a huge, empty, heated hanger that could have easily housed a Boeing 727.

"In the eighties, I ran into fog about half way between here and Gillam, and landed on a bog-rimmed lake to wait it out. It was morning, so I figured the sun would cook away the fog, but the fog got thicker instead. Because of the boggy shoreline, I couldn't pitch a tent or cook a decent meal, so I sat in the Cub or stood on the float for thirty-six hours until the fog finally lifted enough to let me sneak into Churchill. I could have slept on a cactus that night!

"About eight years later I was met at the seaplane base by one of your guys who knew nothing about local people, places or events, but was determined to find out if I'd been 'saved.' That guy really ticked me off!"

Kevin laughs. "I remember him," he says. "We put up with him because we were short of help, but when we found someone who could drive okay and mind his own business, he was history."

My friend Steve Bosnjak sold his Churchill Motel several years ago, so I check into the Polar Inn, then head for my favorite restaurant, the Trader's Table, but they're not ready for supper. I haven't eaten since breakfast, so as my stomach complains, I sit on the steps and slaughter mosquitoes while dreaming of porterhouse steaks.

As if hurried along by the northwest wind, one of the Great White Bear tundra buggies suddenly wheels around the corner and heads toward the airport. The buggy is a descendant of the work of Len Smith, an entrepreneur who took the transfer case from a 2 1/2-ton truck, the engine, transmission and frame from a Ford truck, a differential from a front-end loader, and welded the lot together, then added a 9 x 20-foot body above a set of 63-inch tires. Think "school bus on stilts." Tourists came flocking Len added a bunkhouse on wheels and a diner. Soon he had competition. A decade or two later Sea North tours brought in a thirty-foot aluminum boat to ferry tourists across the Churchill River to Fort Prince of Wales, making stops along the way for whale and bear watchers.

One summer, a friend and I went for a ride in one of the bigger buggies that can roll across the tundra and through shallow lakes with ease. The ride, however, varies with the terrain—smooth at times, then leaping like a bronco when ruts or boulders intrude. Pity the poor tourist compelled to heed a call of nature, only to be catapulted from the buggy's toilet when a nearby wheel vaults a boulder. They don't need seat belts in the buggy proper, but if it were up to me, I'd put one in the john.

Churchill's recorded history should have begun in 1612, the year that Captain Thomas Button sailed up this coast, but Button failed to notice the harbor formed by the Churchill River. That discovery came seven years later (a year before the Pilgrims landed at the comparative paradise of Plymouth Rock) when two ships carrying sixty-four Danes sailed into the bay in search of a water route to the Orient, and were compelled to winter at the mouth of the Churchill River. Scurvy came to call, followed quickly by starvation. When spring returned, only Captain Jens Munk and two others remained. Somehow, the three managed to sail back to Denmark, which quit the field, only to be replaced by Britain, the country that would lose hundreds of men and a score of ships in a fruitless search for a Northwest Passage.

When the Trader's Table opens its doors, I'm the first of a dozen in line. Inside, nothing has changed. Even my favorite placemats are still in use—two polar bears seated across a table, the steam rising from their coffee cups glowing warmly in soft amber light. After scanning the menu, I switch from steak to char. I'll have plenty of fish in the days ahead, but baked char in an almond sauce sounds really good tonight.

The dinner is so delicious that I'm tempted to lick my plate. As I smile at the thought of what the other diners might think, I notice a man at a nearby table looking at me the way that we do when we think we should know someone, but we're not quite sure. When he looks away, I study him and decide he's right, so I walk over to inquire.

"Excuse me, sorry to bother you, but you look familiar. I'm George Erickson. I get up this way now and then from Minnesota."

A smile of recognition spreads across his face. "Sure you are," he says. "Now I remember you, I'm Fred, the guy who took you over to the fort about ten years ago. You wrote me up in that book of yours. Made me look good, too."[TN]

"Nothing but the facts, Fred," I reply, "and who knows, maybe you'll make the next one, too. Do you still take tourists across the river with that Merc' of yours or has Sea North put you out of business?"

"Not really, I just don't do it anymore, but I'll take you if you need a ride."

"Not this time, Fred, but I'll buy you a beer if you'll update me on the belugas and the bears."

"Sounds good," says Fred as he offers a chair.

"Whale numbers are down, and they're still finding too

much mercury in the blubber and milk, which is tough on the calves. It looks like our belugas will be added to SARA—that's the Species at Risk Act—and they don't get on that unless they're in trouble. In the Gulf of St. Lawrence, belugas now have the highest cancer rates of all mammals, probably because of PCBs and other pollutants in the water. I used to live in Sept-Iles, you know (I didn't), when the St. Lawrence Seaway was home to 5,000 of these white whales. But when fisherman blamed declining catches on belugas, our nutty government put a bounty on their heads. Just last week, I read that there are only 350 left. That's less than 10 percent, damn it—thanks to that stupid bounty and pollution-derived diseases."

I shake my head in dismay. I know he's right. Years ago, an article in the *Canadian Geographical Journal* explained that PCBs and other toxins in the St. Lawrence accumulate first in fish, and then concentrate in the fatty tissue of the whales that feed on the fish. As a result, a female beluga can carry most of the toxic, fat-soluble chemicals that she's ingested since birth and then pass a portion of them on to the calves that live on her milk. The result is an increasing number of stillborn calves with high concentrations of PCBs and other chemicals—all released by ignorant or indifferent, anything-for-a-buck humans.

"And the bears?"

"They look about the same, but this global warming's a really bad deal. The ice is going out earlier every year and showing up later. Bears that routinely swam 100 miles from the ice pack to shore have begun to drown because that gap has widened to as much as 300 miles. The bear guys say that the number of bears in this area have dropped 20 percent in the last twenty years, and they're coming off of the ice about 15 percent lighter than ten years ago because short winters cut into the time they can feed on the seals—and they're in trouble, too. A shrinking, short-lived ice pack is bad for seals, which have to come up on the ice to give birth and to nurse their pups. The way it's going, Rankin Inlet or Chesterfield Inlet will probably replace Churchill as the Polar Bear Capital of the World."

"I'm not surprised," I say. "Oil and coal companies have spent millions to persuade us that global warming is just an invention of anti-progress environmentalists. They have bought my Congress. They have almost unlimited media access, and they set up friendly sounding organizations like the Wise Use Council and ICE—that's the Information Council on the Environment—which told lies until it was exposed. ICE folded, but it soon reappeared with a different name and a similar purpose.

"So how about problem bears?" I ask.

"Let's see—last November, a woman got knocked down by a bear as she was walking from a helicopter to the Tundra Lodge. Fortunately, the rest of her crowd was able to drive off the bear. That's rare, though. If I remember right, the last attack that caused serious injuries happened about twenty years back.

"That doesn't mean that we haven't had some close calls. One time, a tourist who didn't realize that a bear was nearby, let his elbow stick out the window of one of the tundra buggies The bear reached up and grabbed it, but the guy hung onto the buggy and hollered like hell while others beat on the bear. We tell people that these bears can have a twelve-foot reach, but that's just numbers to them until some bear stretches up and grabs someone who isn't careful. As one tourist said when he saw his first bears, 'They come in three sizes – big, really big and Oh, wow!'

"Back in the seventies two kids got a hell of a scare. This kid and his buddy were out riding their Skidoos, the old kind with maybe just a ten- or twelve-horse engine, when they spotted a big bear coming over a rise about fifty feet off to the side. The guy in front hit the gas and headed for town, and so did the kid in the rear, who was smart enough to toss his lunch bag off to slow down the bear.

"Fortunately, the bear's top speed of about thirty mph was a shade less than the Skidoos', so these kids, who were only ten years old, made it safely back to town. They kept the story quiet, but a nature photographer had captured the chase, and his photo revealed a bear chasing a Skidoo with one kid's number on its side. When his parents saw it, he said that he was too scared to tell them because they'd have been mad if they learned that he'd almost gotten himself eaten on a school night."

We finish our beer, then head for the door.

"When you're ready to go to the base tomorrow, give me a ring," says Fred. We'll fill your gas bags, and I'll give you ride."

At the Polar Inn, I turn on the television. It's news time. I'm not up on Canadian politics, so a lot of it zips through my head, but I pay attention when I hear the word Iraq. American deaths have just passed 2,700 with at least 20,000 casualties, many with amputations, but the more than 100,000 dead Iraqis are not mentioned. Neither is the fact that we now have more enemies in the Arab world than ever before, thanks to our invading Iraq on trumped up charges.

Before I turn in, I arrange for a 2:00 a.m. wake-up call.

"That's a tad early, eh?" asks the clerk.

"I know," I say, "but I want to see the aurora. You're used to it, but where I live, we're lucky to catch them maybe one night in sixty—and that's if it's clear. You're lucky, you have them just about every other night."

In the northern hemisphere the aurora is usually brightest from early November into January when the long winter nights provide perfect contrast to the evanescent lights. We'd expect them to be most brilliant just above the magnetic pole, but the reverse is true. Instead, the brightest auroras occur in a several-hundred-mile-wide ring that surrounds the magnetic pole, which means that travelers near the magnetic pole can turn their heads in any direction, including south to see the dancing rays. And see them they do, for in Canada's high Arctic, these spectral displays enliven the sky on three nights out of four.

I grab the phone when it rings, mumble a sleepy thank you, pull on my clothes and head outside. To avoid the worst of the streetlights, I walk to a vacant field near the road to the harbor. And there they are, my old friends— mystical, ephemeral, wavering, blushing, shape-shifting friends.

Aristotle, who was hampered by the ignorance of his times, described the aurora's phosphorescent flares as "jumping goats caused by vapors evaporating from the earth and set afire by meteors." He also taught that heavy objects fell faster than lighter objects, but Galileo put an end to that.

Because stroking a dry caribou pelt could produce tiny sparks, the Chipewyans believed that the aurora was made of caribou hair. Some Inuit tribes claimed that when the aurora turned red, it predicted tuberculosis, the disease in which the victim spits blood. When World War II began, others swore that the red auroras had been harbingers of the bloodshed to come.

It's almost 3:00 by the time I get back to my room. Despite a litany of snores from the adjacent rooms, I quickly return to sleep.

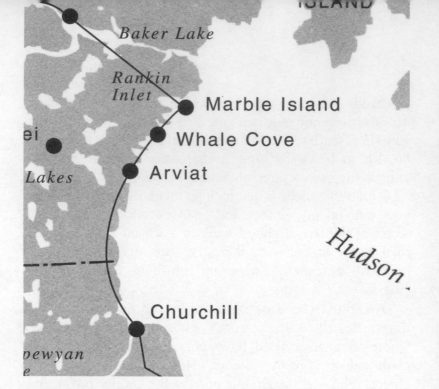

Baker Lake

Rankin
Inlet

Marble Island

Whale Cove

ei

Arviat

Lakes

Hudson

Churchill

pewyan
e

Chapter 3

Churchill to Marble Island, Nunavut

Life is like money.
You can spend it however you want,
But you can only spend it once.

—Anon

"Morning, Fred," I say into the phone. "If you haven't eaten already, I'm buying breakfast."

"Give me thirty minutes," says Fred.

Thirty minutes later, Fred calls back. "How about lunch instead?"

"That's fine," I reply. "Is eleven too early?"

"Nope," he says, "that's fine."

It's fine with me, too. I want to see the beluga movie at the Parks Canada's visitor center, shop at the Arctic Trading

Post and at Northern Images and visit the Eskimo Museum, where my deceased friend Br. John Volant once cared for a fine collection of Inuit artifacts, some of them centuries old. When I stop at Northern Images, I'm pleased to learn (by comparison) that the soapstone carvings I purchased in the sixties and seventies from subsequently famous carvers are almost worth their weight in gold—or maybe silver.

It's 11:00 on the dot when I take a seat in the Churchill Motel's restaurant. At 11:30 Fred arrives.

"Sorry about that," he says. "Got busy all of a sudden. I had to run the Missus out to the airport. She's off to Thompson to visit her mum."

"No problem, Fred."

"So," says Fred, "what's the word on the weather?"

"There's a high to the south. That's good because I'll have offshore winds as far north as Rankin Inlet, which means no fog, but they're forecasting headwinds from Rankin Inlet to Baker Lake. It seems like every time I head for Baker Lake, I'm fighting a northwest wind."

Fred, still in the mood for breakfast, orders coffee and cakes.

"I've got one more bear story for you," he says. "Well, actually it's more about people than bears. You probably know that cabin owners around here protect their entrances by laying planks with spikes driven through them "business-end-up" on their doorsteps. This works just fine, but occasionally the owner forgets about the plank and strolls out the door. That's just what happened a few years back to a guy who walked out of his door barefoot and ended up in the hospital. Got both feet, too!"

Fred adds a squirt of milk to his coffee and two heaping teaspoons of sugar, but doesn't stir it, which puzzles me.

"Why don't you stir it?"

"Oh, no," says Fred, as if I should know better. "If I stir it, I won't have dessert in the bottom of the cup."

When his pancakes arrive, he soaks them syrup, then sprinkles sugar on top. He smiles, and with a wink admits the obvious, "I really like sweets."

Later, with my gas bags bulging with fuel, we head for the seaplane base while Fred describes his prospects.

"I'm officially retired, you know, but I do a bit of this and that to keep from getting bored. After you leave, I'm going to ask Kelsey for a part-time job at the Northern Studies Center, and if that doesn't work, there's the new recycling plant. There's always something somewhere."

Fred waits while I load the Cub, dump the gas into the wings and pump out the floats. A handshake later, I taxi away from the pier, taking pains to avoid the subsurface boulders that keep seaplane pilots alert.

As the engine warms, I turn on my radio and press the push-to-talk button.

"Churchill radio, this is Piper 4855 Mike."

"Piper 4855 Mike, this is Churchill."

"55 Mike is ready for takeoff at Landing Lake. Please open my flight plan to Baker Lake."

"55 Mike, your plan is open. Wind is southwest at four knots. Pressure is 29.98. Call when you're off the water and when you leave the zone. Good day."

The Cub climbs away from Landing Lake, following the river north to Fort Prince of Wales. Built by the Hudson's Bay Company from 1731 to 1746, and armed with forty-two cannons, the fort was intended to protect the HBC fur trade, but it was never properly staffed.

The fort's first commander was Moses Norton, a man despised by all for his brutality and for leading a life that refuted the bible passages he routinely read to his "troops." Samuel Hearne[TN], his second in command, who had walked from the fort to the Arctic coast, thus proving that there was no inland passage to the Orient, condemned him roundly, writing in his journal, "He kept for his own use five or six of the finest Indian girls...He always kept a box of poison to administer to those who refused him their daughters or wives."

After Norton died, Hearne commanded the fort until three French warships anchored just beyond the reach of the fort's cannons in 1782. Hearne, caught with only thirty-nine men to defend a fort that required hundreds, wisely surrendered, and the fort was never staffed again.

In 1787, with Churchill's usefulness usurped by York Factory, Hearne returned to London, where he worked on his journals. As Peter Newman wrote in *Company of Adventurers,* "his magnificent Coppermine journey should have made him an international folk hero," but Hearne's only monument is one that he carved himself at Sloop's Cove near the fort that he once commanded. Chiseled into the granite in elegant script, it simply reads, "S Hearne July ye 2, 1767."

Far below, Sea North's launch suddenly arcs toward a polar bear and two cubs that are lolling in emerald green sea grass at the edge of Button Bay. When the launch is fifty feet from shore, it slows to a stop. Tourists crowd the bow rails, camcorders and cameras held high. At first, the bears ignore them, but then, as if saying "that's enough" the mother leads the cubs behind a huge boulder, out of sight of the boat. Just around the point where the occupants of the boat can't see it, another bear is sitting tourist-like in a broad stretch of marsh grass looking out to sea. When the Cub suddenly appears overhead, it flattens out like a traditional bear rug as if thinking, "If I get down low, I can't be seen."

Button Bay is eight miles across, and because I'm still climbing, I hug the shoreline. If my engine quits, I'll be able to glide to the shore instead of being carried out to sea by the offshore wind. Utility aircraft like the Tundra Cub II can glide about ten miles without power for every of mile of height. The albatross, the long-distance gliding champion of the animal world, does twice as well, but the best of the gliding breed are modern sailplanes that have glide ratios of sixty to one. That's an amazing sixty miles for every mile of height!

Thanks to aerial and satellite photography, my charts are extremely accurate, so when the visibility is good there's never a problem. As I scan the barren plain to the west, I wonder what it was like for men like Hearne who journeyed far from the Bay near the end of the eighteenth century, a time when charts of that region were blank except for four words: "These parts intirely *(sic)* unknown."

Hearne soon learned that those "parts" included the home of barren-ground caribou, animals whose numbers, according to the Inuit, were like the trees in the forests of the white man. But with the advent of the rifle, followed by snowmobiles and the Natives' reluctance to believe government statistics, the years of plenty passed. The Kaminuriak herd, for example, which once topped 100,000, had tumbled to 30,000 by the mid-1980s.

I'm leaving the Taiga, the "Land of Little Sticks," a wandering, hundred-mile-wide transition zone where the forest dwindles, where trees become bushes and bushes become shrubs. This broad transitional zone, the so-called "tree line," can be sixty miles wide if the elevation remains unchanged or as narrow as a mile if it abruptly rises or falls. Beginning in northern Alaska, the tree line wanders southeast across Canada toward Churchill, where it leaps Hudson Bay to undulate north and east through Quebec. The tree line, however, is more than a botanical division. For centuries, it was the dividing line between Inuit and Dene (Indian) cultures.

From here north, the names on my charts reveal their ethnic origins, abandoning English names for Angikuni, Tulemalu, Kaminuriak and Tebesjuak Lakes. Ahead lie the "barren" grounds where plants struggle in a colder climate, driven close to the ground by chilling winds in an attempt to retain whatever warmth they can. In gullies and in the shelter of rocky outcroppings that gather heat from the sun, willows might reach four or five feet, but those that attempt to grow beyond their shelter will be pruned by long and aggressive winters that use blowing snow for shears. And here, on these western shores of Hudson Bay, one unhappy scientist reported five million mosquitoes per acre.

Even so, this is the land that a Chipewyan Native envisioned when he asked a Catholic priest, "Tell me Father, is your Heaven like the land of the little trees when the ice has left the lake? Are the great musk oxen there? Are the hills covered with flowers? There will I see the caribou everywhere I look? Are the lakes blue with the sky of summer? Is every net full of great, fat fish? Is there room for me in this land, like our land, the Barrens? Can I camp anywhere and not find that someone else has camped? Can I feel the wind and be like the wind? Father, if your Heaven is not all these, leave me alone in my land, the land of the little sticks."

Dymond Lake falls behind, followed by the North Knife River, which brings memories of an event that a friend and I experienced while en route to Doug Webber's North Knife Lake Lodge.

We had departed Churchill in my Lake amphibian, and because it was too late to eat lunch at the lodge and our stomachs had begun to complain, we selected a lake with a nice-looking beach, landed and taxied toward shore. As I usually do, I shut off the engine to let the plane's momentum carry us to a gentle stop at the edge of the beach.

After unloading the camp stove and getting a pot of water boiling, I returned to the plane, and was shocked to see an inch of water rising over the floor boards.

"Bob," I yelled, "the plane is sinking. Help me push it into the lake so I can drop the landing gear."

After shoving it out, I climbed in, lowered the gear and taxied onto the beach, where we found a six-inch slit in the bottom of the hull. Wading into the lake, we discovered the culprit—a large rock buried in the sand except for a knifelike projection that had cut a slit in the hull.

We drained the water, ate a leisurely lunch and dried the hull, sealing the crack with a strip of duct tape that extended forward beyond the waterline so it wouldn't loosen during our take-off run. Then, being reluctant to make any nonessential water landings with a duct-taped hull, we headed south to a resort with a landing strip near Ilford, where we put a dent in the walleye population before heading home.

The next 150 miles of pancake-flat coastline contain few lakes that are deep enough for a safe emergency landing, so I climb to 4,500 feet until the *Tundra Cub II* reaches the braided channels of the Seal River. By flying higher and paralleling the coast a mile or two inland, I increase the number of useable lakes tenfold. Farther north, between Arviat and Rankin Inlet, my destination *du jour,* there are hundreds of suitable lakes, so I'll fly that leg much lower to assist my search for game.

The Cub and I are limited to the bottom half of the lowest layer of our atmosphere, the troposphere, the part that's so dear to humans. The Cub poops out near 14,000 feet, but the larger part that we humans can use just barely includes the top of Mt. Everest. Yes, one can live there without bottled oxygen, but not for very long. Even at lower altitudes we can be handicapped by "thinner" air, which is why my wife once became fascinated with her blue fingernails during a long flight over the Rocky Mountains at

13,500 feet and I had trouble doing a simple time/distance problem in my head. Recognizing the symptoms of hypoxia, I made a change of course and dropped to 9,500 feet, where we soon returned to normal.

The Seal River is favored by canoeists who prefer to begin in the forest, transit the taiga and enter the barrens without traveling so far north, but as many have learned, the odds of a polar bear encounter increase, the closer they get to the Bay.

In 1980, a pilot named Bill Clifford, while flying his chopper to Churchill one evening, spotted two airplanes parked on an airstrip near the Seal River and decided to call it a day. Knowing that the tiny cabin was already occupied, he crawled into one of the roomier planes to spend the night. A few hours later, he was awakened by a noise just in time to see a large polar bear smash the bubble of his helicopter with a single roundhouse swing. Turning toward Bill's airplane, it began to pound on the fuselage. The bear then climbed on top and looked in the window, but for some reason didn't smash it. While Bill quivered, the bear pounded away until the pilots heard the uproar and drove it off with shotguns.

The Caribou River, a paisley maze of blue, green and aquamarine channels confined within braided, butterscotch sand bars, blends into Hudson Bay, providing colorful relief to the monotonous plain below. I circle for a photograph - then another and another.

Thirty minutes later, the abandoned post of Nunalla (Egg Island) slips beneath my wings. Every spring, in this far corner of northern Manitoba, at one of the most water-saturated, heavily ponded places on earth, thousands of waterfowl meet to mate and hatch their eggs amidst a seemingly endless supply of small, shallow, oddly shaped lakes, most of them less than a quarter-mile long. This year, as always, the tundra is flecked white by hundreds of molting snow geese, and as the geese struggle to become airborne, I envision the Inuit of centuries past pursuing them across the tundra during the molt, the only time that geese could be caught.

In 1999, when a huge part of the Northwest Territories became the Native-run territory of Nunavut, many villages chose to return to Inuit names. Arviat, which means "bowhead whale" in Inuktitut, is one of those that adopted a Native name. As a consequence, the community that I knew for years as Eskimo Point has gone the way of Constantinople, which has reverted to Istanbul. Some Dene communities have followed suit: Great Slave Lake's appealing "Snowdrift" is now called Lut-selk'e, the place of small fish, but it will always be Snowdrift to me.

As the braided channels of the barely pronounceable Thlewiaza and Tha-anne Rivers weave their way into a sparkling Hudson Bay and the Cub hums its comforting-but-monotonous tune, my thoughts turn to the pioneers of aviation, one of the first being a sixteenth century Chinese scientist named Wan Ho, who strapped forty-seven rockets to the back of his chair and then touched them off, becoming the first test pilot to fly—and also the first to die. Skipping over those who followed, I arrive at William Piper, the man who became the Henry Ford of the aircraft industry. By the end of the thirties, he'd already built the safe and affordable J-2, and then the J-3, both of which, though safe enough, were slow and underpowered. Worse yet, the J-3 was nose heavy, so for solo flights the pilot was required to sit in the rear, something I learned the hard way when, just before my first solo cross country, my instructor said, "Hey, you're light—you can fly from the front seat." So I did.

I found the distant airport and made a perfect landing directly into the wind, but when I turned downwind to taxi back to pumps, up went the tail and down went the nose.

The wooden prop splintered, the engine shuddered to a stop and I found myself looking straight down at the ground. How embarrassing!

To correct the J-3's problems, Piper moved the fuel tank from the nose to the wing, reduced drag with a new engine cowling and added progressively larger engines for better performance. The result was the Piper Cub Special, the plane that I fly.

The *Tundra Cub II* is a primitive but very reliable airplane. It has no starter, generator or battery, which adds to my useful load. Its spartan panel bears a lonely quintet of instruments: an airspeed indicator, a tachometer and an altimeter—three instruments that experienced non-instrument pilots largely ignore because their eyes and ears supply approximations of the data those three provide. Add to these an oil pressure and temperature gauge that wise pilots monitor because the earliest signs of engine trouble are often revealed in lower than normal oil pressure and/or higher than normal engine temperatures.

The Cub also sports a venturi-powered gyro horizon. Were it up to me, I wouldn't have one, but it came with the plane, so there it stays, ready to help me get safely down through an overcast if I ever become so foolish as to fly "on top" without abundant breaks in the clouds.

The Cub's propeller is bolted to the end of the crankshaft, but many of the early aircraft engines were built in a very different way. During and prior to World War I, many aircraft flew with engines that had the crankshaft bolted to the airframe. Around that crankshaft spun a radial engine with a propeller attached to its case, the crankshaft having been hollowed out to deliver fuel and oil to the engine. This "rotary" engine was the first successful air-cooled engine, but it misted the pilot in oil, which explains why those who flew rotaries wore a scarf not for warmth or flair, but to keep their goggles clean. The spinning engine improved engine cooling during taxi and climbs, but its many disadvantages soon sent it the way of the Dodo bird.

Like the Wright's 1903 Flyer, the Cub also relies on a gasoline engine and a fabric skin sewn tightly to stick-like wings. Nevertheless, they look quite different because the Wrights put the propeller behind and the elevator in front, while the Cub does the opposite.

When the Wrights couldn't find a light engine capable of delivering 8 horsepower, they built their own with the help of a machinist friend. The result was a 202-cubic-inch, four-cylinder, water-cooled engine that produced 12 horsepower and weighed 170 pounds. In 1910, their 55-horsepower engine powered their Model R Flyer to a record 70 miles per hour. By the forties, aircraft engines like my Continental were producing 90 horsepower from the same size engine that powered the first Flyer. That additional power and the use of lightweight metals like aluminum (which initially cost $1,000 per pound and was selected by Napoleon III for tableware) now allow aircraft of similar size to carry three times the weight and fly ten times as fast as the Flyer.

The Flyer had no throttle, which meant that the engine ran full bore or not at all. It was light, with a wing loading of only two pounds per square foot. The Cub's wings carry six times that load, which sounds impressive, but the wings of military jets can carry more than 200 pounds per square foot.

The Wrights' success was born of the methods they used. They built a wind tunnel to gather data on lift and drag. Perhaps even more importantly, their study of propellers allowed them to realize that propellers were actually rotating wings that created "lift," which pulled the plane forward. After months of work and many revisions, the Wrights arrived at a propeller that was 66 percent efficient, a huge leap for their time, although modern props can top 90 percent. The Flyer was truly a triumph, but in 1962 a very different aircraft that took to the skies was every bit as unique: it was powered by muscles alone.

It had always been assumed that humans would never fly without help from a motor, but on May 2, 1962, John Wimpenny became the first human to power a heavier than air aircraft, which was fittingly named the *Puffin,* for a flight of 1,000 yards. The *Puffin*'s record was subsequently eclipsed by the *Gossamer Condor* and then the *Albatross,* which was flown (pedaled) across the English Channel in 1977 by an incredibly efficient motor named Bryan Allen. Eleven years later, another supremely fit aviator pedaled a similar aircraft seventy-two miles across the Aegean Sea. Named *Daedalus* for the mythical Athenian who flew too close to the sun, its sixty-one-foot wings were made not of feathers and wax, but of space-age materials.

Arviat (Eskimo Point) appears, and with it, a freighter anchored in water that looks much too shallow. Small boats are ferrying cargo from the freighter to the shore. As I circle, the last of them pulls away from the freighter as water foams at its stern and the ship gets under way. On shore, pallets loaded with canned goods, snowmobiles, four-wheelers and appliances speak of prosperity, but sixty years ago, events at Arviat brought to a close a long tale of deprivation, suffering, hardship and deaths—some by murder—that began 200 miles to the west of Arviat at a place called Ennadai Lake.

For centuries, Ennadai Lake had been the center of the Ihalmiut Inuit hunting grounds. Forty miles long, the lake connects the barren grounds to the tree-lined, southern shores of Kasba Lake, which sits on the Saskatchewan border. At Ennadai's northern end, the Kazan River carries its perpetually frigid waters north to Baker Lake and thence to Hudson Bay.

Like most northern tribes, the Ihalmiut's fortunes varied with whatever nature supplied. When caribou were plentiful, want was held at bay, but when the "deer" failed to appear, or were few and far between, want crept into their lives, bringing hunger and suffering and, all too often, death.

In 1948, a surprise awaited the Ihalmiut that would change their lives forever. Over the eastern horizon came eight Caterpillar tractors, each tractor towing sledges loaded with fifteen tons of construction material. When the ice finally left the lake, a Royal Air Force Canso (PBY) arrived and disgorged a ten-man construction crew that quickly began to build another response to the Cold War— a weather/surveillance station.

In the first years, the Ihalmiut and the army personnel got along quite well, each assisting the other as needed, but despite the army sharing it's limited reserves, starvation occasionally came to call, and in the spring of 1950, the RCMP ordered the Inuit evacuated to Nueltin Lake, which lies ninety miles to the southeast, where they were supposed to survive by working for a fishing company. (A company that was about to give up the ghost.) The Inuit fled, walking all the way back to Ennadai Lake. There the army continued to aid them as best they could. But in 1954, employees of the Department of Transport, who were less liberal with their limited resources, replaced the soldiers.

During the especially hard winter of 1956–7, seventy of the Ihalmiut's seventy-five dogs died for want of food, and by the time an RCMP Otter arrived in May to evacuate the remaining Natives to Henik Lakes, which, being 150 miles to the northeast, would discourage another return, the Natives were surviving on boiled shreds of caribou skin and scraps from the nearby station. At Henik Lake, they were expected to begin a more secure life, perhaps because they'd be closer to the RCMP and the "nearby" (forty-mile-distant) HBC post of Padlei, which was manned by Henry Voisey.

The "evacuation" proceeded quite forcefully and rapidly. Their camp was bulldozed. Five flights carried the fifty-seven survivors to Henik Lakes, but left behind for lack of room or to avoid making another flight, were their kayaks, canoes and tents. One Inuit was even prevented from going to a nearby cache to retrieve his rifle.

At Henik Lake, the Mounties deposited their passengers with their meager belongings and just three dogs. After giving the Natives a few days' supply of food and new tents, the RCMP left, later to conclude that Henik Lake had been a poor choice after all. And so, another move was planned the following spring, this time to a desolate place near Whale Cove called Term Point.

The Inuit began the winter with seven caribou and 1,400 pounds of store food—mostly flour—certainly not enough to carry forty-seven refugees through a long winter unless hunting and fishing were exceptionally good, which, as it turned out, they were not. By December, the dogs were gone or eaten. Starvation and death followed, then murder for scraps of food. The few who were still able staggered inland through bitterly cold days to reach Padlei, where a radio message brought the RCMP and a measure of relief.

One, a woman named Kikik whose tale is artfully told in Farley Mowat's *Walking on the Land,* had farther to travel, having fled from her camp with her children after knifing to death a man who had tried to shoot her. For seven cold, dark December days she plodded on, finally realizing on the sixth that none of them would reach Padlei alive unless she left the youngest two behind. After digging a hole in a drift to shelter the makeshift sled on which the children slept, she pulled a ragged canvas over them, then covered it with a few branches, and as her older children watched, covered the branches with snow.

The three of them made it to Padlei, where Kikik faced a new problem, for when she openly told what had happened, she was charged with murder and with abandoning her children, one of whom was found alive by the RCMP, still sleeping beneath the snow.

Kikik's children, including the snowdrift survivor name Elisapee, were taken from her. She was imprisoned for almost two months at Arviat to await trial. Worse yet, the fact that one of her "abandoned" children had survived was kept from her. When the trial finally began, she had no lawyer, and didn't understand the proceedings, but something good was about to happen, for the judge was a thoughtful man who understood the ways of the north. On hearing the evidence against Kikik, and of her candid support of the facts, Judge Jack Sissons as much as instructed the jury to vote for acquittal.

As Farley Mowat wrote in *Walking on the Land,* "Kikik's external ordeal ended at 9:00 on the evening of April 16. Under the glaring lights of an improvised courtroom, the judge glanced over his glasses at this woman whose face bore the fixed smile of one who does not comprehend what is happening. He spoke gently to her. 'You are not guilty, Kiki. Not guilty...do you understand?' Her expression did not change. She did not understand."

("To walk on the land" means to commit suicide by going out into the cold, a traditional Inuit custom for those who know that their time has come, and not wishing to be a burden on the community, choose death with dignity.)

In the 1990s, after Kikik had died, Elisapee returned to the site of the tragedy with a television camera crew, and there she told her tale.

Years later, when Mowat visited Henry Voisey, the

manager of the Padlei post, he found the aging manager reluctant to dwell on the tragedy, but he had no restraint about expressing his disdain for missionaries. When Mowat asked what the missionaries did to help during lean times, Voisey replied, "Praying, I guess."

That scorn was shared by photographer Richard Harrington, the author of *The Face of the Arctic,* who, during a stop at Padlei, encountered a missionary named Bernard Fredlund of the Northern Evangelical Mission. When Harrington became angered by the lack of aid and the suffering he'd seen, the missionary replied that, "the people were doubtless being punished for their sins."

And the move to Term Point? Although locals advised against it because of its lack of game and its shallow harbor, the government plunged on, not even telling the Ihalmiut where they'd be going until the time to leave arrived. At Term Point, the supply ship, unable to enter the harbor, began to barge supplies ashore, but before their work was finished, a gale arose and the supply ship left, never to return. In October, the Term Point project was abandoned. Many of the Ihalmiut were taken to Rankin Inlet. Some ended up at Whale Cove. Others went south to Arviat, where their long journeying at the behest of the distant white men finally came to a close.

The landscape begins to change as Arviat falls behind. A variety of large lakes, many of them miles long, nestle between rock-strewn hills, bringing relief from the monotony of the heavily ponded terrain between Churchill and Arviat. Deep inlets probe miles into the tundra. Striking, but stark and desolate, it was country like this that Judge Jack Sissons had in mind when he wrote, "In five days the Lord made the earth and all the creatures on it; then on the sixth day He made the Northwest Territories; that done, on the seventh He sat back and threw rocks at it."

Unlike the monotonous coast farther south, where islands are rare, a sudden profusion of islands leads to and beyond Whale Cove, a small town of 300 that straddles a narrow neck of land between Hudson Bay and a lake that's large enough to land on. I'm tempted to stop, but at this time of year many of the "Covers" will be out on the tundra, fishing and hunting. Most of the rest will be "harvesting" arctic char and beluga whales, the latter by being trapped and drowned in nets—250 in one year here and at Rankin Inlet—and I don't want to get involved in that.

Baleen from bowhead, gray, right whales and the other nontoothed whales was still in demand in the early twentieth century, largely for corset stays and similar uses because plastics had not yet arrived. In Hudson Bay and much of the Arctic, the favorite victim was the bowhead or "right" whale, a large, slow animal with long baleen plates and huge amounts of blubber used for oil. Better yet, it floated when killed, which made it the "right whale" to pursue.

Whales are powerful animals. In *Arctic Dreams,* Barry Lopez tells of a bowhead whale that took out two miles (7,000 pounds) of line, pulling the entangled whaleboat down with it. On another occasion, "thirty hours after it had been harpooned, another Greenland right whale was still towing a fully rigged ship at two knots into a moderate brisk breeze."

Imagine the strength of the great blue whale, the largest creature on the planet. According to David Attenborough, its "tongue weighs as much as an elephant, its heart is the size of a car and some of its blood vessels are so wide that you could swim down them." Compared to right whales, blue whales are giants. No early whaler could have taken a blue without the use of explosives.

We humans clear only 15 percent of our lungs with each

breath, but whales can change 90 percent. Combined with muscles rich in oxygen-storing myoglobin, this immense air exchange allows whales to "hold their breath" for incredibly long intervals. The fin-back whale, one of the right whales' more massive relatives, can dive one-third of a mile and remain submerged for forty minutes, but sperm whales like Melville's Moby descend even deeper.

By 1950, whaling has decimated much of the oceans. From Antarctica's waters alone, more than 150,000 whales have been taken. Bays once packed with many species are now empty. During a thousand-mile voyage to and along Antarctica, Peter Matthiesen, the author of *The End of the World,* saw only one whale spout.

Today, whale hunting is widely outlawed, two exceptions being Japan and Norway, which continue to hunt whales despite international pressure, but sometimes we find the reverse. In February 1985, the Russians (the first country to ban polar bear hunting) sent the icebreaker *Moskva* through pack ice to reach a pod of 100 belugas that had become trapped in a "saugssat," a small opening in the ice twelve miles from the open sea. All attempts to herd the whales through the channel failed until someone attached loudspeakers to the *Moskva*'s stern. Blaring classical music, the *Moskva* became the Pied Piper of the Bering Sea and led the belugas to safety.

During the pre-petroleum era, costs mattered little as long as they got the whale. With blubber twenty inches thick, a mature whale might yield twenty-five tons of oil. Add a ton of valuable whalebone, and it's easy to see why the attitude of "damn the cost but get the whale" not only prevailed, but spilled onto the mainland as well. There, it was a common practice to supply Natives with a rifle and 500 rounds of ammunition for one-fourth of the usual price—as long as they brought in the furs. And bring them in, they did.

Imagine what a rifle meant to those accustomed to

arrows and spears. Imagine owning a durable copper kettle instead of a birch-bark pot or a steel ax instead of an angular stone or, if you were lucky, a much softer copper knife. Now imagine gaining access to cloth, gunpowder, metal fishhooks, brandy—and several conflicting religions.

The opening up of the North, like the space program, provided many useful spin-offs, one being frozen food. Attempts to preserve food by freezing had worked well enough even in the late 1800s, but the result when thawed was mushy because slow freezing produces large ice crystals that damage the food's cell walls. The remedy was found by a bright young man who, while working in northern Canada in 1912, realized that fish and caribou frozen in the dead of winter had a better texture and flavor when cooked than those that were frozen in the fall. Over the next twelve years Clarence Birdseye discovered that flash-freezing food eliminated the large crystals. His insight made him wealthy, but he always denied inventing quick-freezing because, as he noted, the Inuit had done it for years.

Gravel roads radiate out from Whale Cove like the legs of a giant spider. Picking one that heads northeast, I leave the town behind and head for Pistol Bay. By the time I reach the Pork Peninsula, which is 90 percent lake and 10 percent land, I've decided to pass up Rankin Inlet. It would be nice to visit Joe Tartak again, but I've never been to Marble Island. Instead, I'll camp with James Knight, the man who served the HBC so well, but lost his life on a fruitless search for a Northwest Passage.

Laying a ruler on my map, I draw a new course line to Cape Jones, the eastern tip of the Pangertof Peninsula.

When the mainland falls behind, I drop lower to search for walrus and killer whales amidst the Mirage Islands, then head for Crane Island, the last bit of stone before the sixteen-mile leap to Marble Island.

The odds of seeing walrus in this region are poor, perhaps because hunters so easily reach the islands, but they're common far to the south in the remote Belcher Islands and among the islands at the top of the Bay. I slow the Cub to 70 mph, open the windows for better seeing and weave from shoreline to shoreline, searching for my first walrus, and for killer whales like those that I once encountered almost too closely in Alaska's Lynn Canal.[TN]

I have plenty of fuel, so I search the archipelago for twenty minutes, but come up empty, which isn't surprising. By 1887, the last year that commercial whalers overwintered in these islands, the number of whales had drastically declined, and by 1905, whaling in Hudson Bay had come to an end. I am, however, surprised at the lack of polar bears, which should be common along this coast. Trying to think like a polar bear, I come up with a possible answer. Why stay here on these barren islets, when my nose senses an abundance of grasses, sedges and berries just a few miles to the west?

As Marble Island looms large, it occurs to me that Knight's death was the culmination of a series of events that began in 1572 when Captain Martin Frobisher made the first of three voyages to the Hudson Bay straits to search for a Northwest Passage—and on one occasion was urged to leave by an Inuit arrow in his backside. Frobisher (the Persistent) returned to England each time with an ever-larger cargo of "gold" ore. The knowledgeable argued that Frobisher's ore contained the "gold of fools," a mix of mica and various pyrites, giving birth to the naysayer's warning about things that glisten and shine—"All that glistereth is not gold." They were right.

Nevertheless, the search for the Passage continued: Henry Hudson entered the Bay in 1610, there to survive a harrowing winter only to be set adrift with his son the following spring by desperate mutineers. They died. The mutineers made it back to England, where they somehow avoided death by hanging. Thomas Button (of Button Bay) followed in 1612, and was succeeded by Jens Munk's almost totally fatal expedition of 1619.

In 1631, Luke Foxe reported sighting an island made "all of white marble" on the western side of the Bay. Once ashore, Foxe discovered "many Ponds therein, and a great store of Fowle, especially water-fowle." Spotting a "tall Fowle" (probably a sand hill crane) he thought it was an ostrich. When the ship's dog pursued a caribou, one of the men who followed the chase claimed that "the Deer shed teares." But after the Foxe visit, close to a century would pass before a new Passage seeker would land on Marble Island in the person of Captain James Knight.

Marble Island is a desolate, eight-mile-long blister of quartzite, which looks like marble when viewed from a distance. Samuel Hearne, who would eventually walk from Churchill to the Arctic coast and back in three life-threatening tries, was accustomed to the Bay's bleak western shore, but he ranked Marble Island among the worst. "Neither stick nor stump was to be seen here.... Indeed, the mainland is little better, being a jumble of barren hills and rocks."

Gretel Ehrlich could have been describing Marble Island when she wrote, "Ice scrapes the earth as if it had claws. Look closely, this is all that is left of the world's body after ice has picked its bones clean."

With Thanadelthur dead and the post at Churchill established, James Knight, then seventy-seven years old, hoped to cap his career by finding the Northwest Passage; so he hurried back to London to raise support for the expedition, which he easily accomplished, setting sail for the Bay in 1719 in two ships, the frigate *Albany* and the sloop *Discovery*. His orders—search the northwest coast of Hudson Bay for the Passage and locate the source of the gold and copper said to exist to the west of the Bay.

Buried within those orders lay an odd restriction designed to prevent Knight, except in extreme emergency, from landing at any company facility south of the 64th parallel—a restriction that included the nearest source of refuge—the outpost at Churchill. Thus began another tragedy in which British lives were lost not because of the task they'd undertaken, but because of poor planning and being saddled with unreasonable requirements by inexperienced HBC committeemen.

In 1767, Samuel Hearne, the Marco Polo of the Barren Lands who was destined to command Fort Prince of Wales, found wreckage from both ships five fathoms deep in a cove on the island's southeastern shore. He also discovered an anvil, muskets, two skulls, side by side, and the remains of a crude 45 x 30-foot house that had been dug into a rare spot of topsoil. Natives told Hearne that the ships had been wrecked by a storm, that fifty had survived the shipwreck, but thirty had died during the first winter. They also reported that the following summer, the crew repaired their longboat, but for some reason, no one tried to reach the nearby mainland or attempted to sail south to Churchill. By the end of the second year only five survivors remained.

The Inuit supplied the five with raw meat and seal blubber but, despite their assistance, three more died. The last two, for "Many days...went to the tip of a rock and earnestly looked to the south and east, as if in the expectation of some vessels coming to their relief. After continuing there a considerable time together, and nothing appearing, they sat down close together and wept bitterly At length, one of the two died, and the other's strength was so far exhausted that he fell down and died also while attempting to dig a grave for his companion."

Hearne also found a large mound of coal and many graves, but when he opened them in search of records he found only "the bons of a Stout man who without a doubt was one of the unhappey Sufferars and ye skulls & bones of Different humane Bodies."

Knight's failure to seek help on the mainland is hard to understand, as is his failure to attempt to reach Churchill—just a four-day sail to the south. And why, I wonder, didn't the HBC try to find Knight and his men, instead being content to merely write off the loss of two ships and forty men as "being castaway to the northward in Hudson Bay..."

Marble Island actually consists of two major islands plus several islets that line up like an arrow aimed southeast toward the center of Hudson Bay. Separated from Marble Island proper by a passage so narrow that I don't see it until I'm almost overhead, is two-mile-long Quartzite Island, the actual site of the Knight tragedy.

Flying low, I skirt the western end of Marble Island, then circle Whaler's Harbor and nearby Deadman's Island, which is littered with eighteenth and nineteenth century graves, more than half of which were caused by the wreck of the whaler *Orray Taft* and the killing winter of 1873. That year, fall storms wrecked one whaling ship and split another in half, leading to lost provisions, overcrowding and exposure to cold. Scurvy killed fifteen harpooners, but the others sealed their fate by refusing to eat foxes—the most prevalent source of meat. Not realizing that scurvy is caused by a shortage of vitamin C, the shipwrecked sailors blamed the water, the air and even the smoldering fires for their bleeding gums, their loosening teeth, their open sores and their deaths. The British navy, on finally learning the true cause, fed their men limes, which is why British sailors came to be called limeys.

Hearne was right. The islands below bear not even one struggling tree, and even the brush looks stunted. Stark and forbidding in appearance, the linear islands remind me of the dirty-white mounds of melting March snow that rim northern parking lots.

The Inuit believed that the islands arose in a single night from deep within the Bay, and that they were once composed of ice that had turned to stone, leaving behind a bottomless sea. Oddly enough, science supports the thrust of their story, for all of the islands, in fact all of the North, once relieved of its immense load of glacial ice—has been rising about one yard per century.

I'd like to camp here tonight, but if I spot a bear, I'll head for Rankin Inlet. I scour the islands for twenty-five minutes, rolling from side-to-side, criss-crossing humps of polished stone and rubble fields of bone-white debris at a height of 100 feet, finding basking seals and shore birds aplenty, but not a single bear. Hooray!

Before I land, I try to radio Rankin Inlet about my change of plans but get no response. Thirty miles at this low altitude is probably too much for my portable radio. I've deviated from my flight plan, which I'd filed for three days in case of weather delays, so I'm extra careful when I set up to land. Were I to have an accident, it would be a long time before anyone would look for me here.

Throttling back, I ease down, nose high with partial power until the floats begin to chatter as they plane across the tips of the Bay's six-inch waves, then nose the Cub into the shallow passage between the islands, sending molting snow geese staggering skyward from the deeper harbor.

Knight's flagship, the *Albany,* was located somewhere beneath my floats by a group of scuba divers in 1979. Split in two, with its superstructure gone, the vessel was so obscured by clouds of silt that the diver didn't see it until he was close enough to touch it. Nevertheless, I taxi back and forth, peering down between the floats while thinking that with luck, good lighting and calm water, I might spot it. The water is placid and the lighting is great, but all I can see is my own reflection peering back up at the Cub.

A dark patch of earth to the east of the harbor marks the site of the Knight disaster, so I rudder the Cub that way and flip the magnetos to "off." As the engine dies, the invisibly spinning propeller reappears as if by magic, then stops, its roaring replaced by the peeping of white-rumped sandpipers scurrying along the coarse gravel beach.

Seized by the scent of the sea, I inhale deeply. I wonder—is my reaction just a natural response to a rare experience for an inland dweller like me? Is it inherited from my ocean-going, Norwegian ancestors or is it deeper still, rooted in the fact that life evolved from the sea? As Loren Eiseley wrote in *The Unexpected Universe,* "The salt of the ancient seas is in our blood, its lime in our bones. Every time we walk along a beach some ancient urge disturbs us so that we find ourselves shedding shoes and garments, or scavenging among whitened timbers like the homesick refugees of a long war."

I drag the Cub tail first onto the beach and secure the wings and tail to three large stones. If the wind becomes oppressive, I'll pile rocks on top of the floats. I've read that Inuit tradition requires first-time visitors to crawl across the beach on their knees and elbows, but when I envision the Rankin Inlet guides smiling at the gullible tourists, I decline. Respecting the memory of those who died is one thing, but crawling crosses the line.

The site of Knight's last refuge lies in a broad depression between a pair of glacier-polished, white-to-lilac quartzite ridges, their pallor reduced by granite inclusions and an occasional ribbon of malachite. A broad patch of dark sod marks the spot where Knight's "house" once stood, and as I climb the gentle, hundred-foot slope from harbor to sod, I imagine fifty worried, desperate men confined within such a structure during ice-bound winters that began in early September and lasted into May—winters that whittled them down from fifty to twenty in one year, then down to five in the next.

On the chance that the archeologists who excavated the site in the early nineties might have missed something, I get down on my knees (perhaps that will satisfy the tradition) and begin to examine the tundra, but unlike the more rewarding search I conducted years ago at Fr. Joseph Buliard's abandoned arctic mission[TN], my probing yields nothing, not even a hint of the ships' oak timbers from which the building was made, not even one square nail.

When it becomes apparent that I won't find any relics, I fetch my camp stove, select a package of freeze-dried beef stroganoff and start a kettle boiling. Thirty minutes later, having feasted on stroganoff, bread slathered with peanut butter, dried apricots and a few cookies, I set off to find the basking seals that I spotted from the air near the north entrance to the harbor.

As I start out, it occurs to me that the polar bears I searched for wouldn't have been very obvious on a bleached stone island, so I detour to the Cub to get my Nikon (say "cheese," bear) and my big, macho hunting knife, which was manufactured by the Pal razor blade company for WW II soldiers. The knife would be useless against a determined bear, and I've no desire to mimic Hugh Glass, the frontiersman they called Lord Grizzly who barely survived going *mano a mano* with a grizzly, but the heft of the knife on my hip feels comforting, if nothing else.

A flurry of eider ducks banks overhead. Looping like jet fighters they reverse direction, descending to land in the harbor close to the Cub. As I watch their orderly procession, I remember a tale in Peter Freuchen's *Book of the Eskimo*. According to Freuchen, every spring the Greenland Inuit collected eggs from the cliffs on which eider ducks and other waterfowl nested. Many eggs were eaten immediately, some cooked, some raw, but most were stored for the winter in lengths of seal gut by making a sort of egg sausage. To accomplish this, women carefully cracked the eggs so they could suck out the white of the egg, leaving the yolk behind. After spitting out the white, they sucked out the yolk unbroken, which they then spat into a length of seal gut that might hold 100 eggs. The "sausage," tied shut at both ends, was then hung in a shady place to dry, after which it is sliced into pieces like candy or stored against the permafrost to preserve it through the warm days of summer for later use as a midwinter treat.

Bird traffic to and from the nest sites was often so dense that the Inuit could pluck birds right out of the air with long-handled nets. Once a dovekie, for example, was caught, they squeezed the bird's heart to stop it from beating. After bending their wings back to braid them together, the birds were stuffed into a giviak, a sealskin bag that had been prepared by removing the heart, lungs, kidneys and digestive tract through its mouth, leaving behind a blubber-lined bag that they stored in a cool place to prevent the blubber from turning rancid. Because the contents of giviaks were considered a great delicacy, they were opened only for special occasions.

The diminutive dovekies, which lay larger than normal eggs, were believed to have magical powers. It was therefore common for a newborn girl to have a dovekie foot tied around her neck so that when she matured she would deliver large, strong children.

When I stoop to pluck an arctic daisy from a patch of lyme grass, I expect a few mosquitoes to meet my hand, but none appear, perhaps because the island is mostly rock, with few ponds to serve as mosquito nurseries. The sky is blue, the air is warm, the breeze is light, and I'm alone on an historic island with very few bugs. How lucky can I be?

I carefully pick my way across the rock-strewn tundra, trying to stay on ledges when I can and carefully stepping between basketball- to softball-size boulders when I can't. Compared to Quartzite Island, Australia's rock-littered Gibber Plains are just broad billiard tables strewn with grains of sand. Step wrong here and there goes an ankle!

In the distance several dogs are barking, but given my aerial search, that seems unlikely. Then I remember Henry Ford, the half Inuit, half white, Baker Lake patriarch who told me years ago that harbor seals can bark like dogs and grunt like polar bears, so perhaps they're the seals I spotted near the harbor's entrance. As I walk, the barking gets louder. When I peer over the top of the last rise, I spot a dozen seals hauled out on ledges at the edge of the harbor. I lie flat on the sloping stone, carefully cradle my rifle/camera and pull the trigger/shutter. One click and the seal is mine, all five feet and 200 pounds of him—or her—trapped on the film in my camera.

Arctic explorer Vilhjalmur Stefansson told of Inuit hunters who mimicked seals in order to get close enough to make a kill. Lying on the ice and keeping their legs together while raising their heads periodically as if to look for bears before collapsing to appear to take a nap, they'd move a bit closer to the cautious seal every time it lowered its head. Well, I say to myself, if it worked for the Inuit, perhaps it will work for me.

Ducking down behind a rise, I head for the shore, then slowly wriggle into the sight of the fifty-yard-distant seals and become a seal incarnate, raising my head to watch for bears, alternately napping, and waddling clumsily ahead with my hands on my chest by using my flipper/elbows. The barking continues, but when I've gained a mere five yards, silence returns. All heads are turned my way, so I lie motionless for what seems forever while the rocks beneath me grow teeth. Still, I lie there. The barking resumes. I gain another two yards, then take another photo. No problem. Then, just as I begin my next advance, my nose begins to itch. Rolling my back to the seals, I rub it. Not good. The tickle worsens. I rub harder, but the sneeze erupts despite my efforts to stifle it, causing a chorus of barks as the seals splash into the harbor. The last picture I take is of a dozen or so curious seal heads protruding from the water, all of them aimed at me.

By the time I return to the Cub and pitch my tent, the tide (that Pytheas first ascribed to the moon in 300 BCE) has ebbed, so I decide to wade across to Marble Island, but as I step into the frigid water, it occurs to me that if the wind comes up and begins to drive breakers through the entrance or the tide reverses, I'd be isolated from my shelter. Worse yet, the rocks are slippery, so I turn back, fire up the Cub and taxi to Marble Island.

Marble Island is a clone of Quartzite Island, but there's a lot more of it. My chart says that the top of three-mile-distant Mount Pitt is only 315 feet above sea level, so it's a gentle uphill climb for most of the way.

As I carefully pace the rocky terrain, I begin to consider the tides. It makes sense that friction from the tides against the ocean bed and shores would gradually slow the earth's rotation, which it does by about 1/1,000th of a second per century. However, I have trouble understanding why the moon has moved farther away as the spin of the earth has slowed. Why should the moon care if the earth spins a little or none at all? The mass of the earth determines its gravitational pull, not its rotation, so it's a mystery to me. I'll hit the books when I get home.

Perhaps I love the unobstructed views of the barrens

because I live in forested country. Here, wherever I look, my eyes reach a distant horizon. To the east and south, an undulating, stony plain trends gently down to a glittering Hudson Bay. To the west and north, the deeply indented coast of mainland Canada is a barely visible strip of stony gray some twenty miles away. As I scan the horizon, I understand why Peter Freuchen claimed that those who have been to the Arctic always long to go back.

In *The Arctic Year,* Freuchen wrote, "The unrest never leaves them…. They have been caught by the arctic [where] all that is superfluous and unnecessary have been eliminated. There are no trees, no houses, no noise; often there are no other human beings than you for scores of miles. You are alone in the world, alone with your thoughts. You feel an undeniable sense of harmony as you stand listening to the beat of nature's heart…and your mind experiences a touch of eternity."

I stroll steadily upward. As I near the crest of Mount Pitt, a white flash suddenly catches my eye. It's too big for a tern or a gull. I think it's my first snowy owl. Taking a page from Vilhjalmur Stefansson, who, when hunting, could take as much as an hour to examine his surroundings with binoculars, I sit down, lean against a boulder and fix my eyes on the spot where the flash disappeared. A minute later, up pops a snowy owl, which quickly flies away. I top the rise, and there on top of a small mound rimmed with feathery cotton grass and hairy-stemmed crocus, is a scraped-earth nest with three chicks and one unhatched egg within it.

I walk off to the side about fifty yards to avoid disturbing the owl, find another boulder to lean on and wait. Minutes later, the owl returns. A ground squirrel, a lemming or perhaps a baby marmot dangles from its talons. She turns and looks directly at me, then looks away. Even at this distance, I'm aware of her great yellow eyes. The gray owl, the great horned owl and Richardson's owl have yellow eyes, but now I wonder—are all owls' eyes yellow?

While I speculate, Farley Mowat's thoughts on the snowy owl come to mind:

"The snowy owl, I've heard it said,
Lives on the entrails of the dead.
It loves to gorge on rotting bowel,
Which spoils it as a table fowl."

Thinking back, I count the number of times that owls have entered my life, the first being when a shriek owl emitted a loud and terrible scream very close to me as I strolled through our Pine Island forest. Being just eight at the time, I tore back to our cabin, fearing that a wildcat was about to attack me.

One harsh winter, a barred owl perched near our living room window for day after day, seemingly oblivious to the activity inside. On another occasion, when my wife and I walked out of a South Dakota restaurant, we were greeted by a tiny, saw whet owl no bigger than my fist. Though patrons stopped to stare and chatter, the owl remained perched on his fence post, totally unconcerned. Finally, there's the great gray owl that raced my snowmobile.

While driving across Lake Vermilion on an ancient Skidoo that could barely top twenty miles per hour, I spotted an owl coming my way from off to the side and behind. Altering its course to parallel mine, the owl easily caught up to me and then slowed to match my pace, flying alongside a few feet above the snow. Then, as if bored with a race it had so easily won, it resumed its original course.

By the time I get back to the harbor, the lichen-mottled shelf leading to my tent is glowing orange in the setting sun; and after securing the Cub I'm soon enjoying a bowl of hot onion soup with crackers, sardines and coffee. I'd like to build a fire, but with twigs as the only fuel, it isn't worth the bother.

My six-mile hike will probably make me stiff in the morning, so I toss down my universal remedy—two aspirin—crawl into my tent and, accompanied by the distant barking of the harbor seals, climb into my wooden shoe and sail away with Winkin', Blinkin' and Nod.

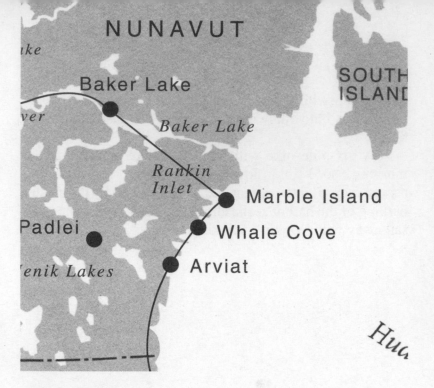

NUNAVUT

Baker Lake

ke

Baker Lake

ver

Rankin
Inlet

Marble Island

Padlei

Whale Cove

'enik Lakes

Arviat

Hua

SOUTH
ISLAND

Chapter 4

Marble Island to Baker Lake, Nunavut

The North gets farther north each year.

—ANON

A strange sound awakens me. I tell myself that it's just the seals barking, only louder. But it's more than louder; it's different. As I analyze the sound, I remember Henry Ford saying that seals can grunt like bears. That's comforting, but because I left my rifle at home, I'm not in the mood to think about bears when I'm alone in a fragile tent. The barking continues, and the longer they huff and bark and growl, the less certain I become that the barkers are seals instead of hungry polar bears.

I fumble for my flashlight to check the time. It's 1:45 a.m., the center of the short span of darkness that these latitudes get in mid-July. I quietly unzip the tent flap and aim my flashlight toward the Cub, only to have the beam swallowed by dense fog. No wonder it's so dark! The fog drifts slowly past, its billows absorbing my feeble light, sweeping it aside.

It suddenly occurs to me that one of Canada's 16,000 polar bears might notice the light and decide to investigate, so I shut it off and tell myself not to do anything else so dumb. I try to avoid thinking about polar bears, but think of nothing else, because, as it happens, I'm loaded with information about Nanook, the Lord of the Arctic, Mr. *Ursus Maritimus,* the peripatetic polar bear.

As I listen to the ruckus, I envision the average Nanook. If a male, it will weigh 1,000 pounds and stand from four to five feet high at the shoulder. The largest of its kin on record, an Alaskan bear that weighed 2,210 pounds, stands eleven feet tall, on its hind legs, in the lobby of the Anchorage airport.

They're powerful, too. One evening, Bennett Spence, a Churchill Chipewyan who had been helping his brother capture live belugas for a zoo, decided to return to the wharf to check on two belugas in a holding tank. When he was about 100 feet from the tank, a small polar bear suddenly heaved a 700-pound whale over the enclosure's four-foot wall and carried it off, "as if it were no bigger than a sardine."

Polar bears were prized at royal courts. When Norway's King Harold was given polar bear cubs for mascots, he rewarded the lucky hunter with an ocean-going ship filled with wood. Romans kept polar bears in flooded amphitheaters to which they added (short-lived) seals, and in 1858 two polar bears were presented to the Emperor of Japan as part of the spoils of war.

A polar bear's body temperature is close to ours, but its insulating fur (plus a layer of back fat up to four inches thick) can make heat retention a much larger problem than heat loss, which might explain the bears' hunting tactics of "stroll, watch and wait." In addition, each hollow hair acts as a light pipe, funneling ultraviolet light to the bear's black skin. Up to a foot long and nine inches wide, the bears' paws, plus their legs and snout, are their radiators, built with a variable blood supply that allows them to dissipate or conserve heat. To their surprise, airborne researchers with infrared sensors found the bears almost impossible to detect from above, though they could easily spot their tracks, which had been warmed by heat from their paws. Thus equipped, even in an ice-filled ocean, a polar bear is as comfortable as Br'er Rabbit in his briar patch.

When the Bay freezes, pregnant females remain ashore, digging dens in drifted snow that collects downwind from hummocks and ridges. They'll need the fat they've accumulated, for they'll lose as much as half of their body weight between August and April. Cubs, usually two, but occasionally one or three, are born in late December or early January. Weighing little more than a pound at birth, the cubs cannot hear for three weeks, and another week passes before they can see. By their sixth week, they're walking, and when mother breaks out of the den in late March or early April, the cubs are ready to roll.

Not all pregnant females excavate dens. Peter Freuchen wrote in *The Artic Year* that pregnant bears often "walked about until they found a place on the lee side of some projection where experience told them that snow would accumulate and pile up on top of them. There, they laid down, curled up and buried their nose in their paws."

For some unknown reason, Churchill bears can be surprisingly docile during the summer. Those who find this hard to believe should view the National Geographic video of a polar bear lying beside a very nervous, chained sled dog that could easily become the bear's lunch. The bear casually rises, drapes a great foreleg around the worried dog as if they were the best of friends and then ambles away.

One Finnish biologist became so attuned to the bears that he could feed them blubber by hand. He even accompanied them on seal hunts, learning that a single bear could consume eighty pounds of blubber at a sitting.

In 1978, after a young Japanese adventurer named Naomi Uemura (who would later die on Denali) finally reached the pole, a bear came to visit. The bear first ate all the dog food while the dogs slept, then sniffed at Uemura as he lay quaking in his tent—and walked away. Uemura was lucky. Even though polar bears are reputed to be "calmer" than grizzlies, they mustn't be taken lightly.

In 1973 a bear killed a tractor operator on the shore of the Beaufort Sea. At Churchill, bears mauled people in '66 and '67, killed a child in '68 and a man in '83. More than eighty bears had to be shot in the Canadian Arctic between 1978 and 1981, and during the 1980s, an average of two bears per year were shot at Churchill alone. Nuisance bears, however, are tranquilized with a dart gun, slung beneath a helicopter and flown far away from town.

One winter, two young men working on an oil-drilling barge north of the Mackenzie River decided to meet at the mess hall for coffee. When only one arrived, his companion and seventy co-workers started a search that revealed scratch marks on the door of the sewage plant where the missing man had worked. Guided by the meager light of the northern winter, they came upon the man's head lying on the ice near the barge. Near it stood an eight-foot polar bear shaking a raglike body. The workers shot it.

Mother bears will fight males twice their size to the death to protect their cubs. If a cub dies, the mother will often remain at its side for days. William Scoresby tells of nineteenth-century sailors who chased a mother and her two cubs across the pack ice. Seeing that her pursuers were gaining, the mother bear held back, first pushing her cubs ahead and them tossing them forward until they escaped.

In *Arctic Dreams,* Barry Lopez told a gruesome tale of hunters who set fire to a pile of blubber to attract bears. In time, a female and two cubs caught the scent and drew near. At first, the female tried to hook pieces of blubber from the fire, but then the men began to throw her pieces of blubber, which she took to her cubs. When she brought the cubs the last piece of blubber, the men shot the cubs. "For the next half hour she laid her paws first upon one and then the other, and endeavored to raise them up. She walked off and called to them. She licked their wounds. She went off again and stood for some time moaning before returning to paw them with signs of inexpressible fondness. Bored, or perhaps mortified, the men shot the female and left her on the ice with her cubs." What slobbering, vicious morons! Where are lightning strikes when we need them?

A new sound intrudes—the hiss of light rain falling onto my tent. A few minutes later, a tiny leak appears despite the rain fly, but it's just above the entrance, which I placed downhill for just this reason. Oh well, at least I don't have to worry about forest fires! The mist turns to rain; the rain drowns out the seals, and I finally return to sleep.

At 9:00 a.m. it's still too foggy to fly, but patches of sunlight are beginning to brighten the sky. As I wash down a Churchill bakery caramel roll with a can of Mountain Dew, pinpoints of light begin to bejewel my tent. When I step outside, I discover that the "jewels" are tiny dewdrops, each one focusing a beam of sunlight into the little "hot spots" that had brightened my tent. I collapse the tent and pack my gear. When I tote my gear to the Cub, I notice that the tide is going out, and the water is already two yards from the Cub.

I quickly fill two of my five-gallon jugs with water and

suspend them from the tie-down ring at the outer end of my right wing strut, then walk around to the left wing and heave up and forward on the struts in an attempt to slide the left float toward the water. It doesn't move. I add another full five-gallon jug to the right wing, and this time, with 150 pounds pulling down on the right wing, the left float inches toward the water when I lift and push on the struts.

While ruddy turnstones patrol the water's edge, flipping stone after stone in an endless search for food, I reverse the process, attaching the jugs to the left tie down and heave up on the right wing struts, slowly inching the Cub ahead with my fitness regime *du jour*. Thirty minutes later, after repeating the cycle again and again to catch the receding tide, the Cub is afloat, and I'm sweating in the humid, fifty degree air. It suddenly occurs to me that as I huffed my load from wing to wing and heaved on the struts, a bear could easily have strolled and tapped me on the shoulder, or worse, before I'd have known it was there.

The Cub's engine warms as I taxi to the north end of the harbor. I switch on my headset, raise the water rudder, push the stick to the left to counter the gentle crosswind and pour on the power. The Cub rises nose high, climbing up onto the steps built into her floats, accelerating faster and faster, then lifts into the air. She's a noisy magic carpet, but the noise is a small price to pay for the wonder that waits in her wings.

I follow the south shore of Marble Island, finding more seals and shore birds, but no bears. Turning west, I climb to 4,500 feet. In velvety air, the Cub seeks Rankin Inlet, which owes its existence to a deposit of nickel ore that we use to harden and "rust-proof" steel, and yes, make nickels.

Nickel was discovered at Rankin Inlet during the twenties, but it wasn't mined until 1955. Today, the harbor is empty, but from 1955 to 1962, the year that the mine closed, ships regularly arrived at Rankin, some for routine commerce and some to transport the ore from the Rankin Inlet mine.

Believing that the Inuit would be unable to properly mine the ore, management at first imported professional miners—who quickly came to dislike Rankin's weather, bugs and remoteness. However, productivity soared when a new mine manager named Andy Easton began to hire Inuit workers to replace the "pros."

When Farley Mowat asked mine captain Paul Proux how he liked working with the Inuit, Proux replied, "Those guys, they are good miners as I ever see. They take big pride in what they do. Now, I think they make better miner out of me."

Mowat, who always sought the Natives' perspectives, also consulted Shinituk, a Rankin Inlet resident of sixty who'd seen it all. "One time," said Shinituk, "lots of seals, plenty deer [caribou]. Then white man come and pretty soon get too many killed. Then everybody get goddamn hungry. People die. Kids die. Maybe police give bags of flour full of bugs. Maybe missions give some old clothes, got bugs in it, too. Now we get work. Can buy good food, good clothes. Can send kids to school."

In 1959, when a freighter scheduled to take the ore to Churchill couldn't arrive before freeze-up, management chartered the *Ithaca,* which was about to traverse the Atlantic from Montreal to Greece. When the *Ithaca* arrived at Rankin Inlet, those who knew ships were appalled by its appearance. Nevertheless, the ship was quickly loaded, and it headed for Churchill, where it left the ore and took on a load of government houses and mining equipment.

As the *Ithaca* steamed past Fort Prince of Wales, the weather began to change. A few hours later, in high winds and heavy seas, the captain of the *Ithaca* headed back to Churchill in an attempt to return to the sheltering port, but the onshore winds made it unsafe to try to enter the harbor. When the captain decided to anchor offshore, its anchor chains broke. The *Ithaca,* in deepening trouble, struggled out to sea, only to have its rudder fail. Helpless, the *Ithaca* was driven ashore at high tide, and as every tourist knows, it's still there, a graffiti-marred reminder of the risks of shoddy maintenance.

Were I flying higher, the community of Chesterfield Inlet, where Native children suffered abuse in church-run schools, would be visible beyond my right wing. Fortunately, those abuses, which were prolonged by government blindness or indifference across much of Canada, are now rare because many of the church schools that fussed about souls while neglecting health and education have been replaced by secular schools in which health and education come first.

When I wrote of these problems in *True North,* I left out stories of missionaries who ordered the converted to shun the unconverted, causing fractured families, great despair and even death when those who needed assistance were deliberately ignored, but I made plain my disgust for churches that tried to avoid prosecution by hiding behind the statute of limitations. My story subsequently brought a letter from an Edmonton attorney whose firm had represented hundreds of the victims of church schools, including the one at Chesterfield Inlet. Yes, he said, many of the churches had tried to hide behind the statute of limitations, but, fortunately, Canadian law prevented that clock from starting until the victims understood that the treatment they'd suffered had been discriminatory, inappropriate or sometimes even malicious. More recently, I've seen notices posted in public areas telling abused Natives to call 1-866-879-4913 or visit www.residentialschoolsettlement.ca to learn if they qualify for any of the 1.9 billion dollars set aside for settling claims of abuse.

All across Canada, children as young as five were taken from their families, their hair was cut short and they were forbidden to speak their language. Parents were rarely allowed to visit. Some schools became havens for pedophiles. In 1997, outraged Newfoundlanders scrapped the old system and adopted a resoundingly successful system of public schooling. In a report titled "Sins of the Fathers," an Anglican publication revealed that eight Indian men committed suicide rather than answer a subpoena that would have required them to describe the sexual abuse they'd endured as helpless children. A few years later, newspapers reported that claims against the Catholic, Anglican, United Church of Canada and others numbered in the thousands. The churches argued that if the judgments ran into the millions, which they eventually did, they'd go bankrupt, but despite the fines and their protestations, the churches are still in business.

Like Henry Voisey, the HBC manager at Padlei, Rankin Inlet mine manager Andy Easton also derided missionaries, describing the community's Catholic, Anglican and evangelical missionaries as "a bloody pain in the ass. They feud like a bunch of castrated hillbillies and don't do a damn thing to help with the real problems of the Eskimos. Which are physical, not spiritual."

This sort of condemnation occurred not just in Canada, but in Alaska, too. Joe Rychetnik, a well-traveled Alaskan state trooper and reporter for Time-Life News Service, was just as critical of missionaries as his Canadian counterparts, writing that many were drawn from "the lower classes of devoted church workers....These adventurous people... would realize they could fairly well write their own ticket up north, and most chose to live a lifestyle well above what they would have attained in West Virginia or Arkansas or the eastern piney hills of Texas. Once they learned the system, they soon acquired the skill of asking for more and better. Often this included maid service and paid help to haul water and collect firewood."

Ray Price, a long-time Arctic resident and man of many occupations, including Baptist minister, had seen what could happen when people took religion too literally. In his book, *The Howling Arctic,* Price told a grisly tale:

Mina, a young, Belcher Island Inuk had been taught by her preacher that the return of Jesus would be accompanied by shooting stars, so when she saw a spectacular meteor shower, she believed that the world would soon come to an end. Mina had also been impressed by the strange behavior of Charlie Ouyerak, who had been telling everyone to "take no thought of the material things." Those who believed Charlie began to kill their dogs and destroy their sleds and rifles. Before long Charlie and Peter Sala, the two most respected Inuit in the band, began to lead revivals. As the passion spread, Mina, who had agreed to become Peter's wife, persuaded some of the Inuit to follow her onto the ice and to remove their clothes so that their children could meet Jesus naked. A few turned back, including Mina, but four children and two women died of exposure.

For a week they were told again and again that Jesus would return until one night Charlie proclaimed, "He's here."

"Where?"

"Here," said Charlie forcefully. "I am Jesus, and Peter is God. You have seen the stars falling." Everyone believed them and swore their allegiance, except for a girl named Sara. One of the believers struck her. Others joined in, beating Sara, who was just thirteen, until she died. When Ketowieak protested, he, too, was murdered. During the next months, the few who dared to speak out were accused of being devils, and were stabbed, beaten, speared or shot.

In the trial that eventually followed, Charlie and Peter were found guilty and imprisoned. Mina was judged insane. When the hearings drew to a close, a bystander was heard to say, "Religion is like alcohol. Most people can handle it OK, but get too much and you go crazy."

So—were there no ethical missionaries who put others before themselves? Of course there were, and their stories have been widely told, including in *True North,* where I wrote about Fr. Joseph Buliard, the self-sacrificing priest who disappeared—possibly murdered—while serving Natives at a primitive, tarpaper shack mission not far from the Arctic Circle. And yes, the Oblate Fathers, the order that established and staffs Churchill's Eskimo Museum (to which Fr. Buliard belonged) was the first organization to give the Chipewyans a written language.

As the climate began to warm at the close of the last ice age, streams began to flow across, through and under the melting ice. Streams became rivers and rivers became floods, each collecting the silt, sand, gravel and boulders that the glaciers had scraped from the frozen valleys, hills and plains. When the rivers finally slowed, the gritty load they had carried settled out in the form of long, meandering ridges called eskers—like the one below that's pointing to Baker Lake.

This esker is just a baby, being only twenty miles long. Dwarf birch, ground pine and stunted willows thrive along its base, painting it Kelly green. On its flanks, mosses and lichens introduce ochre, orange and a pale shade of green. The crest of the ridge has been worn smooth by migrating caribou that use its wind-swept, thirty-foot height to gain relief from mosquitoes and black flies, from warble flies that lay their eggs beneath the animal's hide and from nose bot flies whose larvae can obstruct their nasal passages. As many as 1,000 warble fly larvae have been found in the back of a yearling caribou, and as many as 100 bot fly grubs in the pharynx of another.[TN] Imagine being plagued by both!

The esker below, like all eskers, has another important virtue. In a land composed largely of water, rock and ice, an esker's well-drained, gravel slopes and core provide denning sites for wolves, foxes and other mammals that need to shelter their young or, in the case of ground squirrels, need a safe haven for long winter sleeps. Some might conclude that nature, in its wisdom, is providing for their needs—giving nature a kindly face—but my view is that nature is indifferent and has no intent. Animals that can adapt to their surroundings survive, and those that can't move on or die. Nevertheless, as I follow the esker's caramel-colored ridge top toward the northwest horizon, I'm tempted to side (illogically) with those who believe that Nature wears a provident face.

A few minutes later, Mother Nature begins to whisper in my ear. "Hey, dummy," she says, "You shouldn't have had that caffeine-loaded soda for breakfast." She's right. I temporize, squirming around in my seat while wishing that I had the reserves of our Shetland sheepdog, the camel of the urinary world, who, when I'd take her to the door at bedtime would give me a pained look, as if to say, "What? Who, me? Don't you know it's just Tuesday and I'm good until Friday night?"

Handicapped by the constraints of an aging bladder that won't make it to Baker Lake, but pleased that for once the air isn't rough, which really complicates things, I dig out my plastic jug and find relief. The sun is shining; my body is happy; the Cub is slipping through super smooth air as never before, and for the first time in fifteen tries, I'm on my way to Baker Lake with a tail wind. Thank you, Mama Nature!

My course parallels a 200-mile waterway that connects Chesterfield Inlet to a twenty-mile wide body of water (and a town of 1,500) called Baker Lake The Inuit knew it as *Qamani'tuaq,* which means "where the river widens," the river being the beautiful, placid Thelon that flows through the Thelon Game Sanctuary, the Canadian edition of the Serengeti Plains. Varying in width from half of a mile to twenty, the long waterway is everywhere deep enough to accommodate the barge from Churchill that arrives at Baker

Lake every fall with tons of fuel and supplies. Despite being 200 miles west of the Bay, the elevation of Baker Lake is a mere eight feet, which is a "climb" of four-hundredths of an inch per mile—an easy trip for any barge.

As I run the numbers through my head, I try to envision the sort of technology we'd be stuck with if the Hindus hadn't invented (around 400 BCE) our logical system of numbers. The Hindu system slowly worked its way west through Persia (which is why we call them Arabic numerals) to arrive in Europe around 1000 CE.

What blessings the "new" numbers brought! Before Arabic numerals came into use, (over the objections of the Church which opposed the "infidel numbers") if one needed to write a large number like 238,857, the number of miles to the moon, the Roman figure (CCXXXMMMMM MMMDCCCLVII) could span half a page! Now imagine the length that would be achieved by larger numbers, perhaps the distance to the sun. Worse yet, how would we multiply a Roman number by even a small number like thirty-eight? Multiply it by XXXVIII? And what about division? It boggles the mind. The early Hindu system lacked zeros, but the Hindus soon remedied that. Then, in the late sixteenth century, a late-blooming Belgian tradesman named Simon Stevin delighted merchants, bankers and borrowers who had been forced to rely on clumsy fractions by inventing the next really great thing— decimals. Fractions returned to the schools, and decimals became the tools of commerce and the budding Enlightenment.

The Kazan River splits into multiple channels as it flows into Baker Lake. Beginning far to the south in northern Manitoba

and Saskatchewan, the Kazan flows north through the heart
of the barrens, the cradle of Caribou Inuit culture that
includes Kasba and Ennadai Lakes. The Kazan and its equally impressive neighbor, the Dubawnt, parallel the migration
route of the *Qamanirjuaq* caribou herd, now 500,000 strong,
so to improve the odds of seeing even part of the herd, I
descend to a few hundred feet above the tundra.

Finding nothing but huge flocks of geese, ducks and
shorebirds, I turn toward Big Hips Island, the site of the
HBC post from 1916 to 1926, the year that the Company
moved to the northwest shore of the lake. When I circle for
a photograph, I notice that I forgot to change the film speed
setting on my camera when I switched to high-speed
Ektachrome back near Dymond Lake—a terrible error that
will badly overexpose all of my photos from Churchill to
Baker Lake. Dumb!

Minutes later, Arlug Island, which looks like a piece of
a picture puzzle, falls behind as the Cub begins to glide
toward a beach where Henry Ford and I once hauled ashore
twenty trout, grayling and whitefish in less than ten
minutes—with a net.[TN]

Because my landing and takeoff at Marble Island were
in salt water, which is great for corroding steel, I treat the
Cub to a sloppy fresh water landing. Adding power, I pitch
the nose up and down to give it a final soaking before I drift
to shore near a crowd of gawkers. Their silence, their
sidelong glances and whispered remarks suggest that they
think I'm the worst pilot in Nunavut—if not the world.

Feeling playful, and to give them something new to
consider, I pick up a bucket that's lying on the beach, fill it
with water and throw it all over the Cub. After the fifth or
sixth bucket, I turn to the onlookers and, with a disgusted
shake of my head, complain, "I'm sick of fabric airplanes.
Gotta' wet 'em down at least once a day just to keep them
from shrinking," then stride up to the Northern Store.

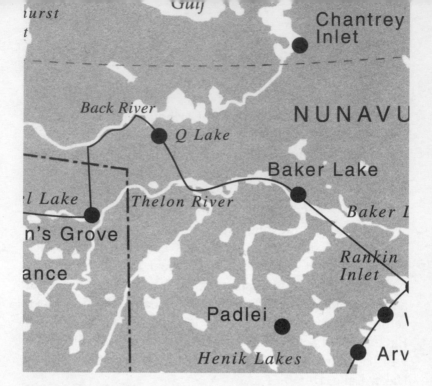

Chapter 5
Baker Lake to Q Lake, Nunavut

Science, freedom, beauty, adventure: what more could you ask of life? Aviation combined all the elements I loved. There was science in each curve of an airfoil. In each angle between strut and wire, in the gap of a spark plug or the color of the exhaust flame. There was freedom of the open horizon, on the open field where one landed. A pilot was surrounded by beauty of earth and sky. He brushed treetops with the birds, leapt valleys and rivers, explored the cloud canyons he gazed at as a child. Adventure lay in each puff of wind.

—CHARLES LINDBERGH

It's been seventy-five years since the Lindberghs refueled their Lockheed Sirius seaplane here at Baker Lake. Headed west to Alaska, they were beginning what would become a record-setting round-the-world trip. The year was 1931, and when they left behind the "three or four white houses" that Anne Morrow Lindbergh described in *North to the Orient,* they wouldn't have believed that in just thirty years, scheduled air service would supplement the yearly barge, or that a hundred homes and businesses would spread along these shores.

At the Northern Store, I ring up Boris Kotelewetz, who seems to have a finger in every Baker Lake pie, including Ookpik aviation, B K Aviation fuel and Baker Lake Lodge.™

"Boris," I ask, "Can someone bring a barrel of fuel down to the beach for my Cub?"

"Sure," he says. "But it'll be about an hour. We're really busy right now."

"That's okay," I reply, then ask him to bring a wobble pump for the barrel.

"Do you know if Durey's around?"

"He's out on the tundra, flying his Maule," says Boris.

"Is that the same plane that got mugged by a polar bear at Wager Bay?"

"That's the one," says Boris.

I'd hoped to meet Orin Durey in case he had news of DeBeers. Spurred by Charles Fipke and Hugo Blusson's Ekati diamond find north of Yellowknife, DeBeers sampling crews are working sites as far south as Oxford House and Attawapiskat, which is near James Bay, and as far north as Baker Lake, where according to Orin, "DeBeers is planning five or six ten-day fly-in camps within a seventy-five mile radius of Baker Lake."

In his last e-mail, Orin noted that DeBeers planned to run "two shifts of a dozen prospectors each during an 18-hour workday, ten days in and ten days out," and closed by predicting that there might be "few takers on the second rotation."

DeBeers isn't alone in the field. Among their many

competitors is Chuck Fipke, the brilliant, controversial, eccentric and now very rich geologist who located the first of North America's many kimberlite diamond pipes far to the north of Yellowknife near a lake called Lac de Gras.™ Since then, according to John Kaiser, the publisher of an investment newsletter, "Chuck Fipke has a stealth program in Attawapiskat, Ontario and there are rumors that he has found the holy grail of the Canadian diamond industry."

Baker Lake has added three new features since my last visit. The first is a prominent sign claiming that Baker Lake, the only inland community in Nunavut, is the geographical center of Canada. The second is the nearby, red-roofed Akumalik Visitors' Centre, so I head there, leaving the third, the Inuit Heritage Centre, for last.

In 1990, when the Kazan and Thelon Rivers were designated Canadian Heritage Rivers, the plans included a Baker Lake Visitors Centre that would describe the natural and human histories of the two waterways. In a successful attempt to retain the spirit of the past, the old Hudson Bay building was cut in half, hauled across the ice by ninety sled dogs and then reassembled close to the Northern Store.

The Visitors Centre features relics of the Caribou Inuit and the community of Baker Lake, including the old HBC store counter, antique trade goods plus displays that focus on the cultural and natural heritage of the Kazan and Thelon Rivers. The centre's most interesting features, however, are a Discovery Table bearing objects from the tundra, and an audio/visual area with video tapes of the Kazan and Thelon Rivers.

The Inuit Heritage Centre, or Itsarnittakarvik, which means "a place for anything old," opened in June, 1998, at the request of elders who wanted to preserve the unique culture of the inland Inuit who moved to Baker Lake, and as I enter the centre, I'm struck by the colorful displays of clothing and the array of tools that kept these people alive.

Historical photographs line the walls, accompanied by audiotapes of traditional Inuit songs.

I spend a half hour browsing, but before I leave I ask the attendant if Henry Ford is still around.

"No," she says, "his son David manages the art gallery since Henry moved away."

"That's unfortunate," I reply. "I enjoyed fishing with Henry a few years ago, and I was hoping he could tell me a bit about Inuit customs and beliefs."

"Well," she replies, "I could ask John Killulark."

As she reaches for the phone, she has a second thought, and instead dials a man she calls Peter.

"Hello, Peter. There's a man from the States here at the centre who needs someone to tell him about the old customs and beliefs. Do you want to talk to him?"

Twenty minutes later, Peter walks up. His deeply creased and weathered face smiling above a spare, five-foot-six body, looks every one of the seventy-five years he admits to, and he acts surprised when I tell him that I'm not that far behind. Better yet, he's a natural storyteller and, with little encouragement from me, he begins at the logical place.

"I was born up on the Thelon, but I don't remember much until I was about six. That's when my brother drowned while we were hunting caribou. We buried him under rocks to make it hard for the animals to eat him."

"I've read about that custom," I say, "but I've also read that personal things were often left at the grave for use in the next world. Did you do that?"

"I don't remember, but when my father died about twenty years later we left him a knife. The missionaries told us not to, but we did it anyway.

"My grandfather taught me more traditions than my father, and most of them were about hunting. He said that all things had spirits, and not just the birds and the animals, but even the stones and the rivers. He said that some spirits were bad, but others were good. If a person treated them badly, he'd get bad luck or maybe die. I remember my mother feeding my sister's baby teeth to the dogs so no bad person could use them to practice magic against her. My mother said that some people had more than one soul, and that the soul of someone who died could be asked to enter a baby. Near the end of the winter she'd beg the spirits to push the darkness back into the caves so it would get light again. My mother also revered the moon, and some still do because they think that the moon receives the spirits of the dead. She told me that when the moon was not visible, it had returned to earth to give spirits to new forms—sometimes to a fish, a caribou or a rock, and sometimes to humans."

Smiling, I tell Peter, "I've read that many Hindus once believed that everyone who dies goes up to the moon. I've also read that some early Christians thought that the crescent moon increased in size as those who died arrived, then later waned when it sent them off to the sun."

As Peter talks, I picture him ladling fresh water into the mouth of a dead seal—a gift to slake the terrible thirst it had acquired during a lifetime in salt water—in the hope that the seal's spirit would advise other seals that here was a thoughtful hunter, a man worth dying for. I see him silently apologizing to a polar bear he is about to kill, explaining his need to feed his family, later rewarding its spirit with a knife or an ulu—human tools that bears surely must covet. Then, as I'm wondering if he'd ever hunted seals or polar bears, he looks at me as if he'd read my mind.

"I never saw a seal or a bear until I was about forty, and then it was on TV. Later, I saw them live at Chesterfield Inlet. You need to remember that only some of us live near the oceans. Others, like me, spent most of their lives following the caribou."

My reading confirms him. Peter Freuchen and Vilhjalmur Stefansson lived with and wrote of the coastal

Inuit, but Farley Mowat wrote of those who followed the caribou in his *People of the Deer* and *The Desperate People*.

"Peter," I ask, "can you tell me anything about a spirit called Kiviuq—or is it Kirviuq?"

"It's Kiviuq," he replies.

"Kiviuq, like Tuktu, the caribou, is an eternal wanderer who walks or travels by dogsled or kayak. Some say he is carried by huge fishes, and that he has lived many lives. They say that his great powers let him overcome anything that gets in his way. Belief in Kiviuq was very widespread. In Greenland he is known as 'Qooqa' and in Alaska he is called 'Qayaq.'

"One story tells of his friendship with the grandson of an old woman. Everyone abused and made fun of the boy except Kiviuq, so the old woman decided to get revenge. With Kiviuq's help, she changed her grandson into a seal and told him to swim out to sea. The men followed the seal to kill it, but before they could, the woman called up a storm and drowned everyone but the seal and Kiviuq. The seal swam back to shore, where he returned to being a boy. Some say that Kiviuq is in his last life now, but before he dies he will return to see his people."

"And what about shamans? Did you know any, and are there any at Baker Lake?"

Peter pauses, looking out over the lake as if searching for a distant memory.

"I'd heard about them but I never saw one until I was about fifteen. We couldn't find the caribou one fall and we thought we were going to starve. One man named Nauja— it's always a man—said that he could see things that others could not, so he said he would fly away to find them. That night he told us close our eyes and not to open them until he clapped his hands. At first we could hear him breathing hard, but then nothing. Finally we heard breathing again and his hands clapping so we opened our eyes, and there sat

Nauja. He told us that he had seen many Tuktu to the south. We had always been told that sleeping people see distant things because their eyes travel, so we believed him. The next day we went where he said and found them."

"Did you ever wonder if he really knew or if you were just lucky?"

"Not really," said Peter. "We were starving and we couldn't just sit there, so we went the way he said. Who knows?"

"What about now? Are there any shamans left?"

"I suppose, but I don't know of any around here."

"And what do you think about the religion that's replacing the shamans?"

He stops to think, then says, "At first the new religion had many bad things. They said that we couldn't hunt or fish on Sunday, but we had to hunt and fish whenever we could or we'd starve when winter came."

"That's awful," I say.

"I know," he replies, "but we'd wait until someone who hadn't heard the preacher went hunting. Then, because the rule was already broken, we figured it would be okay—so we'd go hunting, too.

"My grandfather wouldn't convert because he didn't want to give up our traditions."

"Can you give an example?"

"Yes," he replies. "Some people wrapped baby boys in bull caribou skins to give them skill in hunting or they'd clean new born girls with *sik-sik* fur — that's a kind of ground squirrel — to make them beautiful."

He glances at his wristwatch, a huge thing that looks like a Russian import, and says, "I have to go."

"Peter," I say as we shake hands, "thanks for talking with me, and have a great summer."

A mischievous smile brightens his face.

"Watch out for those spirits!" he says.

When my fuel arrives, I roll the barrel under the wing, unscrew the cap, insert the pump and begin whooshing gas into the Tundra Cub II at about a pint and a half per stroke.

Accompanied by the metronomic rhythm of the pump, I think of Vilhjalmur Stefansson,[TN] the arctic explorer who wrote about shamans in *My Life with the Eskimo*. Believing that illness could be caused by a person's soul having been stolen, an Inuk would hire a shaman to find his soul. If he thought that an enemy had persuaded a shaman to send the sickness, he'd need to secure a shaman-supplied remedy, which might be as odd as having a sick child's mother refrain from changing her socks. And since nature usually cures our ills, the shamans could hardly go wrong. If the illness worsened or the patient died, it was never the fault of the shaman. Instead, there were taboos that the victim had broken, or chants that were not sung quite right, just as Christian Scientists "nurses" and other faith healers have excused their failures by blaming the victims who die despite their earnest prayers.

When Stefansson described the telescopes that let us examine the moon, the Inuit were unimpressed, and asked if we'd been there. That being the early twentieth century, Stefansson said "no," whereupon the Inuit replied that many of their shamans had been to the moon, and had even walked among its caribou before they returned to earth.

On another occasion, when Stefansson described how our doctors could put a person to sleep to repair or remove organs, and that the person would feel no pain, the only evidence of the surgery being the scar left behind, the Inuit countered with a tale of a shaman who, while a person was sleeping, not only removed his entire spinal column and replaced it with a new one, but left "not even a scratch on the skin or anything to show that the exchange had been made."

Like many of today's television preachers, shamans relied on belief, theatrics and a lack of critical thinking. As one Churchill Inuk put it several years ago, "It was all show—and not very useful, but what mattered was that the people believed. They had nothing else to lean on, but today it's different. When people stopped believing, the shamans lost their jobs."

The wing tanks take twenty-five U.S. gallons, and with three five-gallon bags in the rear that's plenty to reach an Artillery Lake fuel cache that I bought last year from a fellow named B. D. Smith when illness canceled his trip. This year, his luck turned worse when a windstorm damaged his plane. After marking the location on my chart, he told me, "There are two, thirty-gallon drums. One has avgas and the other has diesel for a generator. They'll look the same because the guys who flew in the fuel only had used gas drums, but they should be plainly labeled."

B. D.'s luck wasn't much better when I first met him thirty years ago here at Baker Lake. That year, B. D. and a friend were touring the Territories in an overloaded Aeronca Chief. Thanks to winds that had helped them get airborne wherever they stopped, they'd made it to Baker Lake, but when they taxied out to leave, it was calm. Loaded with two people, their gear and extra gas, the Aeronca plowed back and forth, nose-high, snarling and rocking, but couldn't climb onto the step. After a few minutes of straining at full power and low airspeed, their engine overheated and failed. When I taxied away, B. D. and his buddy were crouched beneath their "tent" (a sheet of plastic) in a light drizzle, waiting for parts to be flown up from Winnipeg.

It's noon by the time I'm ready to leave. I'm not very hungry, so I pass up the restaurant, crank up the Cub and radio my route to the Baker Lake DOT. The wind is still south, so I let the Cub sit on the edge of the beach as the engine warms, then pour on the power, take off and head west toward the Thelon Game Sanctuary.

The Thelon River begins hundreds of miles to the south and west in the heavily forested hills that surround Lynx and

Whitefish Lakes. By the time the river reaches Warden's Grove and the inflowing Hanbury River, the Thelon is a hundred yards wide, a clear and tranquil highway for canoeists who seek wildlife and wild country, but not wild water. Flowing east through the diminishing forests of the 26,000-square-mile Thelon Game Sanctuary, the Thelon finally enters the barren lands to flow east through Beverly, Aberdeen and Schultz Lakes. Then, as if sensing its demise, the Thelon cavorts for forty miles, stretching exuberant-but-runable rapids all the way to Baker Lake.

In other years, I've followed the Thelon as far as its Lynx Lake source. This year I'll be taking a more northerly route that will end at Yellowknife, but first I want to visit an unusual lake that's been calling to me for years. After that, I'll cross the Arctic Circle and head north to Bathurst Inlet.

Small, perfectly circular and rimmed with sand, the lake is an anomaly in this rocky country, but in addition to its size and shape, the lake has an out-flowing river despite the fact that no river flows in. When I first saw the outflow, I assumed that it came from deep water springs, but now that I know that the north is peppered with diamond pipes, I'm not thinking of springs—I'm dreaming of diamonds.

By the time I reach 3,500 feet, Beverly Lake, the home of the Beverly Lake caribou herd, once one of North America's largest, is passing below. The Beverly herd, like the Kaminuriak and Bathhurst herds, is just a remnant of its former self. Although reduced to one-fourth of their former size by opportunists with rifles, and later, almost certainly by nuclear fallout absorbed by the lichens on which caribou feed, most of the herds have begun to expand, with some estimates totaling as much as a million animals.

Beyond my left wing tip, the Dubawnt River enters Marjorie Lake from the south. As my eyes follow its sparkling surface, I picture a riverside cairn that marks the site of a tragedy known to most canoeists who have paddled the North.

George Grinnell, in his book, *A Death on the Barrens,* begins the story this way: "It was September 14, 1955.... Thirty-six-year-old Arthur Moffatt was leading five young men, ages 19 to 21, on a traverse of the Barren lands. They had begun at Stony Rapids, Saskatchewan, on June 29 and were bound for Baker Lake."

Big Dubawnt Lake lay far behind, but the men were running late. With hundreds of miles still to go, they began to hurry, squeaking through one rapid after another without stopping to scout them out. Suddenly, what had been an exciting adventure became what Joe Lannuette called the most harrowing day of his life. "It started out...bleak and dismal under a cover of clouds. It was below freezing and the sand was crunchy and hard from its layer of frost and ice.... In a few minutes we heard and saw the rapids on the horizon. At the top, the rapids looked as though they would be easy going...We didn't even haul over to shore to have a look."

Two canoes swamped and the third almost capsized, pitching five men into the frigid water. They managed to get to shore, but everyone was terribly cold. Being the barrens, there wasn't enough wood to make a decent fire, and because they were ill informed about hypothermia they accepted Moffat's trembling assertions that he'd soon be all right. Though they put him in a sleeping bag, they failed to give him hot drinks or warm him with their bodies. And so, to their great surprise and horror, Moffat's heart succumbed to the cold. Arthur Moffat was buried in the Baker Lake cemetery amidst a scattering of crosses that lean this way and that, unable to keep their footing in the cold, thin soil of the barrens.

A narrow fringe of dwarf trees begins to green the banks of the Thelon River as Beverly Lake falls behind, and by the time I reach Ursus Islands, where others have counted up to 100 tundra grizzlies in a single day, the shores and the islands are so thicket-covered that I can't spot even one bear.

When Musk Ox Hill, a sixty-foot frost heave called a "pingo," punctures the horizon, I turn northwest, leaving behind the evergreen oasis created by the Thelon Valley as the terrain reverts to a treeless lace-work of rivers and streams—a flower and lichen-enhanced puzzle of ponds and lakes.

What a marvelously varied world this is! Last winter, during a drive down the windward coast of Hawaii's Big Island, my wife and I stopped on bridges spanning deep ravines lush with one-hundred-foot-tall tulip trees and looked down into their bright orange blossoms. Now, here I am, just six months later, looking down at a very different forest—a subarctic mini-forest of lichens, stunted spruce, willows and birch that creep along the ground.

Forty minutes later, I ease back the throttle and begin a long descent toward a circular, sand-rimmed lake that I first spotted and marked on my chart in 1977.

Shaped like a Q, with an out-flowing stream for the tail at its base, the lake is just as I remember – big enough for a Cub like mine but too small for a Cessna 180. Steep sand banks surround its dark water, the only break being a gap in its southern rim. Through the break flows a stream as clear as space itself. I circle once, reducing power again to set up an approach that will end at the outlet.

Whenever I land the Cub, I become "schizophrenic." One part of me, the right brain perhaps, remains within the plane, sensing changes in speed, engine noise, declining lift and the sound of the slipstream whispering away at the point of contact while sensing the weakening stick forces as I near the impending stall. All of these sensations come together, telling me what I need to know while my muscles do the work.

While my right brain tends to business, its counterpart flies "wingman," sending me images of the descending Cub, always as seen from the left. My mind combines what the right brain feels with images of the Cub gliding down on the waves of wind—images that duplicate every dip, bank and turn until, nose high, my floats touch the water. And then, as if washed away by the splatter and spray, the image disappears.

I shut off the engine and sag in my seat. I've flown at least 400 miles since breakfast, plus I stopped at Baker Lake. I'm tired and hungry. Deciding that "hungry" can wait, I add a second pair of wrap-around sunglasses over the pair I'm wearing, close my eyes and, aided by the tick, tick, tick of the cooling engine, soon drift off to sleep.

I awaken confused and momentarily startled by the tall, dark obstruction that fills the windshield, then quickly sort things out when the extra sunglasses come off. As I stiffly climb from the Cub, I notice that the beach is covered with caribou tracks. Minutes later, a pot of Dinty Moore stew, my favorite quickie meal, is steaming on the camp stove. Beneath a frightfully clear blue sky I begin with an appetizer of honey-laden Baker Lake bread while the breeze defeats the black flies. Fantastic!

The tundra surrounding "Q" lake bears a colorful palette of wildflowers. Tiny, white heather blossoms quiver in the breeze. Daisylike, yellow arnica sway from side-to-side on tall, slender stems beside ranks of red-capped, British soldier lichens and a splash of purple saxifrage. Like the hardy hepatica, the northern Minnesota harbinger of spring, the purple saxifrage, which is aided by green leaves that it maintains through the winter, is one of the first to greet the Arctic spring. But despite its profusion of blossoms, the Arctic is a biological desert when compared to the tropics or even the temperate zones.

A rising wind begins to filter through my cotton parka

as I head toward the lake's northern shore. I consider turning back for a windbreaker but decide I'll be warm enough when I get moving.

I'm suddenly buzzed by an arctic tern, so I've probably gotten too close to its nest. Following the sun almost from pole to pole every year, these terns spend more of their lives in daylight than any other creature. If those who believe that we're reincarnated as other creatures are eventually proven right, I'll pass up coming back as a tern. As much as I like flying, their annual oscillations would be way too much for me. Instead, I'll settle for the chickadee, the amiable, little, black-capped bird that ignores the pushy grosbeaks and perches atop my hat while I fill our feeder with sunflower seeds. Perky, pleasant and tolerant, the friendly chickadee would suit me fine.

My second choice would be a Canada jay because of their ease with winter, their ability to fly and their friendliness. However, if mammals provide the only option, the playful, intelligent otter would be the one for me.

A small stream crosses my path. Along its edge, emerald green moss and short-stemmed flowers pattern the tundra with shades of yellow, russet, gold and blue. I drop to my knees for a closer look. Without exception, the stems of the flowers are hairy, an adaptation that conserves precious heat.

I'm a big fan of lichens, perhaps because, unlike me, they're not in a hurry, some of them growing as little as an inch in several hundred years. Lichens are symbiotic combinations of a fungus and a cooperative alga. The fungus provides the skeleton and the algae within provide the nutrients via photosynthesis. Together, the hardy little buggers live where little else can thrive—on ice-coated rock, on sun-blasted stone, on dead twigs and slate or asphalt shingles, all the while etching away at whatever they live on. Starving explorers who boil lichens for food get little more than stomach pains, but animals ranging from moose to mice eat them whenever they can.

In Antarctica, perhaps the worst place for a "plant" to try to survive, 400 different types of lichens can be found clinging to the continent's icy, wind-whipped rocks. Lichens have even survived for days while immersed in -164°F liquefied air, and their spores have remained viable despite a lengthy dip in liquid hydrogen, which is at –465°F.

The Arctic is a hostile place for those who cannot or will not adapt. Of the world's 3,000 species of mammals, fewer than fifty can endure an arctic winter. There are 8,000 species of birds, but no more than seventy breed in the far north, and fewer than ten will survive a high arctic winter, two of the best known being the snowy owl, a bird that looks like it belongs there, and the raven, which looks like it doesn't.

The hardy ravens can be found as far south as the Sahara. Others winter in the Arctic. When courting begins, they soar in pairs, repeatedly diving in courtship displays that lead to mating a full month ahead of other northern birds. As a consequence, their eggs hatch early because predators, to be most efficient, require a head start. Arctic ravens can brood eggs in temperatures down to zero—a temperature that requires females to stay on the nest, fed periodically by her mate. Not surprisingly, the Inuit and Dene have revered these intelligent birds.

Look at them! How do they handle the cold? Owls and ptarmigan fluff up more than ravens and seek shelter from the wind, but ravens will fly at thirty below in wind chills that must be horrendous. The bills and legs of arctic birds like Brunich's murres are shorter than those of their southern cousins, the Atlantic murres, but ravens can't be bothered. Northern or southern, they're pretty much the same.

As for the mammals, one general rule applies: heat loss is determined largely by insulation and by keeping body volume high and body area low. Thus, arctic animals like the Peary caribou, foxes and even mice generally have shorter legs and smaller ears than their southern cousins.

So what about the bugs? Thanks to the abundance of water and the long summer days, the Arctic hosts some 600 species, and as campers and explorers have noticed, they do extremely well. Ernest Thompson Seton, an explorer who traversed the Territories in the early 1900s, hated black flies with a passion, writing, "black flies attack us like some awful pestilence walking in darkness, crawling in and forcing themselves under our clothing, stinging and poisoning as they go."

Seton wrote glowingly of the sub-Arctic, but its mosquitoes equally dismayed him. "In one five-minute period I counted 254 of these black specs on my hand until I could stand it no longer. Then I smeared them away with my other hand, killing them in a mass of wet blood."

Seton, whom Vilhjalmur Stefansson held in high regard, is relevant today, for Seton was a pioneer in Boy Scouting, the inventor of the merit badge system and the first Chief Scout of the Boy Scouts of America. In fact, a large part of Baden-Powell's *Scouting For Boys* was lifted directly from Seton's Birch Bark Roll.

When Baden-Powell brought the Boy Scouts to the United States from Great Britain, Seton wrote much of the first (1911) manual. According to Canadian author Margaret Atwood, the story of Seton's Woodcraft Indians (the precursor of the Boy Scouts) is a sad one. "Seton developed the organization along democratic lines—grown men were never chiefs, only 'medicine men' or counselors—and the boys elected their own leaders and conferred their own honors upon one another. This movement was later stolen from him by Baden-Powell and converted into the Boy Scouts, with its hierarchy and its quasi-military organization—so useful for producing future soldiers."

Why does this matter now, at the start of the twenty-first century? Because, unlike the Boy Scouts of Canada and the admirable Girl Scouts of America, which don't discriminate against any child for any reason, the federally chartered, publicly funded Boy Scouts of America has refused to admit nonreligious adult leaders or their children, giving rise to a competing, discrimination-free organization called Scouting for All. Oddly enough, the BSA would also have to reject Seton, whose autobiography plainly shows that he, like Einstein, had no interest in personal gods.

I pick up my pace, eager to stretch my legs. What a change this is from bony Marble Island where I admired the sparse flora not for its beauty, but because it had persevered. Here, it's just the reverse. Flowers and lichens seem endless, but try as I might, I remember seeing only two species of lichen on Marble Island. I might have missed some, but on the glaring white of the islands, you'd think they'd have been easy to see.

Many writers describe the Arctic as "fragile," but John McPhee prefers "vulnerable." In *Coming Into The Country,* McPhee wrote that both living and dead tundra vegetation insulates the permafrost from the heat of the summer sun. But when something partially scrapes away or compresses that vegetation, it becomes less efficient. Permafrost melting, ponding and runoff follow, and recovery is unbelievably slow.

According to McPhee, "In the nineteen-sixties, a bulldozer working for the Geophysical Service Inc., wrote the initials G.S.I. in the Arctic Alaskan tundra... Thermokarst (thermal erosion) followed, and slumpage. The letters...are now odd-shaped ponds, about eight feet deep. For many generations, that segment of the tundra will say 'G.S.I.'"

The lake's shoreline slopes steeply down from the tundra for fifteen to twenty feet, providing a good look into its depths. Halfway round, as my boots crunch across the caribou "moss," which is really lichen, I realize that I've left my sampling tools at the Cub. A few minutes later, I'm tiptoeing through sprawling mats of pink azaleas interwoven with clusters of white-blossomed Labrador tea and ground-hugging clusters of blueberry plants. It's a veritable arboretum.

It takes almost an hour to circle my beautiful-but-monotonous lake. Bearing neither reefs nor shoals, its uniform shorelines plunge deeply down, convincing me that I'm standing right on the edge of an unclaimed diamond pipe. Why unclaimed? Because I'm still in the Thelon Sanctuary, and in the sanctuary, development is forbidden. Still, sampling isn't development, and the odds are against me anyway.

Removing, my boots, socks and pants, I wade across the frigid stream and dig out my Rube Goldberg sampling kit. The shoreline's the same wherever I look, so I pick a spot and begin to dig.

Because Kimberlite ore is usually softer than its surroundings, the tops of the pipes have often been scraped away by glaciers, leaving a lake behind. Charles Fipke, the once-struggling but now very wealthy geologist, recommends wading into the lake and then digging down a few feet before digging sideways toward shore to get a proper sample. By the time I'm down just a foot and a half, my legs are beginning to ache. The sand keeps slumping into the hole, which frustrates me by getting a lot wider, but not much deeper. Finally, while my ankles scream from the cold, I shove my war surplus spade sideways and retrieve something besides sand, then dump it into my wife's strainer to remove the coarse material, while saving the "fines" that fall into the bucket below. Next, I dump my precious, five-pound sample into a plastic grocery bag, tie it shut, mark it "Q Lake" and toss it into a float. When I've left the sanctuary, I'll repeat the process at another lake, although I'll probably be wasting my time.

Fipke and his partner, geologist/chopper pilot, Stewart Blusson, sparked Canada's diamond rush when they discovered the Ekati diamond pipe—which produced $491 million of diamonds in just 2002.[TN] That's a pretty good profit for Fipke, who, prior to finding Ekati, had almost zeroed his funds and was selling stock in Diamet for seventeen cents a share. Fipke and Blusson subsequently sold control of their find to Australian mining giant Broken Hill Properties for $687 million Canadian. Fipke no longer needs to search for investors, and Blusson's burgeoning assets have allowed him to donate $50 million to the University of British Columbia. As for BHP, their exploration program has already located more than 100 additional pipes.

At Ekati, the Kimberlite ore is reduced to a sludgelike material. After debris is removed, the sludge (which was originally flown to Reno) heads to Yellowknife, where a high-speed, Russian x-ray machine scans the moving sludge and lights up the diamonds, which are instantly blown into a collecting device by jets of air.

Today, most diamonds are destined for industrial use or for jewelry, but during and prior to the Middle Ages, diamonds were thought to have curative properties. In 1534, when Pope Clement VII fell ill, he was prayerfully dosed with 40,000 ducats worth of diamond dust and other finely ground gems. He died.

Newton, who took a more analytical approach, suspected that diamonds were made of carbon and reasoned that they would burn if he could get them hot enough.

Critics scoffed, but a century later, Lavoisier proved Newton right when he succeeded in burning a diamond. The result was carbon dioxide.

I'd hoped to tour a working mine like Ekati, or even a mine being developed—like DeBeers' Knife Lake project north of Yellowknife or their Victor project near Attawapiskat—so six months before I headed north, I repeatedly asked for permission to visit one of their mines. Neither Fipke nor BHP replied, but I received a response from a woman at DeBeers who asked what I wanted to do. Having already told her what I wanted to do in the first e-mail, I told her again, which ended my dance with DeBeers. That's unfortunate, not to mention bad public relations. (I'd intended to buy my wife a ten-pound diamond for our golden anniversary, but to teach them a lesson, I'm switching to cubic zirconia. My wife will understand.)

The sun's still high, so I hike directly away from the lake in the hope of seeing something new.

I always carry a compass, sealed matches and a candle, plus a poncho if it looks like rain whenever I set out on a hike. I also periodically turn around to see what the terrain should look like on the way back—a precaution that's especially important in the far north where a compass can lead one astray.

I can't believe my luck with the weather. I've flown at least 1,500 miles in the last four days with hardly a cloud in the sky. Aside from the smoke south of Churchill and some morning fog, the weather's been perfect. The blue skies that have smiled on me will probably continue because in this region, summer weather delays are usually brief, largely because the desertlike Arctic receives less moisture than most of North America, about twenty inches per year. Were it not for its rocky nature and the subsurface permafrost that reduces absorption, the Arctic would be drier still. At Thule, Greenland, the yearly total is a meager three to four inches.

Much of Ellsmere Island receives even less. In contrast, most of "dry" Nevada gets seven inches per year.

When my tent has become a barely visible dot and I'm about to turn around, I spot an unusually large clump of sticks about 100 yards away, but because of the clear air and the lack of visual references, the "sticks," which turn out to be half of a set of caribou antlers, are a lot farther away than I'd thought. Fortunately, they're small enough to fit in the Cub, so I lug them back to camp. As the lowering sun stretches out my shadow, I hoist the antler to the top of my head, creating a skinny, antlered shadow at least a hundred feet long.

In the barrens, where the air is clear and the flat terrain provides few visual references, we tend to see what we expect to see, and even seasoned explorers have often been fooled. On one occasion, Vilhjalmur Stefansson was surprised to spot a grizzly lying on a slope outside its den in October, long after northern grizzlies have usually holed up for the winter. Stefansson, who was short of meat, set off to get the bear, but was forced to make a long detour to reach it. Using a ridge to conceal his movements, he carefully stayed down wind of the bear. When he reached his quarry, he was astounded to find not a bear and den, but a marmot beside a heap of dirt it had excavated from its tiny den.

On another occasion he noticed what appeared to be four ravens playing on a distant snow covered hill. Thinking it unusual he reached for his binoculars, and discovered not ravens, but a polar bear lying on its back waving its feet in the air, the "ravens" being the bear's dark foot pads.

On a third occasion, after spotting a distant polar bear with his binoculars and doing his best to gauge its distance, Stefansson hurried off to add it to the winter food supply. When he arrived where he expected to find the bear, he climbed a pressure ridge to scan the area, but the bear was nowhere in sight. Thinking he hadn't gone far enough, he set off again. In fact, he'd over-estimated the distance to the bear and had unknowingly passed it—and the bear was following him. "I heard behind me a noise like the spitting of a cat or the hiss of a goose. I looked back and saw, about twenty feet back and almost above me, a polar bear." The bear's hissing saved Stefansson's life, but it cost the bear its own.

Back at the Cub, I set the altimeter, which is, in effect, a barometer, to 1,000 feet, If the altitude reading is higher in the morning, I'll know that a low pressure area is approaching—and a low can bring troublesome weather. If the reading is lower, I'll expect to see more of the bright, sunny skies that characterize a "high."

I'm hungry for fish, so I dig out my telescoping fishing rod, flick it out to full extension, attach my homemade "church key" lure and cast toward the opposite shore. On my fourth cast, a lunch-size northern pike surrenders its freedom to a stringer tied to my floats. With my main course secured, I walk downstream to a widening in the river where an esker restricts its flow, then cast far into the stream. I wait a second or two for the lure to settle, then begin my retrieve, only to have it stop as if set in stone. I tug, then tug again to no avail, then wade toward the lure to release the snag, reeling in line as I go. To my great surprise, the line suddenly tightens and heads downstream, pulling me along while the line whines out from my reel.

The end is almost preordained. If the hook holds and the line doesn't break, the fish will lose. He stops. I imagine him hanging motionless, considering his options—head upstream, downstream or try for the opposite shore. His mind made up, he suddenly shoots downstream, almost ripping the rod from my hands. Surprised, I clamp down on the reel—and my line falls slack. When I retrieve my lure, the treble hook is missing and the ring that had joined the hook to the beer can opener is now a dangling "C." I would like to have seen that fish!

The northern tethered to the Cub isn't so lucky. As I fillet the northern, tiny capillaries that seem too small and too few to fuel such a vigorous body leak bloody pin points from cream-white flesh. The fillets slowly fall away to each side like the pages of an opening book. With the fillets separated, I slide my knife between skin and flesh, freeing the meat from the skin with a sawing motion. Dipped in corn meal, the fillets are soon sizzling in a buttered frying pan. I wish I had some wine.

Knowing that the wind will go to bed with the sun and allow the bugs to return, I scrounge the tundra for firewood. Twenty minutes later, as my armful of twigs and branches burst into flame, I think of the alchemists' attempts to change base metals to gold—most of them based on fire. Even Isaac Newton tried alchemy, which was one of the few "sciences" to be supported by the early church. Why alchemy? Because any process that could produce gold would be immensely valuable. Newton later admitted that his efforts in alchemy had been "totally devoid of value," but several others who muddled around in early chemistry, which grew out of alchemy, were more fortunate.

One of the lucky ones was a bankrupt German named Hennig Brand, who, thinking that gold might be present in urine because of its color, set out to distill fifty buckets of urine supplied by obedient soldiers. His first efforts produced a vile smelling paste, but further work delivered a translucent, waxy substance that contained no gold, but yielded instead a marvelous new element that burst into flame when exposed to air.

The year was 1669. Hennig had discovered phosphorous, the element that enlivens the tips of our "light anywhere" matches. Unfortunately, making phosphorus from urine was tedious, unpleasant and very expensive, producing phosphorus that cost a whopping $500 per ounce. A century later, an ingenious Swede named Scheele discovered a cheap way to make large quantities of phosphorus, which is why Sweden has led the world in "match making" since the time of the American Revolution. And as my little fire shoots blue sparks skyward, I think of two additional Germans whose work has enriched our lives.

Chemistry students who have used the clean blue flame of a Bunsen burner would probably guess that it bears Mr. Bunsen's name, but few would guess that Bunsen and a coworker named Kirchoff also discovered a way to pick apart the stars. Bunsen and Kirchoff knew that when elements were heated to incandescence, and the light was passed through a spectroscope (a device that sends light first through a slit and then through a prism) the resulting rainbowlike spectrum would be segmented by a series of irregular lines like the lines in a bar code. They also knew that every element displayed a different arrangement of lines. The elements, one might say, had fingerprints.

One night, when a fire broke out in distant Mannheim, Bunsen and Kirchoff decided to aim their spectroscope at the flames, and when they saw the spectral lines of barium and strontium, Bunsen began to think of using the spectroscope to analyze the sun as well, but hesitated because "people would think we were mad to think of such a thing."

Kirchoff, however, had no such qualms, and by 1861, Kirchoff had identified ten elements in the sun that are common here on earth. Shortly thereafter, a Londoner named Huggins trained an improved spectroscope upon the more distant stars, and we learned that they, too, are made of the same materials that permeate our solar system.

My diminutive fire quickly fades, replaced by the after glow of evening and a multitude of brightening stars that are part of this marvelously varied—but understandable—universe that surrounds us.

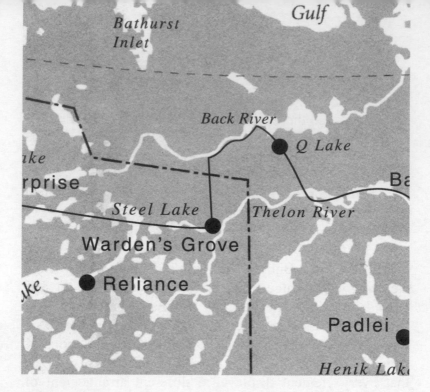

Chapter 6

Q Lake to Warden's Grove, Thelon Sanctuary, Nunavut

"We live in a wonderful world that is full of beauty, charm and adventure. There is no end to the adventures we can have if only we seek them with our eyes open."

—JAWAHARLAL NEHRU

Morning. It's clear, but it's cold and my flapping tent walls proclaim that it's windy. The altimeter reading is up 200 feet, so there might be some weather coming, but it should be flyable for at least a hundred miles. I pump the float compartments and empty two of the gas bags into the wings while wishing I'd done it yesterday when it wasn't so cold. As I zip up my jacket with hands that seem bleached, I think of the Englishman whose whiteness amazed the blacks of southern Soudan. "Were you born under water?" they asked.

While coffee brews, I spread out the charts and begin to plan my day: fly northwest to pick up the Back River, follow it upstream to Beechey Lake and then head north to Bathurst Inlet. As I stow the last of my gear and set the antler on top, a raven begins to orbit the Cub in slowly descending circles. Another arrives, perhaps its mate. They land quite close to my feet.

These two are the opposite of the timid ravens back home that keep their distance from humans. Like black-robed prosecutors, they boldly survey me, and as I toss them bits of bread, I remember a raven that flew low beside my car window as I slowly drove down a rural Alaskan highway. When it persisted, I stopped and opened my door. To my astonishment, the raven slowed, dropped its flaps, landed on my doorframe and uttered a single croak, which I took to mean, "feed me." After carefully lifting a cracker from my outstretched hand, it paused for a moment and then flew away.

These ravens are not quite that bold.

"So," I say, "I know you'd like bread, but how about cookies?"

They cock their heads to the side as I reach into the Cub to retrieve two cookies and toss half to each. The cookies disappear in seconds. As they dwindle, I think of the totem poles that dot the Alaskan and B.C. coasts, many of which featured symbols of Tulugaq, the raven. Some tribes believed that the raven was the source of life. Others called him the "trickster" because of his mischievous ways. Working in pairs, ravens have lured dogs away from their bowls to allow their mates to dine. In another instance, they even learned how to work the latch on the kennel. The dog would lunge at the gate, pushing it open. With the dog outside, chasing one raven, its partner would eat—and then they'd switch roles. The owner locked the gate.

I set the throttle to idle, prime the engine with two shots of gas, turn on the magnetos, step to the front of the float and briskly push down on the prop. The magnetos snap crisply. One more push and the engine rumbles to life. As I settle into my seat, I remind myself that this is musk ox country, so I'll want to fly low today. Besides, now that I'm farther north, I might find a caribou herd.

Barren ground caribou winter near the forest fringe, brushing shoulders with their cousins, the larger and darker woodland caribou that once roamed as far south as Upper Michigan and Minnesota, the last Minnesota sighting occurring in 1892. Hence the Caribou Islands in northern Lake Superior. The Saltaux Ojibwa called this southern range the *Atikaki,* the Country of the Caribou. Every spring, the barren ground females head north to the calving grounds well ahead of the males. There, on the barrens, they deliver their calves in May and June.

The southward migration, however, is led by the bulls. The awestruck Voyageurs called them *La Foule,* the throng. Inland Natives, whether Inuit or Dene, revered the animals, knowing that the herd provided the necessities of life—fur for warmth and rawhide, bones and antlers for tools, its body for food, including the vitamin-rich salad provided by its semi-digested stomach contents, supplemented in summer with blueberries, crowberries and delicious cloudberries.

The Cub's primitive heater warms my feet quite well, but to fight the cold air seeping into its less-than-tight cockpit, I pull a stocking cap over my ears, add the headset, and tie the hood of my parka tight around my face. Were I facing the sun, I wouldn't need it, but the sun is behind me, which is great for spotting caribou, but not for adding warmth.

My compass has become erratic, occasionally turning full circle as if it's lost its mind. It behaves this way primarily because the earth's magnetic field begins to tug compass needles downward as we travel farther north, finally pulling them straight down in the region of the magnetic pole—and what good is that? As it turns out, it is slightly useful, because if you measure the dip angle, the angle the needle points down, you can learn that you are somewhere on circle B, which surrounds the pole, and not on circle A, C or D. To further confuse matters, the north magnetic pole wobbles, tracing out an almost circular ellipse with a diameter of fifty to sixty miles every day, which is another reason why compasses in the Canadian Arctic, where the magnetic pole resides, can be deceptive.

The compass needle, which was at first called the "dry pointer," arrived in Europe from China during the twelfth century. In 1270, after Alfonso the Wise of Spain decreed that all Spanish ships must carry the needle, the economic effects were huge. Within a hundred years, the number of voyages doubled. However, all across the globe, mariners ran up against a common problem: Why, they asked, did compasses point to true north, the geographic pole, only on two pole-to-pole "strips," one on each side of the earth, while in the rest of the world the needles aimed to the right or left of true north, and often by quite a lot?

In the sixteenth century, an Englishman named William Gilbert, who had studied electricity and magnetism, reasoned it out. Using small spheres that he'd carved out of lodestone, Gilbert realized that the earthlike spheres has two poles, and concluded in *de Magnete* that the earth is a giant magnet, and that its north magnetic pole is a goodly distance from the north geographic pole, the pole at the north end of the axis around which the earth revolves. Gilbert, who also understood why compass needles began to point down as they neared the poles, became the first to

explain the "compass dip" that had troubled travelers in far
northern or southern latitudes.

Gilbert, however, had no idea that the north magnetic
pole wavered in place on a daily basis or that it was moving
north about three miles per year, a pace that has increased
to twenty-five miles per year, which will put the pole close
to Siberia by 2050—and it's taking the aurora with it. Those
ideas, he might have accepted, but I doubt that he'd have
accepted without protest another fact—that, in addition to
their wanderings, the poles have reversed many times in the
last 5 million years.

I really don't care what the compass today says because the
visibility is good and my maps are very precise. Instead, I'll
just follow any of the parallel streams that are passing below
because they all head north to the valley of the Back River.

As I search the tundra for caribou, I wish that my old
friend, Wesley Miller, was still alive. Together, we flew all
over Canada, Alaska, Belize and even Australia in a variety
of airplanes. Easy going and restrained, he was a perfect
traveling companion for a twitchy person like me. Flitting
like bees from blossom to blossom, we started every
morning with a routine that was always the same:

"Hey, Wes, what's on your mind for today?"

"Oh, I don't know. You got any ideas?"

"Sure. If we get moving, we could fish the Lockhart
River for grayling and still reach Reliance by noon, then fly
the McDonald fault to Snowdrift, gas there and get to
Yellowknife in time for supper. How's that sound?"

"Sounds good."

Wes, who had needed a new set of bifocals for years,
could barely read a map, so I often led the way. But because

his distance vision was sharper than mine our radio exchanges often went the opposite way:

"Hey George, caribou off to the right."

"Where?"

"1 o'clock."

"Don't see 'em."

"Just to the right of that long, narrow lake."

"You sure? Looks like boulders to me."

And then the boulders would move. Flying closer, I'd watch them grow antlers. Man, how those boulders could run!

In the evenings, while camped on the shore on yet another nameless lake far out in the bush, we'd play cribbage on the top of my camp stove until twilight or until Wes's litany of fifteen-two, -four, -six, plus a double run would close the curtains on another memory-filled day.

While reminiscing about Wes, I spot a small herd of caribou fording a stream. Were it not for the spray flashing in the sunlight, I probably wouldn't have seen them. I power back, grab my camera, open the window and orbit the herd for photos. Then, just as I roll out of my final turn, I catch the scent of gas.

I twist around in my seat to check the caps of the last two bags—the ones I didn't pour into the wing because my hands were getting cold. They're tight, but I still smell gas. Thinking that there must be a pinhole in one of the bags, I roll them over, and there it is—a tiny seepage. Fortunately, there are dozens of lakes to land on, so I pick the nearest and land. Within minutes the fuel is in the tank, where I'd have put it if it hadn't been so cold this morning.

The lingering scent of gasoline brings thoughts of Democritus, the 400 BCE philosopher who, on smelling bread baking in another room, theorized that all things, including bread, must be made of tiny particles that he called "atoms," which means, "cannot be made smaller," and that a few particles of the bread had managed to reach his nose. We can easily smell bread from even a distant room because our noses contain about 5 million olfactory receptors, but dogs have forty times more, which is why they make excellent trackers.

Lady, the starving German shepherd pup that I rescued from beneath Ilford's Gold Trail Hotel, often left me amazed.[TN] We'd be strolling down a forest path, Lady in the lead with her nose to the ground, when she'd suddenly stop and leave the trail at a right angle. Pushing through brush while I followed, she'd stop at the base of a tree and then look up. Thirty feet overhead, I'd see a quiet squirrel, the subject of her search. I can understand how she knew that a squirrel had crossed our path, but I'm astounded that time after time she knew, with apparent certainty, which way to turn.

The Cub slips past Consul Lake, crosses a final ridge and enters the broad valley of the Back River. A few minutes later, I spot a musk ox near the edge of the Jervoise River, a tributary of the Back. Throttled back, the Cub descends, reaching the Back when 200 feet above the terrain, the perfect height for spotting game.

Minutes later, I come upon another musk ox standing beside a gully, then seven more grazing on riverside sedges. The river looks deep enough, so I land, reach for my camera and set off toward the herd.

Musk oxen originated on the central Siberian steppes and on the high plains of northern China.[TN] Their habit of forming a defensive circle around their calves worked well for centuries, but when rifles arrived, their circling became a liability. When one or two adults were shot, which would normally be enough to fill the Natives' needs, the herd would close ranks to defend their dead or wounded, refusing to abandon their kin. Though a hunter might have been satisfied to kill one or two mature cows or bulls, it was often impossible to retrieve the animal without killing the entire herd. Thus, within 100 years of the introduction of the rifle, musk oxen had almost become extinct across much of the Arctic.

These musk oxen, unlike the herd that I once accidentally walked into as they grazed on head-high brush beside the Thelon River, are easy to see, but so am I. As soon as my head tops the rise, the largest bull snorts, sending the herd running into a broad, brushy valley, where they form a circle with the calves tucked well inside.

Called *Oomingmak* by the Inuit, which means "animal with skin like a beard," it's a much better name than the erroneous, English-derived "musk ox" for one reason: They don't have musk glands. Weighing as much as 800 pounds, the hardy musk ox has survived conditions that proved fatal to its prehistoric companions, the mammoths and mastodons. No other hoofed animal can live as far north as the musk ox and the reason is plain to see: its insulating twenty-four-inch hair plus its woolly undercoat, which is called *quiviut,* protect it from frigid winds that often bring sleet and snow. Quiviut, which is finer than cashmere, insulates so well that wind chills of −60°F leave musk oxen unaffected.

Screwing up my courage, I inch closer while reassuring myself that musk oxen rarely charge, snapping photo after photo until they suddenly run away. As they disappear, I remember a friend who aptly called musk oxen "overgrown dust mops with legs."

The Back River begins far to the north of Great Slave Lake. Flowing east through hundred of miles of treeless tundra, the Back finally turns northeast toward Chantrey Inlet, a fisherman's paradise 200 miles north of Baker Lake. I prefer the Dogrib Natives' more descriptive name, the

Thlew-ee-choh, "the Great Fish River," but the Back takes its name from Sir George Back, the man who explored it from start to finish in 1834.

Sir George was lucky to be able to make the trip. A few years earlier, he'd been a member of John Franklin's disastrous first Arctic Land Expedition to the Arctic Ocean, an ill-equipped and badly led foray from Great Slave Lake to the arctic coast and back. During the first days of the expedition, midshipman Robert Hood wrote glowingly of the "long flights of snow geese stretching like white clouds from the northern to the southern horizon," but a few months later, Hood was reduced to gnawing on worn out moccasins, eating the rancid stomach contents of their last caribou and forcing down cooked lichens in a desperate attempt to stay alive.

Of Franklin's party of twenty, more than half drowned, starved to death or were murdered and partially eaten, one of the murdered being midshipman Hood, the man who had been so taken with north country's food-filled skies. Were it not for Native assistance, the death toll would have been even higher.

Franklin, whose naval career included an assortment of adventures and narrow escapes, including being wounded in battle, might have come to believe that nothing could do him harm, for despite his northern debacle, he soon returned to explore the country surrounding the Mackenzie River delta with another expedition that (again) would have fared much worse but for the charity of caring Natives.

In 1833, Lieutenant Back, now on his own, headed north from Great Slave Lake in search of the Great Fish River, which was said to lead to the Arctic Ocean. On reaching its headwaters at Muskox Lake, he turned back, stopping briefly on Artillery Lake to build boats for the following year at a place called Timber Bay, then wintered on Great Slave Lake at Fort Reliance.

Leaving Fort Reliance in June, Back returned to Artillery and Muskox lakes, and set off down the Great Fish River. Weeks later, the expedition finally reached Pelly and Garry Lakes, only to find them frozen. Chopping their way through with axes, they finally reached a string of shallower, ice-free lakes. Ahead lay a long series of immense rapids, the last being the spectacular, nameless chute that roars into Chantrey Inlet at a Native encampment—an encampment that was still occupied when my first *Tundra Cub* taxied through the post-chute whirlpools in 1968. After sailing to the northern end of the Inlet, Back reversed course and began the long trip back to Great Slave Lake.

It was early winter by the time they reached spectacular Parry Falls, a spot of particular beauty on the final portage between Artillery Lake and Great Slave Lake. There, despite his weariness, Back wrote of its grandeur, "The whole face of the rocks forming the chasm was entirely coated with blue, green and white ice in thousands of pendant icicles; and there were, moreover, caverns, fissures and overhanging ledges in all imaginable varieties of form, so curious and beautiful as to surpass anything of which I had ever heard or read." On this long, hazardous journey (that was led by the sensible Back) not a single man died.

Back returned to England, where he was promoted to Captain and ordered to explore northern Hudson Bay in a refitted, 340-ton bomb vessel called the *Terror*. Trapped by pack ice, Back was compelled to winter in the far northern reaches of Hudson Bay. On reaching England the following year in a badly damaged ship, but with his crew alive and well, which was a remarkable achievement, Back was dismayed to learn that his expedition had been labeled a failure by armchair admirals who had no concept of the sort of challenges, risks and hardships posed by Arctic exploration. Only forty-two, he retired and married, becoming a source of advice on exploration, but he never returned to the North.

A decade later, Back's former ship, the *Terror,* joined the *Erebus* (the dwelling place of the dead), to search once again for the Northwest Passage. Captained by the same John Franklin who had twice led men to their deaths, the *Erebus* and the *Terror,* complete with a new and ignorant crew sailed away from Gravesend, England, bound again for the Arctic Ocean where, this time, all 134 men, including John Franklin, died.[TN]

Airborne again, I head west toward Beechey Lake, searching for caribou, but find not a one. I have found the exception to Stefansson's claim that, "The Arctic is lifeless, except for millions of caribou and foxes, tens of thousands of wolves and muskoxen, thousands of polar bears, millions of birds and billions of insects." Were I flying a louder aircraft, the engine might be spooking the wildlife into the gullies that lead to the river, but according to ground observers, the Cub merely utters a quiet snore.

The Back is incredibly clear. In its depths, schools of trout waver in holding patterns below each set of rapids. I'm tempted to stop, but the horizon ahead is becoming hazy, so I fly on. Forty miles later, a blanket of low, gray stratus clouds obscures the river ahead. It's the leading edge of a cold front backed by tall, dark strato-cumulus clouds. I'm going to have to land, but the shoreline here is littered with angular rocks that will damage my floats if the wind comes up. Knowing the beaches are common below a rapids and at the ends of long stretches of water, I fly on, dipping low to scoot beneath the stratus to reach the bottom of the first rapid I find, and then land.

Rainy Lake log boom.

Departure day. Leaving Ely Lake.

York Factory

Former Nelson River islands
ride seas of grass

Owl River - polar bear denning country

Churchill, MB and Hudson Bay

Miss Piggy on the rocks.

Beluga whales
Credit: Mike Macri - Sea North Tours.

Roadside bears
Credit: Dale Walker

Churchill kids and the Town Centre bear

Tundra buggy and author
Credit: Bill Dearlove

GREAT WHITE BEAR TOURS

A napping polar bear

Wes Miller and Samuel
Hearne inscription at
Sloops Cove, Churchill

Sᵗ Hearne
July ÿ 1. 1767

Below: Fort Prince of Wales, Churchill
Credit: Jim Wark

Hudson Bay coast

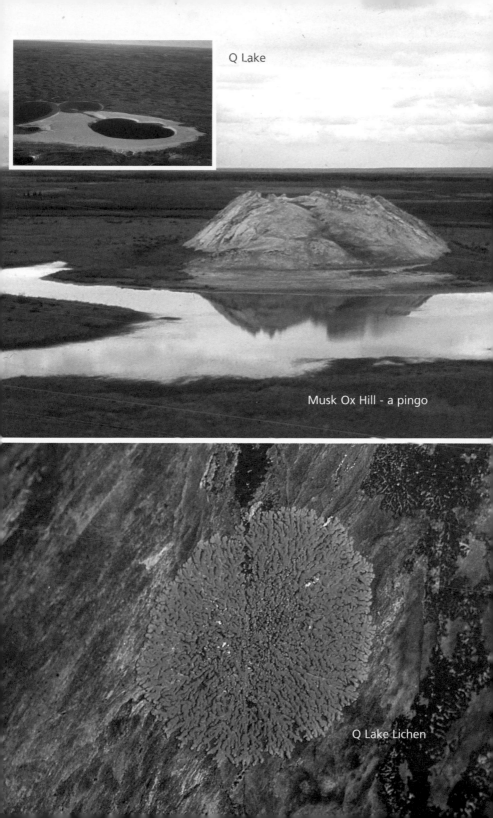

Q Lake

Musk Ox Hill - a pingo

Q Lake Lichen

Fantasy inflight refueling.

Wes Miller and first
"catch of the day."

Wes Miller and second "catch of the day."

My first caribou herd, Thelon Sanctuary

Ten percent of my second caribou herd,
Thelon River

Musk oxen

Char lakes

The Tundra Cub crossing the Back
River barrens.
Credit: Wes Miller

Thelon River *sik-sik*.

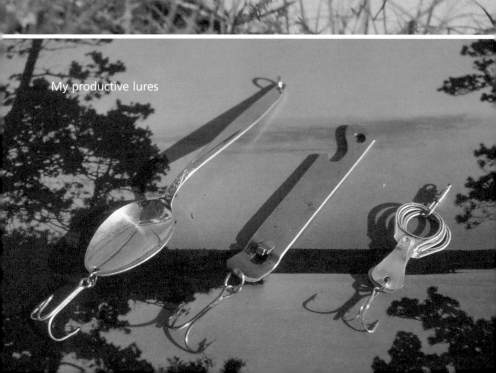

My productive lures

Steel Lake caribou

Lake trout and grayling

Saskatchewan fire scars

A grizzly came to visit.

Glassy water,
northern Saskatchewan

The Athabasca Sand Dunes.

Cree Lake. Sask. - Water as
clear as leaded glass

Black bear cubs

Shadow landing at Comma Lake

Tazin River, Saskatchewan

Three Cubs - northern Manitoba

Lake Winnipeg self-portrait bubbles

Drifting maple leaf

Hudson Strait iceberg
Credit: Mark Helseth

I'm lucky. Tucked between two, parallel reefs below the cascade lies a narrow gravel beach. Within minutes, the Cub is secure, my tent is up and my gear is inside before the first drop falls. An hour passes while I read Stefansson's *My Life with the Eskimo*. The rain continues. Another hour. Still raining. I set Stefansson aside and stretch out on my sleeping bag. Then, just as I'm falling asleep, a huge crash of thunder, which is rare in these latitudes, jolts me awake.

I've never been afraid of lightning, even standing (foolishly, I admit) on the end of our dock to photograph lighting arcing along and inside of ominous, onrushing storms. Nevertheless, I'm glad that my tent has fiberglass poles, and I hope that the nearby ridges will intercept Thor's lightning if he takes a shot at me.

Flash! Lightning brightens the yellow walls of my tent. Another flash! One Mississippi, two Mississippi, three Mississippi—Boom! Three seconds. That's about half a mile. The rumbles continue, and when the next interval between strike and thunder drops to less than two seconds, I open my tent flap and stare through the rain. What the hell, I think. If I get zapped, I probably won't know it, but if Thor throws a near miss, I might as well see the show.

However, this northern Thor lacks the stamina of his prairie cousins, for the show's soon over, and he grumbles off to the east. An hour later, a thin sliver of light brightens the western sky, bringing hopes of spending the night at Bathurst Inlet Lodge. A few minutes later, the wind drops. Wisps of steam begin to form above the rain-soaked tundra. Rising like smoke from a thousand campfires they join vaporous hands to form a blanket of fog, and except for the barking seals, I'm back on Marble Island, waiting for the fog to clear.

I'm lucky to have found this snug little spot before the weather closed in. My moss-covered campsite is soft as a mattress. Better yet, it's level, so I won't have to sleep on a slope. But, most importantly, the Cub is securely tucked between two reefs that will mute both wind and wave.

I decide to fish for grayling. Knowing that there will be plenty of black flies and mosquitoes near the rapids, I pull on a head net and spread repellant over my hands. I've a second church key lure, but it's too big for a grayling, so I clip on an iridescent lure that I inherited from my father, add a sinker and cast it between the reefs. Ten casts later, I walk to the end of the closest reef and cast again.

Something tugs on my line I begin a steady retrieve, sometimes gaining on the fish, then losing when it noisily strips line from my reel. My line is strong, but the lure is light, so I patiently real in when I can and let the fish run when I can't until it tires and comes to shore. It's a beautiful eight-pound trout, but it's much too big for one person to eat. I wait, knowing that the barbless hook will pop loose if he gives the lure a shake. A few seconds later, the trout spits the hook and quickly disappears.

Three more trout take the lure before an arctic char— think big rainbow trout—takes the hook. Speckled orange with crimson fins, it's a stunner. Laying the char on the tape glued to the top of my float, I see that it measures fourteen inches. It's a good char, but nowhere near a record.

While the black flies bug me, I fillet the char and haul my stove and supplies to the tent, then return to the float compartment that contains my canned goods. On my first trip north, I stowed cans in a float compartment to save room in the plane, only to have the labels fall off in the wet compartment. Since then I run a strip of tape around each can to hold the labels in place.

When I open the compartment, I'm surprised to see shining cans, a spattering of soggy labels and disintegrating loops of tape, and then remember that I'd always used strapping tape, but this year settled for cellophane tape. Accepting the fact that I'm going to have interesting menus,

I grab a can. I know it isn't beef stew because of the size of the can. Oh well, I say to myself, whatever it is, I'll eat it.

As the char sizzles on the Coleman, I open the can, hoping for sweet corn, peas or maybe green beans, but my vegetable tonight will be cling peaches in heavy syrup. In a way, it's a lucky choice because the peaches resurrect an event that I'd forgotten for almost sixty years.

When we were fifteen, my friend Norman Pilgrim and I decided to rent a canoe on Lake Vermilion one Saturday, canoe up Bear Creek to camp overnight on Bear Lake and return on Sunday. Neither of us knew anything about the creek, and after paddling eight miles of Lake Vermilion to reach it, we found ourselves in the center of a shallow stream, stuck on a sharp pine knot that had cracked the bottom of our metal canoe. Seeing no other option, we stepped into the mud-bottomed stream, lifted the canoe off of the knot, walked it downstream and dragged it ashore. There, we forced the edges of the break together, intending to seal the edges with the gummy sap that accumulates in balsam tree bark blisters.

Only then did we realize that we'd forgotten to bring containers—not even cups or glasses—so we opened a can of peaches, ate them and went from tree to tree poking bubbles to collect sap. It takes a lot of blisters to make an ounce of sap, but when we finally had enough, we turned the canoe upside down, slathered on the sap, let it become tacky in the sun, and then added a thin layer of birch bark. Turning the canoe over, we repeated the process on the inside, and after laying the tent and our sleeping bags on top of the break to keep the inner patch in place and to counter the force of the water, we gently set the canoe in the river and paddled back to Vermilion.

Thirty minutes passed, and when the canoe didn't leak, we decided to head for Trout Lake, which added an eight-mile paddle and an uphill portage before we arrived (exhausted) at Norway Island. While Normie pitched our war surplus mountain tent, which was white on the inside and khaki without, I started supper. As we ate, we commented on the lack of mosquitoes, only to later discover that they were all in the tent, perhaps attracted to the tent's bright liner because Normie had left the tent open.

"No problem," said I, seizing a smoldering branch from the fire, "I'll smoke them out."

A few minutes later, I emerged from the tent, eyes watering and gasping for air, leaving behind a horde of frisky mosquitoes. Grabbing our air mattresses and sleeping bags, we laid them outside, tied the tent shut and turned in without a single mosquito to plague us.

A distant rumble awakened us just before dawn. Looking to the northwest, we spotted a thunderstorm-studded squall line speeding down the lake.

"Normie," I yelled, "we gotta go NOW or we'll get stuck here and we won't get home on time."

Normie and I, propelled by teenage brains less prudent than those of a chicken, tore down the tent, threw everything into our suspect canoe and headed downwind across four miles of rough water. The wind increased. Lightning lit up the skies and stabbed the shorelines. Exhilarated and scared stiff, we roller coasted down bigger and bigger waves, finally reaching the portage just as the rain began.

Back on Lake Vermilion, we labored against a powerful crosswind for six long miles to return the canoe to its unhappy owner, who demanded ten dollars to repair the canoe. The sun briefly returned while we stood at the side of the road, thumbs raised high, our sodden gear at our feet. Car after car passed by until a gravel truck driver with a full front seat allowed us to ride in the box. It rained. Then it hailed.

Thinking back, it's a wonder we escaped the fate of the two young men who drowned at the border near Sand Point Lake. Perhaps the special providence that some say watches over fools and drunkards took a hand in our lives that day, but I doubt it. Instead, I think we were just extraordinarily lucky. Perhaps the extra energy provided by a big can of cling peaches pulled us through—and maybe not, but tonight, as I dip the last bite of char in my fast-food packet of tartar sauce, I decide that cling peaches in heavy syrup are not only great for retrieving memories, they make a pretty good vegetable.

At eight o'clock it's still foggy. It won't get dark until well after cleven, but when another hour passes without change, I know I'm here for the night. I check on the Cub and turn in, hoping for clear skies tomorrow.

More fog. To kill time, I catch another grayling and cook it for breakfast. Still hungry, I fry three strips of thick bacon and heat up a can that (luckily) contains baked beans. Dishes done, I turn to the Cub. I've promised myself that I'll load the Cub neatly, putting everything in its place each day, but my resolve has dwindled, and entropy has done its thing. My food pack's a mess. My charts—those I have yet to use—are out of sequence, and where did I pack that film? It's time to unload everything, repack and neaten up.

When the Cub is ship-shape, I hike to the top of a nearby ridge to scan the horizon. It's darkest toward Bathurst Inlet, but it's bright to the south. Spotting a finger-thick dwarf birch surrounded by a sprinkling of red rhododendrons at the base of a nearby gully, I'm tempted to count its rings, but I'm caught between wanting to know its age and my discomfort at killing a plant that has struggled to survive for more than a century.

In the end I yield, counting its tightly packed rings with the aid of a wide-angle lens, just as I did a few years ago near

Churchill. To my amazement, the stubby birch has survived almost 200 winters. Convinced I have erred, I do a recount, and then another, but the result remains the same. Then, troubled that I have cut its strivings short, I jam the birch back into the earth, deceiving myself that it will take root once again. As I counted the rings, I recall one of my sons asking why we counted by tens. My guess was that we count that way because our primitive counting tools have always been fingers and toes. I subsequently learned that my assumption was correct, but then I began to wonder why hours are divided into sixty minutes, a minute into as many seconds, and circles into 360 degrees. Years later, I discovered that the Babylonians decided on the sixties system back in 2000 BCE.

At the top of the ravine, I come upon a lichen-encrusted moose rack. Impossible, I think, but then remember seeing moose in the Thelon River Valley, which is less than 200 miles to the south. A moose might have wandered this far north during a favorable summer, but it would have been a mistake, for the waters that surround the Back hold few of the aquatic plants that comprise much of a moose's midsummer fodder. Perhaps a canoeist lugged it along when he portaged from the Thelon into the Back, but that, too, seems unlikely because if he tired of it he'd probably dump it overboard or leave it on the beach instead of hauling it uphill this far from the river.

The antlers bring to mind Thomas Jefferson, who took offense at French claims that New World creatures (including the colonists) were physically inferior to those of the Old. To silence them, Jefferson arranged to have a moose shot, equipped with a huge set of handy elk antlers, and shipped to France. Why elk antlers? Because the moose, which had been shot early in the year, had not had enough time to grow a decent set of antlers. Who in France, reasoned Jefferson, would know the difference?

As I stroll back to the Cub, I envision Bathurst Inlet and

the way that Wes and I found the lodge some thirty years ago. After refueling on Great Bear Lake, we headed toward Baker Lake with a stop planned at Bathhurst Inlet.™ With Takijuk Lakes behind us, we followed the winding Hood River across a caribou-dotted plain. (The Hood takes its name from the same Robert Hood who was shot for meat by one of Franklin's guides.)

After photographing Wilberforce Falls, the Hood's spectacular, 200-foot drop (the highest in Canada north of the Arctic circle) we followed the Inlet south along a back-bone-like string of islands in search of a Hudson Bay store that had closed in 1964, expecting to find nothing more than a scattering of Inuit—if that.

Wes, as usual, was the first to see the red-roofed building. Drawing closer we noticed an oddly lettered sign reading "Bathhurst Inlet Lodge." On landing, we discovered that the store and an abandoned Catholic church that was insulated with caribou skins, had been converted to a resort by Glenn Warner, a retired Mountie, and his wife, Trish, both of whom came down to meet us. As for the sign, its letters were formed from caribou antlers, making it one of the most artistic and graceful works of art we'd ever seen.

The Warners invited us to join them for a home-cooked meal, so we followed them up to the lodge, passing great patches of white-petaled mountain avens along the way. On entering their comfortable diningroom, we received another surprise. Among the guests at this tiny resort, were four people from the village of Round Lake, Minnesota, a small town just fifteen miles from our homes. We knew them all.

Their interest in waterfowl and ours in "snooping," had, against all odds, brought us together, unaware of each other's plans during one of their three days at a new resort on the edge of the Arctic Ocean. That evening, when David Meech, the naturalist of arctic wolf fame, arrived in a de

Havilland Beaver chartered by the National Geographic Society, Wes turned to me and asked, "What's next?"

Later, Wes and I walked past racks burdened with drying trout, char fillets and strips of caribou meat. Spotting fish eggs spread out to dry on a flat-topped boulder, I popped a tapioca-like sample into my mouth and squeezed it between my tongue and palate.

"Well?" asked Wes.

"Fishy," I replied.

A nicely antlered caribou head lay near one of the racks. To the great amusement of Boyd, the Warners' young son, I hoisted it in front of my face and asked Wes to take my picture. That photo of a creature with the head of a caribou and the body of a man standing in a field of arctic cotton always brings a laugh, but whenever I see it, I remember not the mini pom-poms of arctic cotton, but the stench of the caribou's neck, and my telling Wes, "Hurry up! This thing stinks."

When we returned to our Cubs the following morning, we discovered we'd just missed the tide. With larger aircraft we'd have needed to wait for high tide, but with Glenn, Boyd and some Inuit helpers, we easily slid the Cubs across the twenty-foot beach to reach the receding waters of Bathurst Inlet An hour later, we picked up the Back River and turned east, later to come upon Father Buliard's fate-filled mission at Garry Lake.[TN]

The clouds lift just enough to reveal that it's flyable to the south, but the ridges to the north and west are still obscured in clouds. I wait a final hour, worrying all the while that my hole to the south will close and I'll be stuck here all day. The bright southern sky hangs in there, but so do the clouds toward Bathurst Inlet. Decision made, I fire up the Cub and leave the Back behind, heading south to brighter skies and the center of the Thelon Sanctuary.

Forty minutes later, the first trees return. Stunted and widely scattered, they're the vanguard of the open forest that gives the Thelon its parklike beauty. The *Tundra Cub II* intersects the Thelon just south of Hornby Point, the site where three unprepared adventurers starved to death in the winter and spring of 1927.[TN]

Map in hand, I descend to watch for caribou, musk oxen and the elusive tundra grizzlies. In thirty summers of flying the north, I'd seen hundreds of grizzly bear tracks, but only one grizzly. That bear, which I had imagined snapping up salmon from some northern rapids or sniffing the Cub, was sitting on its rump beside a highway (unperturbed by tourists who stopped to take photographs) dining on sweet-stemmed, fireweed blossoms between Whitehorse and Haines Junction. As cars slowed to a stop and shutters clicked, the bear grazed on, giving the lie to tales of ferocious grizzlies.

I scan the map to see what lies ahead. There's Grassy Island, usually a good spot for musk oxen. And then I notice Cosmos Lake, the site of a huge military operation that began in January 1978, when a ten-thousand-pound, nuclear-powered Soviet reconnaissance satellite named Cosmos 954 scattered radioactive debris across a 600-mile swath of the Northwest Territories from Great Slave Lake into the Thelon Sanctuary. One fragment fell onto the Thelon's frozen face, where campers wintering at Warden's Grove discovered it. Like good citizens, they reported their find, expecting a few days or perhaps a week of disruption. Instead, their isolated winter home became the setting for a massive military intrusion.

Heavy equipment arrived on ski-equipped aircraft to bulldoze a runway across newly named Cosmos Lake, the closest lake to the fragment. In time, the whapping of helicopter blades yielded to the whine of turbo props. Camp

Garland sprang up on Cosmo Lake's shoreline. Soldiers needed accommodations; dignitaries and officials had to be housed, and the campers' solitude slowly changed to circus. Flown to Yellowknife for medical checks, they chafed to return, though one, for a time, found the media attention irresistible.

Weeks later, the government flew the campers back to their base, which had been used and somewhat abused by the military. They'd hoped to recover their pre-Cosmos serenity, but their sense of seclusion had slipped away. The midwinter carnival had altered their moods, and things were never the same.

The Canadian Government sent a $15-million bill for the cleanup to the Soviets, who paid less than half. Of the thousands of fragments that fell to the surface, many were potentially lethal, but less than 1 percent of the radioactive material was recovered. The rest lies buried in the tundra or in the depths of thousands of lakes, causing one wag to warn tourists like me to watch out for three-eyed trout.

Cosmos Lake is less than two miles across, so I orbit it twice while searching for the remains of Camp Garland. I'm flying at 200 feet, so any ruins should be easy to spot, but no matter how hard I look, I find nothing. Rolling out of my final orbit, I head for Grassy Island while wishing that Wes, my sharp-eyed game-spotter was here.

My canoeist friends have told me that they always find grizzlies near Grassy Island, so I scan the four-mile island, flying up its center and down its sides twice to no avail. Disgusted, I continue upstream. A few miles later I encounter a flotilla of four canoes. Their occupants wave their paddles madly, but when I land, it's obvious that they only want to talk to someone different, having been without a change of company for more than three weeks.

After introductions, I ask how the trip is going. Chuck, who is obviously the oldest, replies, "Pretty well. Bob here (pointing to a sandy haired man who stays seated in his canoe) sprained an ankle while portaging Helen Falls, and I'm temporarily reduced to one-handed paddling because I grabbed a frying pan that I thought had cooled, but hadn't. Other than that, we're in good shape."

"Well," I say, "you're going with the flow, so you should do alright. By the way, have you seen any caribou between here and the falls?"

"Not a one," he replies. "Just a bunch of musk oxen and a single tundra grizzly at the edge of the river that sat down to watch us just like we'd watch a parade. Quite a sight, that was."

As I get ready to leave, one canoeist hands me a letter to his father, explaining that his father had paddled the Thelon forty years ago, and that he'd love to know how the trip had been going.

"Sure," I reply, "and you can do me a favor, too. When you get to Baker Lake, tell the Department of Transport you saw me near Grassy Island on my way to Artillery Lake. That way, if I turn up missing, they'll now I got this far."

By the time we part company; it's getting late. The country to the west is rocky, and I'm reluctant to leave the Thelon's sandy shores, which are kind to aircraft floats, so I fly upstream to Warden's Grove, a frequent caribou crossing site, a great place to cast for trout and a perfect spot for camping.

The beach at Warden's Grove is wider than I remember, perhaps because it's been a dry year and the Thelon is running low. I tail the Cub onto the trackless beach in line with the nearest tree, only to discover that my ropes are too short to reach from tail to tree. That shouldn't be a problem unless a big wind comes up. Nevertheless, in order to sleep easy tonight, I retrieve two three-foot ground anchors from a float compartment and screw them into the beach beneath each wing to secure the Cub. As I tie the final knot, I try to imagine what it would look like here in the spring when the Thelon's in flood, when house-size blocks of three-foot-thick ice override the shorefast ice, bulldozing heaps of gravel, ice and boulders ashore.

Warden's Grove consists of a log outhouse and three dilapidated log cabins, the first of which was built in 1928 to house a warden who had the lonely job of patrolling the sanctuary. None of the cabins are fit to stay in, so I find a level spot, cook supper and, as the sun angles down to the northwest horizon, carry my gear to the tent and begin to clean the bugs from the Cub.

The front of the cowling and the leading edges of the wings, struts and tail are plastered with the gritty remnants of mosquitoes and black flies. The windshield's not as bad, because I clean it every day. When the outside is finished, I climb into the Cub to remove the bugs I've crushed against the windshield, and then lean back in my seat to enjoy the view. As I exit the Cub, I glance at the opposite shore. There, slowly wandering along the beach is a tundra grizzly and her cub.

I freeze. One hundred yards of water separates us, and the wind is blowing downstream, so they're not likely to scent me, but now I wish that I hadn't left my rifle at home. Head down, she ambles along the edge of the brush, stopping periodically to sniff the air. My camera's in the tent, but I don't want to attract her attention, so I just stand there. I'm like the woman who, when confronted about her messy house, replied, "They say that housework won't kill you, but why take a chance?"

The poor grizzly has had bad press from the day that it was named *Ursus horribilis* by a taxonomist who'd never seen one. Relying on the description of another person who also hadn't seen one, he damned it: "He is the enemy of man and literally thirsts for human blood." A few minutes later, vicious mom and junior quietly amble around a bend in the river and disappear. Rats! After thirty summers of searching for them, I finally see my first tundra grizzly and I don't even have a photo…grumble, grumble.

It's too early to head for the sack, so to entertain myself while I keep an eye out for the return of Mrs. Grizz, I dig out my *Herter's Professional Guide's Manual,* climb back into the Cub and close the doors and windows to keep out the bugs.

In 1967, I prepared for my first flight into northern Canada by reading every survival manual I could find, including two wonderfully entertaining books titled *Herter's Professional Guide Books, Volumes 1 & 2.* Useful for greenhorns, but often amusing to those who knew the bush, the books were packed with advice, some of it practical, all of it optimistic and none of it modest. In fact, Herter's encyclopedic books and catalogs claimed to provide the very best of everything, including advice on "how to enjoy eating raw fish."

As the mosquitoes bump against my windows, I sample Herter's bits of wisdom, learning that I shouldn't take heavy clients on horseback hunts because their bouncing stomachs can affect their hearts and cause shortness of breath, and that caribou, because of their hollow hair and back fat can be floated to camp, which is much easier than carrying if a river or lake is available. Bugs a problem? Wear red because red shirts are said to repel black flies. Lost with no compass? Spruce sap oozing from beneath the bark is clearer on the north side of the tree than on the south, and on cloudy days the sun can be located by holding a knife vertical with the edge pointing away from your face. Despite the clouds, the sunny side will be brighter. Keep turning until the brightness is equal or the difference is maximal. (I tried that one. It didn't work for me.)

Out hunting and you need to light a fire, but your matches are soaked, leaving nothing but your rifle? No problem! Just remove the bullet from a casing and pour the gunpowder onto the small heap of kindling. Then take a small piece of frayed cloth and push it into the cartridge. Fire the gun straight up. The rag should ignite, and it can be used to ignite the gunpowder-sprinkled tinder to start the fire.

Your flashlight dead? Your candles lost? Again—no problem! Knowing that smelt are fatty enough to make a passable candle, the Herter folks advise you to light one of the well dried smelt that you've been using for bait. Those who desire a smaller, less aggressive fire might want to stick a wick in the mouth of the smelt and light it. I wonder—should a smoker use a burning smelt to light his Camel?

Herter's catalogs reeked with immodesty. All of their products were deemed the BEST, in every regard. Ads for their "Famous Wilderness Canoes" claimed that their nonskid keel made them "unaffected by cross currents or wind…. Hit any aluminum canoe with a hammer and the hammer head will go right through it. Hit our Wilderness canoe with a hammer with the same force and it will not dent. Our Wilderness canoe is an adult canoe, not one that will stand only romancing in city park lakes. Our canoes are not designed by self-styled experts whose canoe experience consists of canoeing in city parks and talking canoeing, not doing it."

The Herter company is no longer in business, but their guidebooks linger on, advising and entertaining people like me who will never hunt in Africa, but still might want to know the best way to call in a lion or skin a crocodile.

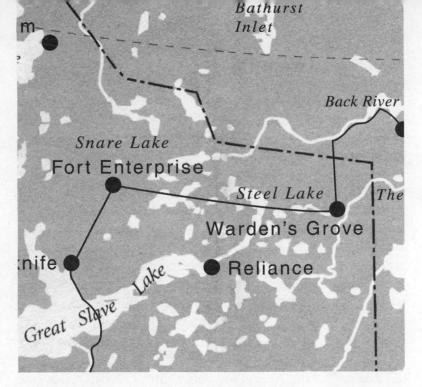

Chapter 7

Warden's Grove to Fort Enterprise, NWT

Learn as if you were going to live forever.
Live as if you were going to die tomorrow.
—MOHANDAS KARAMACHAND GANDHI

It's still dark when I crawl out of the tent to check on the Cub. The first thing I notice is that tonight, the first clear night I've had since leaving Churchill, someone has turned off the northern lights, leaving an obsidian sky shot through with brilliant stars. The second is that I need to crank my age-stiffened neck toward vertical to find Polaris, whereas back home I just look to the north and up a bit to find the polar star. The moon has yet to appear, and on this cool, calm night, the Milky Way seems brighter than ever before.

In *Bright Galaxies, Dark Matters,* physicist/astronomer

Vera Rubin wrote, "Less than 400 years ago, Galileo™ put a small lens at one end of a cardboard tube and a big brain at the other end." In so doing, Galileo learned that the sky-crossing band of lights that we call the Milky Way consisted of millions of stars, but until Galileo pointed his optical tube skyward, a host of other ideas prevailed.

The Greeks believed the Milky Way to be the breast milk of Hera, the wife of Zeus, but subsequent generations imagined the lights to be the souls of the dead. Some Inuit tribes saw the snowy path of the Raven god who traveled between heaven and earth. Muslims envisioned a path for pilgrims to follow to Mecca, while the Chinese imagined a great river that led to a pool in which the sun and moon bathed their children. Less poetically, Russians described a trail of straw that fell from the cart of a thief.

Except for our Milky Way, only three other galaxies can be seen from the earth by the unaided eye. Of the three, the Andromeda Galaxy is the nearest full-size spiral galaxy. Perhaps it's the one we like the most because it's shaped like our Milky Way. Since Galileo's time, refinements in optical telescopes and radio astronomy have shown that our Milky Way, with its billions of stars and potential planets, is just one of billions of similar galaxies. In short, we are probably not as special as our egos would have us believe. As Chet Raymo asserted in *The Virgin and The Mousetrap,* "Our galaxy, our star, our planet and even our life and intelligence are cosmically mediocre."

When the moon peeks above the horizon, I wish I were farther north, preferably north of 72 degrees, in the region where the moon sometimes misbehaves, remaining in view for days on end, occasionally appearing during a portion of the day, and then disappearing below the horizon for just as long as it was in perpetual sight. The farther north one travels, the longer those periods become.

To further confuse matters, the full moon phase occurs

during the winter months, which is handy during the long, cold months of sunless travel. The reverse is true in the summer, when the tiny sickle-shaped new moon rides low, if at all, in the daytime sky. Because summer in the high latitudes is a time of continuous daylight, a thin crescent moon can be very hard to see. Thus, if some northern traveler claims to have guided himself through the high latitudes by the light of the full summer moon, you will have reason to doubt his story, and perhaps the rest of his tales.

Snug in my parka and resistant to sleep, I count shooting stars until the oncoming sun begins to brighten the sky. The predawn, indigo horizon slowly purples, and then shifts through pastel shades of red, orange and pink "Look here!" commands the brightening sky. "The sun is bringing a brand new day!"

It's no wonder that people have worshiped the sun. There it is! Feel its warmth! We who live in the north truly admire the sun, looking forward to the soothing, sun-spawned, summer highs that dim our memories of the winter's egregious lows.

It's time for a really good breakfast, so I unpack the bacon and eggs that I bought at Baker Lake, fire up the Coleman, and after stirring a handful of blueberries from the nearby bushes into my pancake batter, whip up a delicious meal. As I flip my first flapjack, something chirps near the edge of the bushes. At first I think it's just a bird, but out pops a sik-sik, a northern ground squirrel that's related to our chipmunks.

I've camped with these critters before. This one, unlike the sik-sik that Wes and I once photographed at the Garry Lake mission, is surprisingly tame, perhaps because

Warden's Grove is a frequent stop for campers. As Wes slowly approached the Garry Lake sik-sik for a photo, it ducked into a hole, then popped out from an alternate entrance several yards away. Wes slowly moved closer, only to have his quarry scurry underground, then pop up elsewhere to sit calmly in the sun.

Unwilling to be outwitted by a rodent, I stretched out on the ground a yard from one entrance as Wes advanced on the other. A moment later the sik-sik emerged, indifferent to my motionless form, and sat boldly erect, surveying his kingdom. When my camera shutter clicked, he scrambled into his hole and didn't return.

Sik-siks, unlike the musk oxen and polar bears that combat the cold with fat and furry insulation, avoid it altogether by hibernating. Slowing its pulse, the sik-sik adopts a technique used by hedgehogs, whose heart beat falls to 2 percent of its summer pace. My chirping sik-sik, by lowering its winter metabolism, adds summers of life with long winter sleeps. Far to the south, its lazy cousin, the Mohave ground squirrel practices both hibernation and estivation, a state of torpor induced by extremes of heat, sleeping away much of the winter and the summer. I decide to name my sik-sik "Sam," and as Sam and I scarf down our bacon, eggs and pancakes, I recall a cousin of Sam's that I met years ago in a tent beside Ferguson Lake.

I'd been heading for Baker Lake when I spotted a tent with a boat nearby. A canoe wouldn't have piqued my interest, but finding a boat so far inland on such a remote lake meant that its owners were more than tourists, so curious George throttled back and landed to see "what gives?"

There, I found three prospectors. As we lunched on tea and biscuits and I updated them on the world they'd left behind, a sik-sik suddenly scampered into the tent, climbed into an empty coffee mug and calmly accepted a cracker from one of the men. The sik-sik, they explained, was a pet, brought along from a camp near Chesterfield Inlet. They planned to take it with them to Artillery Lake, then on to Yellowknife, making it the most well traveled rodent in the Northwest Territories.

My early rising and a big breakfast have made me sleepy, so I set my wristwatch alarm for 7:30 and return to my sleeping bag. I awaken at 9:30! Yikes! Hustling to make up for lost time, I'm back in the air in less than thirty minutes.

The forested Thelon falls behind as the Cub crosses Steel Lake™ where, years ago, I walked through a herd of caribou that paid me no more mind than if I were a stick. The odds are a million to one that I won't be so lucky again, but as I begin to cross an island near the center of the lake, I suddenly realize that it's covered with caribou, a few of which have just entered the water.

The island is a confusion of felsenmeer, the geologist's word for frost-shattered rock, but there's a small gravel beach on its eastern shore, so I pull in there, jump out and hurry uphill toward the herd They're nervous at first, but when I sit on a rock, they calmly graze past, their ankle bones clicking in the characteristic tympani of caribou herds. The largest, the bulls, would reach 350 pounds, and their antlers span six feet.

When a caribou pauses to look at me, its bristly muzzle reminds me that I'm back in Chipewyan country, a land where women refused to eat a caribou muzzle for fear of growing beards. Young men, in turn would reject bear's feet for fear of offending the dead bear's spirit, which would slow their running.

Like the Inuit, the Chipewyans harbored a host of beliefs. From birth to death, all Chipewyans wore an amulet containing a piece of their umbilical cords as a protection from harm. Good people who died traveled to idyllic islands in boats carved from stone, but sinners were doomed to capsize and swim forever. Fishnets must be widely spaced so that no net would become jealous if another net caught more fish and then stubbornly refuse to catch any fish at all. Following a successful hunt, the tongue and fat of the first caribou killed would be hung on a branch as a sign of respect and thanks to insure another good hunt. In the winter, hunters used snow from the soft bottom of drifts for drinking water, believing that it made them fast runners who could better pursue game. Foolish hunters who ate the harder crust would be slowed and suffer the consequences.

One Chipewyan legend tells of a woman who mated with a doglike animal she had rescued, later giving birth to an immense being so tall that his head reached the clouds. With his walking stick he drew the earth's lakes, rivers and islands—and then killed his dog-father, tearing him apart so that the entrails would become fish, the skin birds and the flesh caribou. Another legend describes two giants, who fought until one mortally wounded giant fell down, covering the straights between Siberia and Alaska. Across his body, all of the Dene tribes migrated into North America.

Because the Chipewyans were sandwiched between the Cree to the south and the Inuit to the north, and different people were feared, the Chipewyans were among the last to benefit from western technology, relying as they had for centuries on innovations like birch bark containers, their seams sealed with spruce gum for cooking pots. To heat the contents, hot rocks from the fire were picked up with antlers and lowered into the pot. Caribou tongue and a caribou fetus were considered delicacies, as was the semi-digested contents of the animal's stomach. To avoid becoming snow-blind, Natives fashioned "sunglasses" by cutting narrow slits in birch bark or bone that they trimmed to fit their faces.

As the last of the caribou splash into Steel Lake, I pause

to enjoy the sweep of this sub-Arctic paradise. Fluffy, sheeplike cumulus clouds slowly graze through royal blue skies. An amber esker snakes for miles across the southern horizon. On a day like today, I can see why the Natives wanted to live nowhere else—but that's on a day like today.

When I return to the Cub, I'm stunned to see that one side of the fuselage is slathered with oil from cowling to tail. Opening the cowling, I discover that the oil filler cap (with dipstick attached) has come loose, allowing oil to be sprayed out of the filler tube. I can't believe that I didn't tighten it properly when I last checked the oil, and because it seems tight when I screw it on again, I wipe down the Cub, replace the missing oil and give it another try.

Three orbits of Steel Lake later, I land again, this time at a mainland beach. Once again the oil filler cap is rattling around and my freshly cleaned Cub wears a new coat of oil. When I check the cap more carefully, I notice that the gasket seems unresilient, so perhaps that's the cause. To prevent the cap from rotating, I laboriously drill a tiny hole in its metal rim with the point of my knife, then run a steel fishing line leader through the hole, add more oil, replace the cap, tie the leader to a nearby brace to prevent the cap from rotating, and clean the Cub again. Three orbits later, I land again. The Cub is clean and the cap is secure. My problem is solved, but when I get home, the dip stick will need a new gasket!

It's one hundred miles to the fuel cache near the end of Artillery Lake, and when the lake finally creeps into sight, I begin to worry that someone might have found the cache and, thinking that the fuel had been abandoned, used it all. The cache, however, is located well away from the beaten track, and it's hidden in the head high brush, so I tell myself, "Relax—it'll be there." If it isn't, I'll just head for Yellowknife and leave the side trip to Fort Enterprise for next year.

As I taxi through the narrows that lead to the beach, I

recall B. D.'s admonition: "Don't worry if you don't see them right away. They're about a hundred feet into the bush, with brush on top, so they won't be easy to spot. Just follow the little stream that flows down to the beach and you'll find them."

The drums are right where he said, but the labels are gone, leaving only a few small chips of faded paint on their rusty exteriors. I've no idea which drum contains gas or which contains fuel oil, but one thing's for sure—these drums are old! They might even be relics of the DEW (Distant Early Warning) Line, which was built after World War II.

I don't carry a bung wrench, but I've used pliers to open these barrels before, so I spread the handles wide, engage the jaws of the pliers with the protrusions in the bungs and give them a twist. Nothing moves. Same for the second barrel. I strain at both repeatedly to no avail.

In an attempt to halve my work load, I try to detect the presence of fumes at bungs, but sniffing fails, and I can't tell the contents of A from B. They're too heavy to lift, and even if I could, I'd be straining so hard that I wouldn't be able to gauge their relative weights (gasoline is slightly lighter), so while the breeze bugs the mosquitoes, I sit on one of the barrels and try to think of a way to learn which of the drums contains gas. And then, like Archimedes, I have a "eureka" moment.

When King Hiero II asked Archimedes to determine (without deforming the crown) if his crown had been adulterated with silver, Archimedes found the solution while reclining in his bath. After weighing the crown, he immersed it in water to see how much water it displaced. He then compared the result to the volume displaced by an equal weight of pure gold. Though they weighed the same, the crown displaced more water than the equal weight of gold, which proved that the goldsmith had cheated the king—poor goldsmith!

It's said that when Archimedes reasoned out the answer, he leaped from his bath and ran through the streets of Syracuse naked, shouting, "Eureka, I've found it." That's fine for Archimedes, but not for me. Here, the rocky terrain negates naked running, and mosquitoes make strolling unwise.

The barrels almost propel themselves down to the lake, where they slowly bob side by side. It's immediately obvious that their contents are either different or that one of them is less full, so I beach them, tip the lighter drum on its end and contemplate its rusted bung. Opening a pair of pliers wide so that the jaws engage the lugs of the bung, I insert my big hunting knife between the handles of the pliers to increase my leverage and give it a careful-but-forceful twist. The barrel begins to rotate but the bung holds firm. To prevent its rotating, I sit on top of the barrel, bung between my legs, determined to drive my knife through the top of the barrel if one more try fails to loosen the bung. With my pliers in place and my knife betwen the handles for extra leverage, I strain against the bung, which finally yields, and within seconds I'm reassured by the scent of gasoline.

As I fill the Cub's wing tanks, I envision combining a photo of an Air Force jet tanker with a photo of the *Tundra Cub II* taken from the same perspective, making the Cub appear to be refueling from the probe that trails from the tanker. I already have a good photo of the tanker, and I can easily get one of the Cub. With my computer, I'll marry the two. Eased into my slide presentations about bush flying, the image will provide a good laugh for those who recognize the absurdity and gasps of amazement for those who don't.

While the Cub climbs westward toward the Snare River and Fort Enterprise, I stoke my fires with a few Oreos, some dried apricots, a can of pop and a *Bit-O Honey* candy bar that I carefully try to separate from its wax-paper wrapper, but, as usual, I fail.

I'm skirting the edge of the tree line, which is moving north every year, bringing robins to coastal communities where they've never been seen and yellowjacket wasps to Arctic Bay, a village far north of the Arctic Circle. To my right, 200 miles of barrens lead to the Arctic Ocean, but just thirty miles to my left, the earth is covered with trees. Beneath the Cub flows the parklike taiga, the open forest. Neither barren nor packed with trees, in my eyes it's the belle of the northern ball.

The advancing forest has already begun to encircle Courageous Lake, and when the Cub lands on Winter Lake, a twelve-mile widening of the Snare River, I'm back in solid green. Near the doorstep of Fort Enterprise, Winter Lake discharges a three-mile set of rapids downstream to Roundrock Lake, and to save a long walk through thickets of alder and birch, I taxi as close as I dare to the brink of the rapids, shove the nose of the Cub into the willows, and secure it as fast as I can.

The location of Fort Enterprise—with the word "abandoned"—is plainly marked on my map. I've been told that others had great difficulty locating the overgrown site, and then found nothing of interest, so I'm not expecting much. Nevertheless, I'm here, just miles from where midshipman Hood was murdered, so I might as well look around. Thirty minutes later, after having at least as much trouble locating the site as my predecessors, I come upon what might be the site of Fort Enterprise, but I'm far from sure because the site is hugely overgrown.

To salvage the stop, I return to the Cub, clip a lure to my line and try to attract a grayling. On my third cast, the peacock of fresh water fish, a two-pound grayling comes my way and soon lies flopping at my feet. With its sail-like dorsal fin and iridescent red and purple spots flashing brightly against its shimmering dark gray sides, the grayling's so striking that I'm tempted to set it free.

However, this grayling, gorgeous or not, will supply my supper, condemned to death by an excellent flavor that exceeds the taste of its cousins, the many varieties of trout.

The wind has switched to the northwest, putting me on a sheltered shore that's swarming with black flies, so I hop in the Cub and taxi across the Snare. Why clean fish while feeding black flies bugs when a two-minute taxi to a windy point will blow them all away?

While I fillet the grayling and toss together a decent meal (mushroom soup, bread, squeeze butter, coffee, peanut butter, grayling, more fresh blueberries than I should probably eat plus three oatmeal cookies from the Northern Store) I try to imagine what it must have been like in the winter of 1821–22 when the survivors of the first Franklin expedition staggered back from the barren coast of the Coronation Gulf to these wooded, sheltering shores.

As the party trudged south toward Fort Enterprise, they were down to eating boiled scraps of shoe leather and *tripe de roch,* a lichen that provided little nutrition but excelled at causing stomach pains. By early October, they had divided into two groups, the least feeble forming an advance party, with the remainder trailing behind. George Back, the leader of the advance section, limped ahead to search for food, finally coming upon the rotting corpse of a caribou, which was instantly devoured when the rest of his group arrived. In the meantime, events were going from bad to worse for those who trailed behind.

On October 11th an expedition member named Michel returned to camp with what he claimed was a piece of wolf meat, though it really had been cut from the bodies of two crewmen who had fallen behind. A week or so later, Michel and midshipman Hood agreed to stay in camp while the rest of the party gathered *tripe de roch.* Hearing a gunshot, they rushed back to camp, and found Hood lying beside the fire, shot through the head—supposedly a suicide. Waiting until

Michel was gone, the remaining men examined Hood and discovered that he'd been shot through the back of the head. Only then did they realize that Michel, who had become increasingly hostile (and always carried two pistols, a bayonet and a knife), presented a threat to their lives. A conference was held. Decision reached, Dr. Richardson, the senior officer present, shot Michel at the first opportunity.

Most of the original twenty-two men managed to reach Fort Enterprise, but once there, they died one by one until three Copper Indians sent by George Back arrived with food. With their strength restored, the survivors headed south with their saviors, arriving at Fort Confidence on Great Slave Lake in mid-December. Captain Franklin subsequently wrote in his logbook, "Lieut. Back, Dr. Richardson, John Hepburn, Augustus and I returned to York Factory on the 14 July. Thus terminated our long, fatiguing, and disastrous travels in North America, having journeyed by water and land (including our navigation of the Polar Sea), 5550 miles."

The grayling's so tasty that I decide to catch another for breakfast. Returning to the top of the rapids, I cast far out into the still water just above the first ripples of the down-stream run. When I cast again, my eye follows the lure toward the opposite shore, where I notice something move—something really big—right where I'd parked the Cub while I searched for Fort Enterprise. Just as at Warden's Grove, it's another grizzly. The bear appears to be grazing. Since the wind is blowing toward me, I stand my ground for a while, but then retreat to the Cub. I had planned to camp here, but now it seems foolish when there's an equally nice beach just a few miles up the lake.

When the Cub roars to life, the grizzly lifts its head, then rears up to full height and dashes into the willows. It's tempting to stay, but I want to sleep easy tonight. Minutes later, I'm eight miles away, tucked into a quiet cove rimmed with fragrant pines. Not bad for a guy without a reservation!

Wes and I overflew this very spot about twenty years previous. Earlier that day, we'd arrived at Port Radium, the Great Bear Lake site of The Eldorado mine that provided the uranium for the bombs that wrote an end to World War II. And as I scaled the 120 steps between the pier and the lofty offices of Echo Bay Mines to file a flight plan to Reliance, I thought of the ziggurats that ancient astronomers climbed every night in a fruitless attempt to get close to the stars.

Reliance is located on the eastern tip of Great Slave Lake, and because we always allowed extra time in case we decided to camp or if weather slowed us down, I filed a flight plan for three days. As it turned out, we flew straight through and camped just a few miles short of Reliance that evening. The following morning, just as we were about to leave for Reliance, the drone of an oncoming aircraft preceded a twin-engine Otter that was flying along the shore. We dismissed it, thinking it was just a charter flight. The Otter, however, banked toward us and began to orbit overhead. On both sides of its fuselage, large orange letters spelled out the word "RESCUE."

The Otter had wheels and couldn't land, so I climbed into the *Tundra Cub,* flipped on my portable radio and punched in the emergency frequency.

"Rescue Otter, this is Piper 4745 Mike. What can I do for you? Please reply on 121.9." (To keep the emergency frequency clear.)

"45 Mike, this Rescue. We're wondering what we can do for you. According to your flight plan, you were due at Reliance yesterday—three hours after departing Port Radium."

I instantly knew what had happened. Accustomed to flight plans and flight notes that rarely exceed a few hours, the agent who took our call from Port Radium wrote down "hours" instead of "days."

"Rescue Otter, we filed for three days, not three hours. With these Cubs, we couldn't even get here in three hours."

"Okay, 45 Mike. Glad there's no problem."

As his "Have a good flight," came through my headset, the Otter banked away toward Yellowknife.

"Wow," said Wes, "how's that for efficiency?"

"It's great," I replied. "And it's nice to know that the system works."

Later that day, when we stopped to refuel at Reliance, weatherman Jake invited us to come up to the station for a cup of coffee. Thirty minutes later, as I finished my second cup, the cook arrived with a surprise—a steak dinner complete with baked potatoes, escalloped corn and apple pie. While we ate, Jake told of their mid-July "ice-out," of a forest fire raging east of Yellowknife, and about a drowning the previous week. I asked Jake if he'd read *North of Reliance,* a book by David Oleson, a native Minnesotan, fellow pilot and professional sled-dog musher who lives with his wife on the nearby Hoarfrost River, but the book was news to Jake. He'd met the man, but he'd no idea that Oleson had written a book.

The breeze is strong and blowing onshore, so there won't be a problem with bugs. I collect firewood for my evening fire, placing it well away from my gasoline-filled, fabric-covered Cub. In my fire-starting kit, I carry a few stubby candles, which will also do if my flashlight fails. Whenever I fall back on the candles, I think of Edison's, "We will make electricity so cheap that only the rich will be able to burn candles."

I also carry several other fire starters, and because I like to try alternatives to Mr. Scheele's phosphorus-tipped matches, I've occasionally lit my fires with the sun and a camera lens or with sparks struck from a flint. I've read that you can even start a fire with clear ice that is shaped like a magnifying lens. Someday I'll try that, but because I've never used friction, and there's an abundance of dry driftwood and materials for the bow, I decide to give the friction method a whirl. Besides, the sun is still up and the day is hot so it just might work.

After cutting a two-foot piece from the beach-rimming alders, I make a bow by bending it into an arc with twenty-pound braided line from my tackle box. With a cup-shaped chunk of dry wood ready to receive the business end of my "whirling stick," I twist the string around the pestlelike stick, kneel down on the sun-baked sand and go to work, pressing down on the stick with a fist-size piece of green wood in my left hand to keep the palm of my hand from blistering.

Like the firewood that warms us twice—once when we cut it and again when it burns—I quickly get hot, but so does the wood. Within a minute, the tinder I placed in the "cup" begins to smoke, and I'm close to dripping with sweat. A tiny glow appears on the tip of a pine needle, and then spreads to a clump of powder-dry moss. Bending low like a Muslim at prayer, I gently blow on the tiny embers, breathing them into life. A quarter-inch flame beams up at me like a newborn infant, then quickly seizes thin strips of birch bark and a small heap of resinous spruce needles. Dry, thin, wing bone-like sticks follow. Bursting into flame they ignite scraps of finger-thick driftwood. I've made a friction fire! But as I congratulate myself, my conscience intrudes, saying, "Okay, hotshot, let's see you do it when it's thirty below or with wood that's wet."

I've an answer for the wet wood dilemma. Find some dead wood. Even if it's raining, the inside is usually dry, so split it and make dry shavings. The objective is to expose as much fuel to as much air as possible, so cut the shavings fine and arrange them loosely. Think about it—kerosene burns poorly as a liquid, but spray it into a mist and it becomes a torch. Plunge a lighted match into flour and it will be extinguished, but (do this outside) sift a small amount of flour in the air above lighted candle and watch it explode, which is why dust-laden grain elevators sometimes turn into bombs.

Contrary to my prediction, the wind begins to drop. One by one, female mosquitoes begin to follow the scent of my exhalations, seeking the big bag of blood beside the fire. To thwart them, and to extend my outdoor evening, I stand in the smoke while trying to be philosophical. After all, they only want a tiny part of me, and their cause is just. They seek my blood to give their eggs a start.

Mosquitoes can survive on nectar alone, but a blood meal will multiply egg production a hundred fold. When neither nectar nor blood is available, mosquitoes in Israel's Negev Desert search out the "sweet spots" that aphids leave behind. Known as honeydew, it's really just aphid waste, but because it's sweet, Negev natives treasure it as candy, probably not realizing that these deposits are the Bible's "manna" from heaven.

Feeling charitable, I let one feed on my arm. She swells like an expanding balloon, then staggers into the air. Another arrives, and I'm suddenly beset with bugs. As they accumulate, I remember the tale of an outraged mine camp worker who, aided by an excess of gin, decided to kill mosquitoes with his .44 Magnum while in the outhouse, sending nearby workers running for cover as he improved the john's ventilation. Stories like this abound, but because they rarely involve Natives, I wonder if those who grow up in the bush are less severally troubled by the bugs or are they just stoic, quietly tolerating that which they cannot change?

Unlike their smaller, southern cousins that have a noticeable sting, these bumbling mosquitoes draw blood quite painlessly. As I watch them, they take advantage of my rolled-up sleeves. Drawn like iron filings to a magnet, they search for the mother lode. I let them probe for a moment, then squeegee them off with my hands, rolling their bodies into gritty little balls.

As I retreat to my tent, I begin to understand geologist George Camsell who, when pushed close to panic by mosquitoes, felt himself wanting to run. "I pulled up and made a small fire so that I could get some relief in the smoke. I could easily imagine a man going off his head if he should have to endure such torture for any length of time." Camsell was lucky that his attackers weren't black flies, because black flies, unlike mosquitoes, aren't bothered as much by smoke. The only good thing about black flies is that their season doesn't last very long.

The Inuit have nothing good to say about *Kiktoriat,* the mosquito, but Havelock Ellis (who can avoid them) offers a softer view: "If you would see all of Nature gathered up at one point, in all her loveliness, and her skill, and her deadlines, and her sex, where would you find a more exquisite symbol than the mosquito?" Male mosquitoes certainly agree, following the distinctive whine of the Joni One-Notes to their source so effectively that when a Canadian power station began to emit just the right sound, thousands of males literally gummed up the works, causing it to malfunction.

Ellis aside, it's probably true that no animal on earth, not even tigers, grizzlies or crocodiles, have had such a profound impact on the human race. Some say that mosquitoes serve no purpose, living only to perpetuate their species, but they're wrong. Mosquitoes feed our aerial friends, the dragonflies, the hummingbirds of the insect world, and several species of bats and birds that scoop them out of the air—one dainty in-flight meal at a time. In addition, the mosquitoes' unsinkable, unwettable, quarter-inch-wide egg rafts, which contain up to 300 eggs, nourish aquatic creatures from larvae to fish.

Worldwide, there are 1,600 kinds of mosquitoes, of which less than one-tenth dwell in North America. Those that plague the far north have not been known to carry disease. Their southern cousins, however, host to a long list of woes. Malaria, which was once thought to be caused by bad (mal) air (aria), West Nile Virus, Dengue fever and encephalitis all travel via the mosquito, but the worst was yellow fever, which, though rare these days, ravaged Philadelphia in 1790, killing 10 percent of the city's 55,000 inhabitants. Sixty years later, yellow fever destroyed 9,000 lives in New Orleans, taking another 11,000 from the surrounding parishes. Unfortunately, mosquito-borne organisms like the malaria plasmodium continually evolve, becoming so resistant to one drug after another that millions still die of malaria.

Few people realize that the United States was as good as given the Panama Canal by the lowly mosquito. In the 1880s, when the French attempted to dig the canal, they were defeated by malaria and yellow fever, a mosquito-borne combination that killed 1,200 workers in just one year. Because the workers had been given clean housing, and the mosquitoes were thought to be just an annoyance, the baffled French blamed the disease on immoral living and shortcomings of character that weakened the body. In an attempt to demonstrate that no one of good character would be affected, one engineer brought his entire family, only to have them die one by one, with the engineer the last to perish—one of the 30,000 who died during the French attempt.

When the U.S. began to dig in 1904, drainage ditches were included to reduce the number of ponds in which mosquitoes matured. As a consequence, only 2 percent of American workers were hospitalized at a given time, far less than the crippling 30 percent experienced by the French.

Most of the mosquitoes inside my tent have lost interest in me, attracted instead by the rosy glow of the Winter Lake sunset. As they whine against the netting, they become easy targets for a few sweeps of my hand. Minutes later, silence reigns, and I no longer care what happens outside.

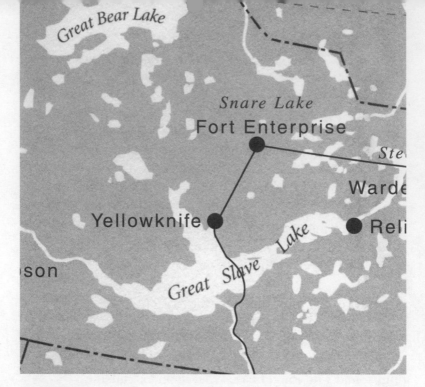

Chapter 8

Fort Enterprise to Yellowknife, NWT

"Where are we?"
"If you really want to know, I'll tell you."
"Never mind. Here aloft we are not lost, but found."
—ERNEST K. GANN, FROM *FLYING CIRCUS*

A south wind sighs through the mosquito netting. Outside, lingering wisps of fog drift low over Winter Lake. Razor and toothbrush in hand, I crawl out of the tent and discover a set of grizzly tracks leading to the Cub. I survey the area like a wide-eyed child, but see nothing while promising myself that I'll NEVER leave my rifle behind again. Kneeling down, I place a spread-fingered hand inside a huge paw print, losing it within the indentation while remembering the joke about how one tells black bear scats from those of the grizzly: Black bears stools are smaller and often contain the seeds of berries, but grizzly stools, they say, besides being larger, are studded with pieces of bone *and cans of pepper spray!*

Twenty yards upslope, my cooler still dangles from a tree branch where it spent the night. I follow the tracks, noting the impressive claw marks that adorn each print. The tracks approach the Cub, and then turn away. Not scenting food, the bear shuffled off to the south. That's fine with me. After a thirty-summer dearth of grizzlies, I've had my fill.

When it occurs to me that the bear might return, I pack my gear, fire up the Cub and leave Winter Lake. Promising myself a proper lunch in Yellowknife, the newly proclaimed Diamond Capital of North America, I make do with a handful of fig bars, a can of sardines, a few slices of cheese and a soda—probably more than many people in some parts of the globe will eat all day.

I'm almost straight north of Yellowknife, but I'll need to fly a course of 150° because my compass points to magnetic north, which lies far to the south of true north. To correct for that deviation, which in this area is 30°, I'll fly a heading of 180° minus 30°, or 150°. Were I flying above the clouds or on instruments and I'd neglected to make the correction, I would miss Yellowknife by more than fifty miles. However, because I always fly by "finger on the map," my error would soon be revealed. If the two pilots who left Coppermine for Norman Wells in 1956 had been just as careful, they could have avoided causing a harrowing "adventure" that put Search and Rescue pilots at risk.

The October weather was decent enough, with overcast skies, but good visibility, when the pilots of two Cessna 195s left Coppermine with full loads of fuel. Had the pilots been competent map readers, reaching Norman Wells, which is 360 miles southwest of Coppermine, should have been a breeze. But as the ceilings dropped lower and map-reading grew more difficult they slowly became confused. Without reliable compass readings or radio-navigation aids, they wandered around for hours before finally selecting a lake and landing, now very short on fuel.

When the weather finally improved, they drained the fuel from one Cessna into the other and took off for a look around, only to realize that they'd landed at Sherman Lake, almost 70° and hundreds of miles off course. As a consequence, when Search and Rescue flights combed their intended route, they drew a blank.

Neither aircraft had enough fuel to risk another takeoff, so one passenger volunteered to hike seventy-five miles to the nearest settlement, arriving there nineteen days after the planes left Coppermine. With no chopper available and one of the stranded passengers suffering from a cut hand and subsequent blood poisoning that might require removing his arm, a seaplane piloted by Jim McAvoy bounced across the newly frozen face of Sherman Lake, then landed in the lane of shattered ice. Thanks to luck and Jim McAvoy, they all survived, but if the commercial pilots had been decent map readers, they'd have arrived without incident at Norman Wells.

Because of my skill at map reading, I've been seriously lost just once, not in the north, but on the other side of the globe while accompanied by Wesley Miller.

All travelers have good reasons to head for Australia— some to dive the Great Barrier Reef, some to brown their bodies on the Gold Coast beaches of Queensland and New South Wales, and some to cast aside a former life. Wes and I, having signed up for a fly-it-yourself tour in rented Cessnas, were there for the wildlife, eager to photograph emus, bowerbirds, wallabies and kangaroos. But most of all, we wanted to visit Australia's Mecca, the massive 230 million-year-old, sandstone tortoise shell called Ayer's Rock—the ochre pupil of the desert's awesome eye.

In Australia's Red Center, just as in the Arctic, the country dominates the people and colors their language: the Dry, the Wet, the burn, salt-bush, ghost-gums and the gibbers (stones) of the Gibber Plains. There, aborigines cook emus in pits with the head exposed, knowing that when steam issues from the birds' nostrils, the flesh is done. And there, not far from the Rock, I met a sun-tanned eight-year-old who had never seen rain.

After checking out in the Cessna Skylanes in Melbourne (pronounced "Melbin" by proper Aussies), we began a two-week circuit that included stops at Broken Hill, Andamooka, Ayer's Rock, Alice Springs, Mount Isa, the Gulf of Carpenteria, Cairns and Brisbane.

On the first legs of the tour, abundant landmarks made navigation by map alone a breeze. However, on leaving Broken Hill as the eighth aircraft in a ten-plane flight, our takeoff was delayed to allow another aircraft to land, and we lost sight of the plane we were supposed to follow. After takeoff, we soon discovered the futility of trying to correlate a map to what had become a featureless plain below.

Our Cessna was equipped with an ADF (automatic direction finder) that might have led us to the next airport, but neither Wes nor I had ever used one, so on we flew, trying vainly to locate ourselves over the blank-faced outback with a map that might as well have depicted the ocean. Riding in the cool air a few thousand feet above the realities of the desert, Wes and I began to consider our limited options.

When the lead planes radioed that they had reached the airport and were landing, we still had nothing in sight. Trailed by the two aircraft that had followed us, we eventually stumbled onto a gravel runway that our tour leader had told us to avoid except in an emergency because it was an airport restricted to those who had business on a reservation for aborigines. Having come closer to an emergency than we wanted, we radioed the tour leader and landed. Fifteen minutes later he arrived to lead us back to the fold.

That night, Wes and I got out the manual for the ADF, having learned that navigating by finger-on-the-map, which had worked so well in the Arctic, was a wonderful way to get lost over Australia's unadorned outback plains.

If nothing else, our brief disorientation taught us to avoid relying on the other guy's navigation and to have a little charity when a worried voice reaches out on the party line of the airways to ask a fellow traveler, "Where in the hell are we?" So far, whenever I've heard those words in my headset, they've always sorted it out, slowly refining "about here" to "Oh yaa, here we are."

In my case, whenever the terrain and the map don't seem to agree, I assume that my eager mind has gotten ahead of the airplane. To outwit my impatience, I draw the Cub's track on the map as I proceed, writing down the time wherever I cross an easily identified landmark. Later, if things look wrong, I check the time of my last fix on the map. If it's just twenty minutes ago, twenty minutes at ninety mph should take me thirty miles past the last checkpoint. On comparing the map to the terrain below, I always find that the Cub is right where logic requires, but well behind my brain.

As Roundrock Lake falls behind, I think of John Steinbeck, who was frequently lost—and even faked it when he wasn't as a way to begin a conversation. In *Travels With Charlie*, Steinbeck wrote, "A man who seeing his mother starving to death on a path and kicks her in the stomach to clear the way, will cheerfully devote several hours of his time giving wrong directions to a total stranger who claims to be lost." Unfortunately, my experience echoes Steinbeck, making me wary of directions from well-meaning locals, especially those who have little acquaintance with east, west, north and south, and rely on landmarks. I'm even more cautious with those who begin with "Oh, that's easy" or close with the deadly "You can't miss it."

It's 170 miles to Yellowknife, so I settle back for a two-hour flight. Far off to the west lies Indin Lake where, a decade ago, I came upon a human skull protruding from the tundra. The size of the lichens adorning the skull implied that it was hundreds of years old, but a more recent adventure in the same area involved a fiery death and taught a careless radio operator a lesson about properly doing his job.

Bush flying in the old days was risky enough when everyone tended to business, but things could get hairy if someone dropped the ball, especially during the winter. One such fumble happened in 1942 when Alf Caywood, Jack Rennie, and a passenger left Yellowknife on a flight to Coppermine, which lies on the Arctic coast, with a stop planned at Great Bear Lake's Port Radium.

When Alf was an hour or so out of Yellowknife, a front forced him to cancel the Great Bear stop, so he changed course, heading directly for Coppermine after first alerting Yellowknife of the change. Unfortunately, the Yellowknife radio operator didn't write down Alf's message—and then forgot about it.

In most cases, it wouldn't have mattered, but an hour or so later, Jack, who was flying co-pilot, began to shift around, ducking down to look beneath his seat. When Alf asked what was wrong, Jack replied, "I don't know, but the back of my legs feel warm."

When Alf swung open the door to the cabin, he saw, to

his horror, the entire cabin engulfed in flames. In a flash, Alf dove for the tundra as hundreds of rounds of ammunition destined for Coppermine began to explode, spraying bullets everywhere, ripping holes in the wall between Alf and the burning cargo—not to mention the passenger, whom they couldn't see because of the smoke. According to Alf, they hit the frozen lake so fast that they skidded for almost a mile.

Alf and Jack leaped from the burning wreckage, ran to the passenger entrance and ripped open the door. The body of their passenger tumbled out, peppered with bullets and burned to death.

Had the Yellowknife radio operator done his job, Alf and Jack would have been found within hours, but because of his error, nine very cold days passed before they were finally spotted, having sustained themselves on the tinned beef and the centers of deeply burned turkeys.

As for the missed stop at Great Bear Lake's Eldorado mine, no one really cared, and the cargo was soon replaced. But if that flight had been detoured the following year, it could have had larger consequences, for by then a new and much more important project was underway. Shrouded in secrecy, its discoverer, a knowledgeable prospector named Gilbert Labine, lowered his voice while he and famed bush pilot Ernie Boffa rode the dozer to the Eldorado mine.

"Ernie," said Gilbert, "there's big things going on—the biggest thing since the birth of Christ. It's called uranium, and it just might end the war."

Ernie was right. Uranium did end the war, but it wasn't uranium that put Yellowknife on the map. It was a yellow mineral that the Slavey Indians called "rock fat," though the rest of us call it "gold."

In late 1933 two prospectors named C. J. Baker and Herb Dixon became the first to realize that the Yellowknife region had tons of gold in its basement. Word leaked out and the rush was on! Southern headlines trumpeted "gold nuggets as big as a man's thumb," and the headlines, for once, were right. At that time, decent ore could be expected to yield a quarter ounce of gold per ton, but the Burwash strike on Yellowknife Bay brought in 13.6 ounces per ton. That's fifty times the average!

In 1932, a British immigrant named Tom Payne arrived in Ft. Smith, where he drove bulldozers for a few years before heading north, ending up as a destitute watchman on a mining property at Beaver Lodge Lake—a dead-end job if ever there was one. So in 1935, Tom moved farther north to a scattering of shacks called Yellowknife. There he maintained machinery for several of the budding mines while keeping his eyes open for signs of the Mother Lode, which he eventually stumbled upon, only to learn that his find had already been staked. However, the absentee owner had failed to develop the property, and if he didn't begin within a few months, the claim would be up for grabs. Tom quietly waited, hoping that the many feet that crossed his finding day after day would accompany eyes that rarely looked down.

Tom was lucky. In the rush to stake out the abandoned land, which had just become public knowledge, Tom was the first to reach his find a few minutes after midnight. A year later, Tom and his partners sold a 60 percent interest in the property to Consolidated Mines for $500,000— a huge sum for 1937. Tom, who had struggled to feed his family, would never be poor again.

Tom's buddy in this affair was a man named Gordon Latham, a former teacher, then clerk, who had decided to go to Yellowknife to build a hotel. After working for Wop May's Canadian Airways, he rode the Athabasca and Slave Rivers downstream to Fort Resolution, then boarded a barge for the hundred-mile crossing of Great Slave Lake. As the barge labored in to Yellowknife Bay, Gordon spotted a few shacks at Burwash Landing and a scattering of tents on a small island that would come to bear his name, for it was on that island that Gordon Latham built Yellowknife's first "tent hotel," later adding wooden walls and a real roof to his Corona Inn, a building that was often so full that latecomers were required to sleep beneath the trees, paying a dollar each to use the Corona's primitive "facilities."

Liquor, though illegal at the time, was always available—if the price was right. Medicinal alcohol, however, was allowed, which caused critics to complain that most of the hotels, including the Corona, were so well stocked with booze that they might as well have been hospitals. As Ray Price wryly noted in *Yellowknife,* "Diseases that only alcohol could cure were rife." In his book, Price described a typical evening in the full-as-a-tick Corona: "Lying in their eiderdowns [sleeping bags] in a corner of a large room were two Roman Catholic priests; a step or two from them a card game was in progress; on the table was plenty of rum and money; over in another corner a dentist was working on a tooth with a treadle-powered drilling machine...One of the priests stirred, caught the attention of a card player and said, 'Give me a shot of your rum.'"

A few years later, the Yellowknife Hotel appeared, eventually managed by another wonder of the north, a hardy fellow named Vic Ingraham who lost both legs and most of his fingers in a fire on Great Bear Lake. Ingraham, not one to take his problem too seriously, toured U.S. army hospitals to show young amputees how well he managed with his artificial limbs. "Hell," he'd roar, rapping his wooden legs with a stick, "these things have some real advantages. For example, those damn mosquitoes never bother my ankles any more."

One might think that the arrival of the second hotel would have ended the crowding, but Yellowknife continued to boom. As late as 1945, the fourteen-bed Yellowknife Hotel was still "plagued" by too many guests, occasionally moving up to twenty-five beds into the "beverage" room, thereby breaking the old rule that falling asleep in a beer parlor will get you thrown out the door.

As the Cub flies on toward Yellowknife, I scan its primitive panel. Fifty-eight years old, the faded faces of its oil and temperature gauges bear permanent "shadows" behind needles that have rested on zero for most of their lives. It took a few months, but I finally learned not to be startled when a glance at the gauges revealed zero oil pressure because the "shadow" at zero was more prominent than the faded oil pressure needle that closely matched its background.

Next comes the altimeter, a gift from Evangelista Torricelli and Blaise Pascal, two Italians whose work led to the first practical barometer, which is the basis for altimeters. The first westerner to suggest that air might have weight was a first century Greek philosopher named Heron (Hero) of Alexandria. However, progress in science soon stalled and in some cases reversed due largely to the efforts of antiscience, Christian zealots. In *Lost Discoveries,* Colin Ronan wrote, "On the advice of the Bishop of Alexandria, who detested all pagan [non-Christian] learning with a pathological vengeance, the Emperor Theodosius ordered the great Library [of Alexandria] to be burned." The 500,000 to 700,000 works that went up in flames constituted a huge loss to the western world. Cyril, the Bishop in question, was later declared a saint. So thorough was the church's eradication of secular knowledge that by the fifth century, St. Chrysostom would proudly boast, "Every trace of the old philosophy and literature of the ancient world has vanished from the face of the earth." The Dark Ages followed.

Centuries later, Evangelista Torricelli and others began

again, with Torricelli devising "an instrument which will exhibit changes in the atmosphere." Building on Torricelli, Pascal created the barometer, which proved that air had weight. In fact, an average room at sea level contains about two pounds of air.

Two centuries after Torricelli, an English physician devised a leech-powered "tempest prognosticator" to warn of oncoming storms, the logic being that leeches often became more active whenever the air pressure dropped. Not surprisingly, the doctor's leech barometer found little "suck-sess."

As I sit in my airborne enclosure inhaling and exhaling billions of air molecules with each breath, it occurs to me that because of the diffusion of air molecules it is quite possible that any of us, myself included, might occasionally inhale a few of the molecules that once enlivened Heron, Torricelli or Newton—or maybe Jack the Ripper.

The ignition switch on most Cubs is mounted on the cockpit's left sidewall, where, at my discretion, it permits or prevents the flow of electricity from my engine's magnetos ("generators") to its spark plugs. That current exists because of the work of an English genius named Michael Faraday[TN] who thought to spin a magnet within the arms of a horseshoe-shaped coil of wire, causing the wire to become electrified. Faraday had just invented the generator, without which our civilization would instantly collapse. Imagine a life without electricity. No electric lights, radio, computers, televisions or phones. No subways, cars or diesel-powered trains or buses. No central heating or air conditioning. No x-rays, CAT scans or MRIs.

Faraday's invention was based on the work of a Dane named Hans Oerstad who, during a public lecture, noticed a magnetic field surrounding an electrified wire while performing an experiment designed to prove that no such field existed. When Oerstad brought a compass close to the wire, he was surprised to see the needle align itself with the wire. Oerstad, who understood that science must be self-correcting, simply admitted his error and moved on.

On many aircraft, a temperature probe extends through the windshield, but the Cub makes do with a thermometer taped to the strut where it's easy to see. My thermometer, which is accurate to one or two degrees, is far superior to Galileo's water-filled thermometer that, besides being useless below freezing, had no markings. In time, markings were added, leaving one final challenge: how to make a glass tube with a constant diameter bore.

At the suggestion of Isaac Newton[TN], some early thermometers used zero for the temperature of melting ice and twelve for body temperature—the two standards that were commonly available. A few years later, Gabriel Fahrenheit invented the first alcohol thermometer and then the mercury thermometer, the two that we use today. Fahrenheit placed 0 degrees at the coldest temperature he could reach with a mixture of salt and ice, which turned out to be 32 degrees below the freezing point of water. On the same thermometer, the boiling point of water arrived at 212 degrees. Then came Anders Celsius, who saw the logic of having 100 degrees between the freezing and boiling points of water, but for some reason Celsius put 100 degrees where water froze and 0 degrees where it boiled—an odd arrangement that lasted until Celsius died, and then it was quickly revised. Now much of the world uses the Celsius (centigrade) system, but a few societies (like mine), still cling to an outmoded, illogical system of weights and measures that includes the Fahrenheit scale.

Picking up the Yellowknife River, I follow it south while

watching for the aircraft that are sending a stream of transmissions to the Yellowknife tower. To the west lies Rae, the
site of a Hudson's Bay Company post opened by John Rae in
1852 and the home of the Dogrib Dene, one of several Native
villages that received national attention when Mike Thomas
began to criticize the government's Indian policies. While
running a trading post at Lac La Martre, Thomas had come to
understand and admire the relatively stable, centuries-old patterns of the Natives' lives, but according to Thomas, when the
government became involved "everything changed."

Thomas, as quoted in Shirley Matheson's *Flying the
North,* argued, "the white man decided that these kids had
to go to school, which meant that the mother had to stay
here [with them]…The old man can't go out on the trap line
without his family. It was a family affair.

"I saw total destruction of the northern Indian in twenty
years…in Snowdrift, Lac La Martre, you name it.

"Now you've got schools and these kids go to about
grade six. Some even made it as far as Yellowknife to the
residential schools. Okay, they say, now we've educated
you. Go back to your people…Their own people called
them 'goddamned white men.' We don't want you back
here. You don't know how to trap. You don't know how to
fish. You don't know nothing. You can't drive our dogs.
You're no good to us.

"Our society didn't want them. Who would hire grade-
nine kids? So they'd migrate to the cities. They'd end up on
back streets doing whatever they could to survive, the
loneliest people you'll ever meet in your life. Nobody
wanted them. And there's nothing worse than being
someone no one wants, eh?"

Looking west, I strain to see the raised beaches that rise
stairlike beyond Great Slave's northwestern shore, but
they're just too far away. Like their counterparts that
surround much of Hudson Bay, the beaches were created

when the last Ice Age waned, the land rose, and Great Slave Lake could again flow out through the valley of the Mackenzie River.

At Prosperous Lake, I listen to Airport Advisory Delta, switch to the tower frequency, wait for a break in transmissions and call the tower.

"Yellowknife tower. This is Piper 4855 Mike."

"Piper 4855 Mike. Go ahead."

"Yellowknife tower, Piper 4855 Mike is a PA-11. 20 north at 1,000 [feet] with Delta for landing Back Bay."

"Piper 55 Mike, continue approach. Report on three mile final for Back Bay."

The Cub descends while I scan the skies for traffic. I'm number four to land behind a Twin Beechcraft, an Otter and a Beaver—all of them "heavy iron" compared to my Cub.

What a change they represent! Today no one gives them a glance, but in 1929, the year that bush pilot Wop May brought the first air mail to Great Slave Lake from Fort McMurray, any aircraft created a scene. Philatelists, hearing of the coming "first" swamped May with a thousand letters. Farther down the Mackenzie, May was met by an incredulous Native who exclaimed, "I don't believe it. The wings don't flap."

In 1987, Yellowknife, then just a town of 8,000, became the capital of the Northwest Territories, which constituted a third of Canada. By then, the Dene had named Yellowknife the "money place," which it certainly was, but it was also the only government center where, in the true pioneer spirit, city cleanup was left to volunteers. Now past 20,000 and growing, Yellowknife boasts good hotels (the Explorer and the Yellowknife Inn are but two), art galleries, an attractive $25 million Northwest Territories' Legislature building, and a hugely busy seaplane base and harbor called Back Bay.

As usual, the Spur dock is occupied. If they had space, I'd buy avgas, but I end up so far from the facility that I decide to get car gas with my collapsible bags. Avgas costs more than car gas, so using a nearby station will easily cover the cost of the cab.

Most of the docks are occupied by commercial operators like Air Tindi and Wardair, the airline that Max Ward envisioned in 1946. Starting life as Polaris Air, Max's "airline" began with a single de Havilland Fox Moth, an odd-looking biplane with an open cockpit for the pilot, who sat above and behind his enclosed passengers. For about a year, things went well for Max, but just as he began to prosper, the Air Transport Board informed Max (surprise) that he needed a license to fly for hire.

To keep the feds happy, Max partnered with a licensed pilot, but times turned tough and Polaris went bust. Max returned to southern Alberta where he shingled roofs on hot summer days while dreaming of flying the North. Carpentry paid pretty well and Max was thrifty, so he finally saved $96,000, which was just enough to purchase one of the finest bush planes ever made—the de Havilland Otter. Returning to Yellowknife, Max formed Wardair, the hugely successful airline of the western provinces and Northwest Territories. Years later, while waiting for a flight from Honolulu to Maui, I watched a beautiful Boeing 747 taxi up to the main terminal. Emblazoned on its fuselage was a name I'd seen on countless 180s, Beavers and Otters all across the North—Wardair.

I'm starved! I've been feeding myself since Churchill, and it's time for a decent meal, so I head for a nearby cabin that houses the Wildcat Café. Built of logs in the thirties, later remodeled (and needing it again), the Wildcat, which is a "summer only" operation, echoes Yellowknife's pioneer days. It's not quite noon, but when I step inside, the place is already packed. All of the benches are occupied; so I wait until someone leaves, then take his place at the end of a bench. I scan the menu, which features the usual fare, but it also lists caribou steak. I've never had caribou, so today's the day.

With my order taken, I turn to my neighbor, who's been flying for a charter service contracted to one of the mines. "Bill" is totally bald and powerfully built—a Caucasian version of Odd Job, the stocky, oriental hit man who wielded a lethal steel derby in one of the James Bond films. If Bill had lived here a century ago, the Natives would have called him a "slippery head" because of his lack of hair. (Being bald is rare among North American Natives.) When we've disposed of the weather, Bill glumly allows that he's just been fired, not for incompetence, he says, but for telling off a big shot from one of the mines.

According to Bill, a director wanted him to make a "little detour" during a return flight from one of the company's mines. Bill, knowing that the detour would deplete his fuel reserves, told the director, "I have an hour of fuel in reserve, and a detour that long will use up most of that fuel. That's unsafe, and it's also illegal, so I'll have to stick to the plan."

"Listen," said the director, "I know you guys carry plenty of gas, so make the change or I'll have you canned!"

Fed up, Bill told the director what he could do with his "little detour."

The next day, Bill was fired. However, if his flight record is as clean as he claims, he'll soon be flying again.

Bill's lament reminds me of Bob Ellis, as Alaskan bush pilot whose company sent coded messages between Juneau and Fairbanks to keep the competition guessing. During a slack period of flying, Ellis decided to break the code, which he did, receiving a message a few days later that said, "Fire Ellis!"

The caribou, done medium-well and served with

broccoli, mashed potatoes and gravy, is delicious—better than venison, which I like, but not enough to go deer hunting.

Bill departs, promptly replaced by Jason, a self-confessed "new guy" to the North who works for Northern Transport. When I ask if the Igloo Inn is still in business, he looks puzzled, then asks the diner to his right if he's heard of an Igloo Inn.

"Yaa," he replies, "but now it's the something Coach. Same place. A little nicer, but more money. You should try the Explorer. It's spendy, but it's first rate."

Ed and his neighbor begin a conversation about bar hopping—which places they like and which to avoid—placing the Black Knight, the Raven's Pub and Barkley's at the Explorer on the A list.

When I ask where I shouldn't go, Ed replies, "Just stick with Barkley's. It's a good crowd and not too noisy. Me, I'm done with the noise and rough stuff. Just last week they had a big fight outside of one of the other bars. Even the ladies got involved."

"Really!" says the neighbor. "Wish I'd seen that."

"Wish I hadn't," Ed responds. "Suddenly there was knives out and people running everywhere. One guy falls, another lands on top of him and the guy on the bottom comes up bleedin' and his eye hangin' half out."

"Oh, wow," says the neighbor, "maybe not."

The Explorer, as it turns out, is fairly close to the harbor, so I can easily check on the Cub. It's the height of the tourist season, but they still have plenty of rooms, including one on the top floor, which I prefer for the view—and because no one can stomp on my ceiling in the middle of the night.

Nick, the YK cab driver, picks me up at the door and we head for the nearest gas station, where gas is just a dollar per liter—about $3.50 U.S. per gallon. Two trips later, the Cub's tanks are full.

"Where to now?" asks Nick.

"First I'd like to see that Thelon River mural. The last time I was here, it was falling apart, but they say it's been redone. After that, you can drop me off at the legislative building. I should walk back to the hotel, but if you can be back at five, I'll ride."

Lauren Sinnott's mural, which is painted on the side of a small, garagelike building, features a mixture of wolves, musk oxen, caribou and tundra grizzlies backed by the winding Thelon. The colors are vivid and the sweep is grand, having been painted by an artist enamored with the sights she'd seen. Unfortunately, her first effort weathered badly, so a few years later Lauren replaced it with materials that can stand up to the tools of time.

As Nick heads up Franklin Avenue, I ask if he knows any good stories about Yellowknife characters.

"Sure," he says. "Have you heard about light-fingered Joey Veitch?"

"No."

"Well," says Nick, "this guy had sticky fingers. He came to Yellowknife around '38 with a few supplies and a team of sled dogs that he slept with, claiming that they kept him warm and were good for washing dishes. Folks soon realized that when Joe was around, they'd be wise to keep an eye on their stuff. Because of Joe's 'problem,' he often landed in jail.

"On one occasion, when he was sentenced to cut wood for the town, Joe deliberately cut every piece just a little too long to fit into the firebox, but he was arrested again and forced to cut them in half.

"Years later, Joe moved to Norman Wells on a barge that carried a fancy, wood-burning stove. The stove lids, however, were missing, and without the lids, it couldn't be sold. A few months later Joe offered to buy the stove for a fraction of its usual price, saying, 'I think I have some lids that might fit.'"

The NWT capital is impressive, and at $25 million, it should be. Set on the shore of Frame Lake near an antique drilling rig with an equally elderly Wisconsin engine, the building houses a circular assembly chamber designed to inspire the consensus approach to government.

From the government center, it's just a short walk to the Prince of Wales Northern Heritage Centre, a fascinating showcase of the north's people, land and animals. The outside of the Centre bears artful renditions of caribou and musk oxen. Inside, are an assortment of attractive exhibits plus a huge assortment of northern photographs that can be viewed on the facility's computers. Hours pass. As my tour draws to a close, I come upon a weathered wooden yoke— the sort that's used to carry pails. Close to the yoke is a bronze bust of Tom Doornbos, the namesake of Doornbos Street in Yellowknife's Old Town.

Yellowknife has had plenty of characters, but one of its favorites was Tom (Tjar) Doornboos, a tall, Dutch immigrant who left his intended behind when she refused to come to Canada's western plains. There, in 1934, the prairie wind blew Tom from job to job until he headed north to Fort Smith and then to icebound Yellowknife in 1941. By then WW II had turned attention away from gold mining, and Yellowknife, which was just four years old, had little to offer a fifty-year-old immigrant with marginal English.

One job led to another until Tom decided to carry water, and carry water he did, trudging the Yellowknife streets for years with a yoke across his shoulders from which dangled two five-gallon pails. Charging 25 cents per pail, Tom trudged from home to restaurant to hotel to bar, becoming an essential fixture in a town with no municipal water supply. Despite Tom's appearance of poverty, some say that he became as rich as those who found Yellowknife's gold. That poverty, whether real or imagined, led to stories of Tom occasionally ordering a cup of hot water at the Gold Range Café. Adding generous amounts of sugar, pepper and catsup, he'd create the Doornboos version of tomato soup.

Tom's first home in Yellowknife was a six-by-six-foot dugout with a tent for a roof and an "air-tight" heater to fight the cold. As he trudged the winter streets in his long black coat, some called Tom the King of the Ravens, perhaps a term of respect, given that many North American Natives revere that crafty bird. One tarpaper shack after another followed Tom's dugout until he finally moved into a senior residence in 1971.

With such a background, I was surprised to learn that Tom loved poetry. One of his favorites, which he showed to journalist Gorde Sinclair not long before he died, seems to refer to the love he left behind.

> Oft in the stilly night
> ere slumber's chain has bound me
> Fond mem'ry brings the light
> Of other days around me.
> The smiles and tears of boyhood years
> The words of love then spoken
> The eyes that shone, now dimm'd and gone
> The cheerful hearts now broken.
> Thus in the stilly night
> ere slumber's chain has bound me
> Sad mem'ry brings the light
> Of other days around me.

There's no cab in sight when I step outside, so I hustle off toward the harbor while a raven—the symbol of Yellowknife—circles overhead. It's a long hike, but it's pretty much downhill. Besides, I need the exercise, and if I take a cab, I won't be able to justify eating another restaurant meal. Fifteen minutes later, I puff into Barkley's Dining

Room, the Explorer's comfortable restaurant. An hour passes, and I emerge more slowly, feeling guilty for having eaten more than I should.

To ease my conscience, and knowing that the sunset arrives past eleven, I stroll down to the harbor to check on the Cub, and then head for the Bush Pilots' Memorial. Ten years ago, I briskly climbed the big granite dome that supports the memorial's obelisk, arriving at the top in comfort, but this year, hampered by the additional years and a substantial meal, I arrive puffing, glad to lean against the tall, cool obelisk while I catch my breath.

Hearing voices, I walk to the opposite side of the monument, where I find a man, a woman and two teenage children. Ted Nelson, his wife and two grandchildren have driven up from Edmonton in a rented car. In a few days, they'll fly back and another couple will fly up to return the car. Ted, a retired geologist with rock dust in his blood, has worked all over Canada, including Yellowknife and Red Lake. As a consequence, he likes to visit towns like Yellowknife, Thompson, Lynn Lake and Sudbury where the community's lifeblood flows up from well beneath the ground. He's also a pilot, and as we begin to swap aerial tales, Mrs. Nelson and the grandkids head for the Explorer's pool.

Ted spent twelve years in Yellowknife in the sixties and seventies, and then moved to Red Lake until he retired. I ask if he knew Lennie, but he doesn't remember the name. However, when I ask if he'd heard the story about Marius Madsen, he responds, "Everyone in Red Lake knows that one. In fact, I'll tell you a similar story. The fellow's name was Fred Giauque (pronounced Jakeway), and he made it big right here at Yellowknife."

Ted and I, two pilots past our prime, lean back against the obelisk, and as an assortment of seaplanes taxi to and from the docks like bees tending their hive, Ted begins.

"A lesser man than Fred Giauque would never have

made it to Yellowknife, but Fred was tough. When no jobs could be found, he started a lumber business, and when sales turned bad, he shipped his mill to Goldfields—that's on the north side of Lake Athabasca. Maybe he figured he wouldn't go broke in a place with a name like Goldfields, but go broke is what he did.

"Back at Fort McMurray, Fred took a job managing a saw mill, then quit in disgust after two years of being paid only in groceries. Before he quit, Fred built a forty-foot boat to float his gear up to Fort Smith. He arrived flat broke, but at an excellent time. The freighting company that carried goods around the Slave River Rapids needed help so badly that they agreed to portage his boat and cargo free if he and his three sons would work the portage for just one week. At the end of that week, Fred and his sons headed down the Slave toward Yellowknife, which was 300 miles away.

"Yellowknife, like many mining towns, had cycles of boom and bust, and when Fred arrived, a bust seemed imminent. By February 1943, he was deeply in debt, with a mortgage on his boat, but he owned the only caterpillar tractor in Yellowknife, which he kept busy until World War II and an upswing in mining reversed the trend. Securing a contract to float telephone poles down the Mackenzie River from Fort Smith to Norman Wells, that's almost 800 miles, Fred built the longest log boom ever constructed and ended the year with $17,000 in cash and a line of credit. And then his fortunes really took off. On a trip to Gordon Lake...you know where that is?"

"Sure. About sixty miles northeast. I passed it coming down."

"Okay. Well, at Gordon Lake, Fred spotted a good showing of gold, staked it, and then sold his claim for $12,000 as soon as he got back to Yellowknife. A few days later, Fred hired a plane to take him and two of his sons to a different lake, telling the pilot to come back in two weeks. Unfortunately, the agent who booked their flight was replaced a few days later and the pilot flew off to the States for a holiday.

"Everywhere they looked, Fred and his sons found gold. They staked twenty-four claims and then sat down to wait for their plane, which failed to arrive. A week passed. Still no airplane. Having run out of food, they ate whatever they could kill, including some hawks that they said tasted like chicken.

"When Fred's third son got back from Norman Wells, he finally tracked down the pilot's mechanic who happened to know where they were. When the plane finally arrived, Fred hardly knew which emotion to vent: 'Where the hell have you been?' or 'Son, we are going to be very rich!'

"Back at Yellowknife, Fred sold their claims for $100,000 plus 10 percent of whatever the claims produced—and in the forties, $100,000 was very big money! In just a few years Fred had climbed quite a ladder, going from being a destitute farmer's son to a bankrupt sawmill owner, then from a laborer paid only with food to being one of the wealthiest men in Yellowknife. Some might say that Fred was just lucky, that he was just in the right place at the right time—and you can't argue with that—but Fred was a worker who kept his eyes open and his mind active, always looking for a way to get ahead. In my view he was at the right place at the right time because everything he did made it possible."

A Piaggio Royal Gull amphibian passes noisily overhead, heading straight for the Yellowknife airport.

"I flew one of those once," says Ted. "They move right along, but those supercharged Lycomings sure are loud."

Turning, he tilts his head back and looks up toward the obelisk's peak.

"You know," he says, "I'm surprised that so many of

those early pilots survived, what with marginal maps, bad weather forecasting and aircraft that were nowhere as reliable as the planes we fly today."

He pauses, then says, "Well, I'd better be getting back."

"I'll walk with you," I say. "How about a drink at the bar? I'm buying."

"No thanks I gave that up when my kids were teenagers—quit smoking at the same time. It wasn't easy, but I made it. I should have done it sooner."

A handshake later, I head for the bar, which is quiet, perhaps because it's early. It's been years since I've ordered a mixed drink. Unlike the Pilgrims, whose decision to land at Plymouth Rock instead of sailing farther south was partly motivated by a shortage of beer, a six pack will last me a year, as will a bottle of wine. But tonight I order a whiskey sour to celebrate my tenth trip to Yellowknife, the first occasion being in 1971, when I arrived in a beautifully restored Piper Family Cruiser on new Edo 2000 floats. Equipped with a 150-hp Lycoming, my "Sand Piper" was a great performer. I should have kept it, but a Lake amphibian caught my eye. My Sand Piper went to Alaska, flown there by a one-armed ferry pilot who picked it up on the Mississippi River in downtown St. Paul.

The ice cube jingling in my glass turn my thoughts to Doctor John Gorrie, who, while searching for the cause of malaria in Apalachicola, Florida, in the mid-1800s, began to think of ways to make ice, which cost a dollar per pound when shipped south from Boston. (The HBC, in one of its less successful enterprises, once paid Stikine Indians to "harvest" British Columbia ice to be shipped to California. After turning a small profit, they tried a run to Hawaii, where most of the ice arrived as water, having melted along the way.)

Gorrie knew that compressed gases cool as they expand. Why not, thought Gorrie, with the aid of a compressor, use cool, expanding gas to lower room temperatures, which he did in his hospital ward. Next, he used his machine to cool brine to below freezing, then pumped the brine through pipes immersed in water—which froze! Gorrie obtained a patent, but the public wasn't impressed. The *New York Times* scoffed, "There is a crank down in Apalachicola, Florida, who claims that he can make ice as good as God Almighty." Gorrie's process eventually found wide use, but by then he'd died, some say a victim of the malaria that he'd been trying to cure in his air-conditioned ward.

The reading material in my room consists of the local newspaper (the *Yellowknifer)* and two magazines: *Up Here* and *Canadian Diamonds*. All three are interesting, but the article that catches my eye involves a Yellowknife company called Sirius Diamonds. Using gems from the Ekati mine, Sirius has begun marketing "Polar Bear Diamonds" that have been microscopically laser-engraved with the image of a polar bear, the word "Sirius" and an identification number. So where can I buy a Polar Bear diamond? Oddly enough, not in Yellowknife. They only engrave them here.

Turning on the television, I skip through the usual fluff until I come upon a program critical of companies that constantly pressure the public to buy products designed to keep us scrupulously clean—perhaps too clean for our own good. In support of the program's thesis, I remember that while I practiced dentistry, and was constantly exposed to a host of viruses, I had the flu just once and rarely caught a cold, but after I retired, I soon rejoined the rest of the world that periodically coughs and sneezes.

As the program progresses, I turn on the shower to remove my post-Churchill grime while sympathizing with people who feel compelled to wash their hands repeatedly or use an endless list of antibacterial sprays, liquids, powders and wipes. It's overkill. We host trillions of bacteria both inside and out. Many of them are beneficial, most are indifferent, and only about one in a thousand can cause us harm.

Nevertheless, it pays to be reasonably clean, especially when a break in the skin is involved. Clostridium, the organism that causes gas gangrene, can reproduce in just ten minutes. Do the math, and you'll discover that, given enough to feed on, one bacterium could produce more offspring in a single day than there are drops of water in the ocean. Worse yet, some organisms are incredibly tough!

A streptococcus bacterium was found living inside a camera that had been on the moon for two years! Some are almost immune to radioactivity. As Bill Bryson wrote in *A Short History of Nearly Everything,* "Blast [their] DNA with radioactivity, and the pieces immediately reform like the scuttling limbs of an undead creature from a horror movie."

I know from experience why surgeons respect the staphylococcus crowd's ability to persevere. When I was fourteen, a severe staph infection in my ankle laid me flat for months. I recovered, thanks to surgery and the advent of penicillin, but thirty years later, the same organism flared up in the same site, requiring more surgery followed by months of treatment with new antibiotics like Keflex and Minocin. By then, the medical community had learned how wildly wrong the Surgeon General had been when he stated in the sixties, "The time has come to close the book on infectious diseases. We have virtually wiped out infection in the United States."

The sun has yet to set, but I'm done with TV and I'm tired of reading, so I head for bed. Just twenty-four hours ago, I was working up a sweat with my fire-starting sticks on the beach at Winter Lake. I appreciate the hotel food, the comfort and the conversations, but short term, I'd rather be out in the bush. Long term, I don't think I'd make it. How lucky I am to be able to enjoy the best of both worlds.

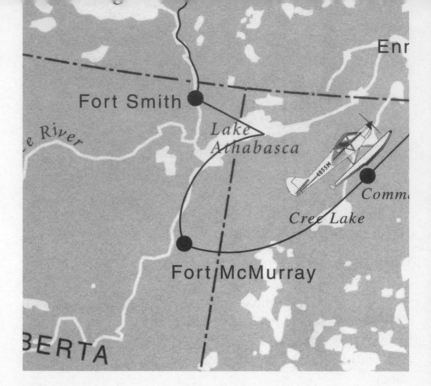

Chapter 9

Yellowknife to Fort McMurray, Alberta

Where the telescope ends, the microscope begins.
Which of the two has the grander view?

—VICTOR HUGO, *LES MISERABLES*

The harbor is alive with boats and seaplanes by the time I
get back to the Cub. I pack my gear, pump a few ounces
of water out of the floats, fire up the Cub and then listen to
the Yellowknife Airport Advisory while I taxi away from the
pier. I've already phoned in my flight plan to Fort McMurray,
requesting three days for what could be a six-hour trip.

"Yellowknife Tower, this is Piper 4855 Mike."

"4855 Mike, Yellowknife Tower."

"Yellowknife Tower, 55 Mike is ready for take-off Back
Bay with information Zulu."

"55 Mike is cleared to take off. Traffic is a Cessna 206 five miles to the west and a twin Beech on final for Back Bay. Report leaving the zone."

The Cub crosses Yellowknife Bay, heading southeast over the same rocky outcroppings that caught Fred Thompson's eye in 1938 during a flight to Yellowknife. Fred later returned with his partner, Roy Lundmark, in a Waco seaplane. Within hours Fred and Roy found a veritable "garden of gold." Fred and Roy staked twenty claims, naming their properties "the Waco group" in honor of the airplane that carried them there. So rich was their find that one magazine labeled it "Aladdin's storehouse without a roof; the most spectacular find of surface gold in Canada's history."

I climb to 4,500 feet for the crossing of Great Slave Lake. If my engine pops a cork, I can easily glide to any of the islands that lie just off to the east. The Continental, however, continues its steady drone, and as the sun pours in through my windshield, offsetting the early, 50°F air, I enjoy the warmth that burst free from the sun some eight minutes ago. Speeding across the 93-million-mile gap between sun and Earth while I flew just twelve miles, it warms my face, my hands and chest, giving birth to an appreciative smile.

Most people understand that that the sun is huge, but in 450 BCE, when Anaxagoras argued that the sun was not a god, that it was bigger than all of Greece, and that moon shone by reflected light from that "big, hot stone," he was charged with irreligion and imprisoned. Shortly thereafter, Aristarchus concluded that the sun must be at least seven times as large as Earth, and that it was absurd to believe that the larger sun would orbit the smaller Earth. He was right, but it took about 2000 years for the facts to prevail over the egocentric, earth-centered solar system that the churches preferred.

Perhaps the sun looks so small—no larger than the

moon—because it's hard to visualize how distant it is. The sun contains 99 percent of the mass of the entire solar system, but that's also hard to envision, so I think of Jupiter, the king of the planets, which can swallow 1,300 Earths. The sun, in comparison, could consume a million Earths with room left over for more. However, compared to its siblings, our sun is mediocre. For a really big star, try Betelgeuse, the second brightest star in the constellation Orion. Replace our sun with Betelgeuse, and the orbits of Mercury, Venus, Earth and the asteroid belt would lie well within its 800,000,000-mile diameter.

Years ago, when I wondered if the sun would fit between Earth and its moon, I got a big surprise. Even though the moon is a quarter million miles away, just a third of the sun would span that gap, leaving the remaining 615,000 miles of its diameter projecting into space.

Because the sun radiates in all directions, and because it's so distant, we receive only about two-billionths of the energy it produces, which is enough to allow plant life to survive, but not enough to drive off our atmosphere. In the array of planets that surround our sun, we lucked out, with Venus, the intolerable hothouse of searing temperatures, no water and a poisonous atmosphere, being much too close to the sun, and frigid Mars, too far. We northerners are also fortunate that the earth's elliptical orbit places us a bit closer to the sun during northern winters and farther from the sun in our summers. As a consequence, our northern hemisphere receives about 7 percent more radiation in the winter and 7 percent less in the summer. Sorry about that, Australia.

King Louis XIV, who declared himself the Sun King and had himself painted as the Sun God Apollo, was merely repeating an Egyptian belief that the pharaohs were the Gods of the sun. Across the Atlantic, the Aztecs claimed to be the "Sun's Chosen People," and to be certain that the sun would return every day, the emperor periodically placated the gods with an abundant supply of "precious water"—the blood of sacrificial victims.

In the 1500s, when Copernicus™ restored the sun to the center of the solar system (the Greeks had placed it there 1,800 years earlier) and demoted the earth from its church-ordained importance, the Catholic Church banned his work for more than 200 years. The clergy railed against him, Martin Luther saying, "This fool wishes to reverse the entire science of astronomy. But sacred scripture tells us that Joshua commanded the sun to stand still, and not the earth."

The sunspots that Galileo reported—and the churches rejected—had been recorded by the Chinese 1,600 years earlier, but powerful churches that could trump eyewitness evidence had no interest in other cultures. Despite the Church, Galileo continued to observe the forbidden sunspots. On noticing that they seemed to move across the face of the sun, he concluded that the sun must rotate, which it does, making one revolution every twenty-seven days. And though the sun is incredibly hot, Galileo's "spots," many of which are larger than Africa, have turned out to be 3,500° cooler than the rest of the surface. From those spots, great bubbles and arcs of energy leap far into space as solar flares, causing our marvelous northern lights.

Chinese technology and science, which had been recording eclipses as far back as 4000 BCE, often preceded that of the West. The Chinese invented paper around 100 BCE but the West did without until the twelfth century. They were the first to use petroleum as a lubricant and as fuel for fire. Philosophers in India were teaching that Earth was round and that it orbited the sun 1,000 years before the Greeks came to that conclusion, but Christian Europe clung to the flat Earth concept until the 1500s despite knowing that the Arab and Oriental nations considered it spherical. As Cyril Aydon wrote in *A Book of Scientific Curiosities,* "In the early 9th century, when the Emperor Charlemagne could barely write his name, the caliph of Baghdad and his scholars were exploring and extending the boundaries of mathematics, astronomy, geography and medicine." Unfortunately, the rise of Islamic fundamentalism brought about their religion-dominated Dark Ages, from which they are slowly and painfully emerging today.

Knowing that it's just an hour or so to the lovely beaches formed by the Talston River where it enters Great Slave Lake, I skipped the hotel breakfast, buying instead a few strips of bacon and several eggs from Barkley's agreeable chef. Now, with Great Slave falling behind and the wind in the south, I reduce power, land toward shore and taxi up to the beach.

The morning sun sends my shadow wavering across the rippled beach toward a haze of emerald willows as I set up my stove with a view of the lake and examine the makings of breakfast. This morning sir, the waiter advises, we are offering golden pancakes with maple syrup, eggs scrambled or fried as you like them with a side of thick bacon and coffee. That sounds great, and I'm soon enjoying a marvelous view of Great Slave Lake while enjoying an excellent breakfast exactly as advertised.

Fort Smith, my next stop, is 110 miles to the south. That's just ninety minutes away despite the headwind, so with time to burn, I fall back on a favorite diversion— beachcombing. As I stroll, I remember a Yukon beach surrounding a small oval lake, its lapis water gleaming darkly up from within its sandy rim like the pupil of a gigantic eye. I envision the beach in the Churchill harbor where, in 1967, maroon rivulets of warm blood ran down to the river from the "throats" of garroted beluga whales, and I recall Hawaiian beaches on which reflected sunsets coursed up and down with every swell, occasionally bejeweled by colorful glass balls from the nets of Asian fishermen.

Great Slave Lake mirrors the rivers that feed it, being almost opaque where the silty Slave and Hay Rivers supply its southern shores, but to the north and east the lake is as clear as leaded glass. Why, I wonder, does adding opaque lead to glass improve its clarity? As I ponder the seeming contradiction, I come upon a bottle protruding from the sand. Using care in case it is broken, I scoop it free. The label is gone, but the bottle's shape, its light green color and the indentation in its base say "wine." Like the old "ashes to ashes, dust to dust," this bottle was being slowly reclaimed by the material from which it was formed.

All glass begins as sand. Pure sand makes great glass, but the melting point of sand is inconveniently high. As a consequence, glass was rare until a thousand years ago, but when someone noticed that adding soda lowered its melting point, glass production soared.

By coincidence, my bottle wears the same shade of green as a paperweight that sits on my desk. Made in Venice on the island of Murano (where glassmakers were compelled to work to reduce the risk of burning Venice), my green orb was crafted by the descendants of well-paid artisans who were, for four centuries, prisoners of their occupation. From 1200 to 1600 CE, when knowledge of the secrets of Venetian glass making was deemed as good as gold, the penalty for flight was death.

So what should I do with my bottle? Dump it in the trash at Fort Smith or insert a note, seal it and heave it into Great Slave? Tearing out a page of my notebook, which bears a few red splotches where mosquitoes have died, I write a brief note, trim a candle stub to fit the bottle's neck, seal it by dripping wax from another candle into the recess and heave it into the lake. Carried offshore by the southerly wind and west by the current, my bottle might be spotted by tourists ferrying across the

Mackenzie River to Fort Providence, Rae and Yellowknife. If it stays afloat it could bob past Fort Simpson and Norman Wells or even reach the ocean. I hope that someday, someone will find my bottle and the note it contains, which reads: I began my voyage on Great Slave Lake at the mouth of the Talston River. E-mail tundracub@mchsi.com. And call 218-744-2003 or write George at 4678 Cedar Island Drive, Eveleth, MN 55734.

I follow the Talston River upstream through sixty miles of boring, boggy terrain toward Fort Smith, the most southerly city in the Northwest Territories, and then pick up the Slave River near the Rapids of the Drowned. One hundred years ago, steamboats plied this river with the heaviest cargo (bags of lead shot or cement) loaded onto the bow. If the boat ran aground, the bags were carried aft, raising the bow enough to let the boat back off.

I'm skirting the eastern border of Wood Buffalo Provincial Park, the 17,000-square-mile sanctuary of mixed woodlands and wetlands that straddles the NWT—Alberta border. Within its boundaries, endangered whooping cranes nest and the world's largest herd of bison run free. One summer, while Wes and I were crossing the park, we were attracted to what looked like patches of smoke, but on drawing closer, we realized that "smoke" was dust raised by buffalo rolling around in their wallows.[TN]

As the Cub slips across the border between Fort Smith, which is in the Territories, and its nearby seaplane base, which is in Alberta, I'm surprised to see that much of the twenty-mile portage on which Fred Giauque and his sons labored is still visible.

The Cub replaces a Beaver that is leaving the Loon-Aire Pier. If I'd remembered to buy oil at Yellowknife, I wouldn't have to stop, but I've used the last of my oil and I like to keep a quart in reserve. Besides, if I refuel here, I can pass up Uranium City.

While Jim, the gas "boy" tops the tanks, I ask if he knew the fellow who had his job ten years ago, but Jim, like many other northerners, is here just for the summer, working a different job every year to pay for college, as I once did.

"So what's your major?"

"Forestry," he replies, "especially fire control and prevention. I'm taking flight training too, because it might help me land a job. If nothing shows up with forestry, I might be able to get a job as a bush pilot."

While Jim tops the tanks, I head for the office to phone my wife. The phone is still where it always was, but Georgia, the gorgeous centerfold who once adorned the wall, is gone, replaced by a bulletin board.[TN]

When my wife answers, I adopt my best telemarketing voice.

"Good morning, I'm calling for the Society for the Prevention of Cruelty to Animals. (My wife loves dogs.) May I speak to Mrs. Erickson?"

"Oh, baloney," she says. "Where are you?"

"At the Fort Smith seaplane base."

"Where's that?"

"You know, in northern Alberta."

She updates me on the grandkids, the weather, the garden, and on the progress of Bush's "Mission Accomplished" war, which is going down the drain.

"Where do you go next?"

"Down to Lake Athabasca, then probably to Fort McMurray. I haven't been there in years. You doing alright?"

"Sure. How about you?"

"I'm good. The fishing's been great, but I didn't make it to Bathurst Inlet, so maybe next year…"

"Okay. Call again when you can."

Jim, accompanied by a squadron of horse flies, returns with my bill.

"Getting warm," he says.

"So what's the record around here? Ninety-something?"

"More," he says "Try 103."

"Wow."

I shouldn't be surprised. The farther inland one goes from the temperature-moderating oceans, the greater the weather extremes. Besides, I've seen ninety degrees at York Factory when the wind wasn't coming in from the Bay.

The south wind becomes a crosswind when I turn east toward Andrew Lake, the last lake in the northeastern corner of Alberta and a site of a beautiful campsite that Wes and I chanced upon in 1969. After refueling at Uranium City, we'd headed toward Fort Smith. It was late in the day when we came upon Andrew Lake's long, broad beach that could hold fifty campsites.[TN]

"Wes," I radioed, "let's stop here. It's just an hour or so to Fort Smith, and we could eat breakfast there tomorrow."

Three hundred yards of spotless beach welcomed us. We pitched our tent amidst birch and pines, sleeping well, accompanied by calling loons and the complaints of two hungry eaglets in an eight-foot-wide nest set high in a nearby pine. The morning sun warmed our tent, bringing a day so perfect that we abandoned the restaurant breakfast and, after catching a northern, dined on fish and pancakes beside the pristine beach. An hour later we overflew Fort Smith, bound for Fort Simpson and the Nahanni River Canyon on a wandering, whimsical trip that would take us to Norman Wells, Coppermine, Bathurst and Chantrey Inlets plus Baker Lake before heading home via Churchill and Norway House.

Mile-wide Pelican Rapids falls behind. Off to my right, the equally impressive Cassette Rapids marks nearby Fitzgerald, where the portage road to Fort Smith begins. As the noontime sun beats down through my windshield, I leave the Slave River valley behind and re-enter the beautifully rugged, lake-splattered country that extends to Hudson Bay.

It's hot! The vents are open, but they aren't up to the job, so I open my yard-long window and peel of my clothes until I'm down to shoes and shorts. As the swirling air cools me, I envision a nearly naked pilot suddenly faced with a forced landing in a populated area. His explanation: Abducted in mid-flight by aliens? So poor that he had to choose between clothing and fuel for his plane? He's a wanna-be model for Haines?

Years ago, I crossed this region when it was ablaze with forest fires, weaving back and forth between flaming hills in acrid, smoke-filled skies.[TN] The fires seemed like cancers gnawing the flesh of the land, but, in reality, the fires were beneficial, releasing a flood of nutrients from whatever they consumed, making way for the forest now passing below. Near the end of the day, I landed on a lake beside an earlier burn. Only three weeks had passed since the fire had died, but fireweed, sedges and yellow bluebeard lilies had already begun to push up through the ashes.

When Andrew Lake appears, I fly along the beach to look it over, then land and taxi to shore. The beach and the lake are still the same, but the eagle-nest tree is gone, and a stump has taken its place. Some of the trees have been cut for firewood, and that's understandable, but the campsite is strewn with debris. A half hour later, my garbage bag is full and the beach is almost clean. Disillusioned, I leave Andrew Lake and enter Saskatchewan. I'll drop the bag at Uranium City if I stop there or at Fort McMurray if I don't.

Where should I camp tonight? I have two great choices. The first is the nearby Tazin River, which bears dozens of beautiful campsites. The second is Cantara Lake, a small, oval lake about a mile inland from Lake Athabasca's southern shore. My choice is Cantara Lake, but to be sure that I'll have fish to eat, I decide to stop on an L-shaped lake in the Tazin

River that bears the crème de la crème of northern campsites—a high honor, given its many competitors.

A few minutes later, the Cub skids to a stop at the base of a long esker that points a sandy finger toward a cliff on the opposite shore.[TN] Reeds extend far into the lake along its moose-tracked southern shore. In contrast, its northern shore, an expanse of crystallized butterscotch sand, rises abruptly from the depths to level off amidst well-spaced birch, aspen and pine. Lichens, moss, wintergreen plants and bearberries cushion the level ground. Were I to camp here tonight, I'd feel like a gourmet confronted by a large menu of excellent choices, wondering,, should I pitch my tent here where no wind can reach me, or there, where the morning sun will warm my tent, or maybe over there to view the eleven-thirty sunset through the netting?

I spin the Cub around and drag it part way ashore. Retrieving my fishing rod, I tell my complaining stomach— be patient! I know it has been a long time since breakfast!

At the tip of the esker, I wade thigh-deep into the lake and cast my teaspoon lure toward the distant limestone cliff.

A three-pound lake trout hammers the spoon on my third cast. It's a beautiful fish, but it's just a minnow compared to the world-record, ninety-two-pound lake trout caught at nearby Lake Athabasca, the Dene's Lake of the Hills. Then with lunch secured to the cleat on my float, I cross over to the esker's southern shore, wade out to the edge of the reeds and cast again.

The lure strikes the water. A second later, the water erupts as a huge northern leaps skyward in a shower of spray. For five minutes we battle, see-sawing back and forth. I crank in line again and again, only to have it stripped from my reel until the northern finally lies at my feet, its gill plates flaring like a panting athlete who's completely out of breath.

I'd like to take a photo of the northern, but my camera's in the Cub, so I back across the esker, releasing line as I go. As I reach into the Cub for my Nikon, the line snags in the rudder cables. I hurriedly free it while hoping the northern is vain enough to want its picture taken. It waits. A shutter click later, the northern is free, sculling slowly away through the reeds.

My lunch will be fried lake trout, tartar sauce, bread and peanut butter plus coffee and whatever comes from one of my cans. I'm expecting fruit, but out come peas, which would please my wife, who always serves peas with fish, and who believes that vegetables that are served with A shouldn't accompany B or C. Feeling lucky because of the peas, I open another can for dessert I'm hoping for fruit, but I get wax beans, which I pour into a plastic bag. It's wax beans for supper tonight!

With my stomach happy and my dishes clean, I heave the remains of the trout into the Tazin, prop the Cub to life and head for the Athabasca Dunes, the Mohave of the North.

As the Cub approaches Uranium City, I resurrect a conversation with Captain Larry Daudt, a retired Northwest Airlines pilot whom I met following my Bush Flying for Beginners forum at the Experimental Aircraft Association AirVenture convention in Oshkosh, Wisconsin.

Captain Daudt had flown for NWA for thirty-six years, the last eighteen or so flying from the United States to Asia and Europe on routes that took him across Canada at least 350 times.

"Larry," I said, "I can't tell you how many times I've watched jet trails streak across the sky and wished that I were up there sharing your magnificent view instead of being down low fighting a head wind."

In response, Larry described a flight on which he'd aided a lost pilot near Uranium City. When he was finished, I asked him to send it to me so that someday, perhaps in a future book, I could pass it on, and here it is:

"I logged many hours over the Canadian wilderness— all of it at 28,000 to 37,000 feet... While you were flying low, envying my speed and view, I longed to be down there in a Cub or a Seabee, just flying free, camping and fishing at will. I retired in 2001 and, thanks to your *True North,* my interest to seek an adventure like yours has been renewed.

"You'll probably remember that we talked about the requirement to monitor the emergency frequency. It's good to know that a pilot on an adventure like yours can always call on 121.5, knowing that some airline pilot will respond with assistance. It was on just such an occasion that my story begins.

"It was a clear, smooth morning at 37,000 feet above the Yukon and Northwest Territories one day in June, 1987. The crew of NWA 747, flight 18 from NRT [Narita, Japan] to JFK, had just rechecked the INS [Inertial Navigation System] coordinates to continue southeast across Canada to our destination Edmonton. Air Traffic Control had already cleared us to fly directly to Uranium City and to continue on course.

"Most of the passengers were sleeping when the flight attendant entered the flight deck with our meal service and another cup of coffee. The first officer and second officer were eating their meals and I was tending the store, so to speak. I was monitoring 121.5 as well as 126.7, the Flight Service Station frequency in northern Canada.

"As we neared Uranium City we heard a discussion between Fort Nelson FSS and a Cessna aircraft, the general drift of which caused me to pay close attention. It seemed that the Cessna pilot, who was looking for a landing strip, had become disoriented and was concerned about his fuel situation. I advised FSS that I had been monitoring the conversation and asked the operator if I could be of assistance. He responded immediately in the affirmative and so I went to work.

"First I asked the Cessna pilot for his aircraft type, his fuel on board, and the number of passengers he was carrying. He stated that he was flying a 172 on wheels. He hesitated to say that one tank showed empty and the other read below 1/4 tank, but that these gauges weren't very accurate anyway and he was sure that he had more fuel on board, and that he had four on board including himself.

"I then asked if he knew where he was and he said, "not exactly." I then asked if he had a low frequency navigation receiver on board. He replied that he did and he was sure that it worked quite well although he hadn't turned it on yet.

"I told him to look at his compass and tell me which direction he was flying. He said that he was on a heading of about 330 degrees. I then asked him to turn his radio to a frequency I had on my map and tell me which way the needle pointed. He did and I drew a line on my map. I then asked him to tune another frequency and tell me which way the needle pointed. Drawing the second line pinpointed his location where the two lines crossed. Ahh, I thought, he's somewhere beneath my aircraft, heading northwest.

"Our position was about sixty miles west northwest of Lake Athabasca so I asked if he wanted to land and he said, 'Yes, as soon as possible.'

"I told him that if he turned to the east and looked up in the sky he would see my contrail, and that we were going to cross Uranium City where there was a sizable airport. I also told him that he would soon see a really big lake and that he should stay on its north shore. I then told him that there should be a gravel strip about fifteen miles west of Uranium City, should he need it. He soon confirmed that he had the lake in sight and would stay on the north side, then thanked me as we continued on to JFK.

"We laid over in New York that night and the next day flew flight 17 back to NRT on a flight plan that took us over the very same route that we flew the day before. When we were near Fort Nelson, the FSS operator asked if we were the same crew that had assisted the Cessna the previous day, and on hearing that we were, told us that the Cessna had landed at Camsell Portage without enough fuel to make

Uranium City, then thanked us for our assistance and wished us a Bon Voyage.

"I never heard from the pilot, but I later learned that he was from Winnipeg, and was heading to a small landing strip near a camp in the Northwest Territories. After paying about $7.50 per gallon to have fuel flown to Camsell Portage by helicopter, he continued his trip as if nothing had happened."

Uranium City mushroomed during the fifties in response to demands for atom bombs and nuclear power stations. By the seventies, it had become a community of 10,000 with modern homes and businesses, a first-class school and a new airport. But in 1982, times and priorities changed. The mine shut down and the town's economy collapsed. A few years later, I landed at the seaplane base and walked up the steep road to town, where I met an eerie sight—an almost empty city. No children; no laundry flapping on the lines. Just two parked cars and one dog. Until a pickup rumbled by, no city sounds reached my ears. Since then, I've flown this route several times, but I haven't stopped. Old ghost towns intrigue me, but Uranium City is just too new.

When the last Ice Age waned, flood waters from melting glaciers carried immense amounts of sand to a low region south of the Athabasca Hills, and when the icy barrier finally withdrew, the lake's excess water could once again escape to the north, exposing the hundreds of square miles of sand bars that now comprise the Athabasca Dunes, the largest area of sand dunes in Canada.

The Dene elders, however, have offered a different tale: A long time ago, a giant went hunting for beavers that had built a dam across Lake Athabasca, so to find the beavers, the giant broke the dam to lower the water level. Coming upon a very large beaver he speared it and, thinking that he had killed it, threw it onto the shore. The beaver, however, was still alive, and as it died it began kicking big heaps of sand ashore, forming the massive dune field to the south of Lake Athabasca.

Submerged swirls of caramel and bronze-colored sand rise from the lakes depths as the dunes come into sight. To the east, the MacFarlane River limits the dunes' progress, trapping the wind-blown sand, which it carries into the lake. An intensely green boreal forest forms the river's eastern shore, but to the south and west of the river lies a vast sea of sand.

Circular Cantara Lake is bisected by a long, narrow esker. I scan the lake to check it for snags, then begin to descend, crossing raised, stair-step beaches that march inland from Lake Athabasca. Unlike jumbo jets that howl down from the sky like streamlined space platforms to land with a thud and a roar, the Cub whispers earthward in a long, protracted glide. Nose high, the keels of its floats cut long slits in the water. Slowing, the Cub becomes boat-like and motors up to the beach.

Cantara's shoreline disputes the barren dunes beyond, bearing bright yellow tansy blossoms, white chickweed, beautiful sea thrift with tiny pink flowers and, to my great surprise, an abundance of rose-colored lady slippers in beds of reindeer moss.

Eight years ago I camped beside Yakow Lake[TN], which lies twenty miles to the east. The lake's steep, sandy slopes made getting my gear up to the campsite difficult, but here, the shoreline rises gently, and within minutes, my tent is set amidst a scattering of bunchberries, my gear is stowed inside and I'm ready to begin another of my passions—photographing sand dunes.

I've always loved sand dunes. Years ago, my wife and I

stumbled onto Colorado's Sand Dunes National Monument, where magnificent dunes have accumulated over the centuries as high-country winds dropped their gritty loads at the base of the Sangre de Cristo Range. The dunes can be seen from a distance, but their grandeur is reserved for those who leave the main highway and venture into the park. There, the film began to spin through my camera—close-ups of herringbone sand patterns, wide-angle shots of curling dunes, and an endless array of curvaceous, nudelike crests under deep blue, contrasting skies. As I climbed dune after dune, I imagined myself Antoine de St. Exupery, lost, parched and hallucinating after crashing in the Libyan Desert. Later, when I returned from my sun-baked climb of several miles and 1,000 vertical feet, I hardly needed imagination.

The Athabasca dunes are not as dramatic. Few reach 100 feet, but their contours are just as graceful. It's just a matter of scale. Before I set out, I fill a half-pint bottle with water. With the bottle in a pocket and my compass clipped to my belt, I head out across the dunes.

I walk for more than an hour, weaving between the dunes on pebble-strewn flats, passing trees with roots suspended in air, exposed by "blowouts" that carried away the sand. On my previous visits, I'd found an abundance of insects, spider webs and bird nests in the branches of sandblasted trees. This year, however, they're barren, as if an exceptionally strong wind has carried them off, leaving behind a lonely and lifeless void.

When the terrain becomes repetitious, I climb to the top of a dune and stretch out along its crest. Without snakes, scorpions or Gila monsters to worry about, I direct my attention upward. Six miles above, a swept-wing jet draws a contrail across the sky. It's a wide-body with four silhouetted engines—probably a 747. Could it be Larry Daudt's flight 17, now captained by a younger pilot? I wonder if she, like Larry, might be dreaming of sharing my intimate view. Her next stop—Anchorage? Japan?

Rolling onto my side, I survey a scene lifted from Lawrence of Arabia. Were it not for the scattered islands of sand-blasted jack pines, birch and forlorn tree skeletons, much of David Lean's epic could have been filmed right here.

A solitary thunderstorm peers above the western horizon. Years ago, when a friend doubted that thunderstorms could be seen from a hundred miles away, I pointed out that an average eight-mile-high thunderstorm at 100 miles, with a height/distance ratio of 1 to 12, would be much more obvious than a thirty-story office building that's easily seen at ten miles despite a height/distance ratio of only 1 to 150. The logic was compelling, but my friend's first-hand knowledge of 100 horizontal miles dwarfed his ability to envision eight vertical miles, and, logic-be-damned, he refused to concede.

Back at camp, I break the bleached bones of a jack pine into pieces and begin to assemble my evening fire. I've no paper to burn and I'm short on patience, so I drain an ounce or two of gasoline from the *Tundra Cub II,* toss it onto the pile and throw in a match. Pow!

Supper tonight will be wax beans from the bag plus Spam, the canned meat product that my generation came to dislike during World War II. Tonight, however, a fried Spam sandwich with a touch of mustard should taste just right beside a bowl of soup. With a handful of cookies and a cup of butterscotch pudding, I'll enjoy a decent meal. Soup, however, presents a problem because of my anonymous cans.

Returning to the Cub, I line up my eight remaining cans on top of a float I know that four contain soup and four hold beans, corn, peas or fruit. I shake the cans, hoping that the sound will give me a clue, but that doesn't work. So, employing the next best thing, which involves three geniuses called Eenie, Minee and Moe, I select and open a can. Out comes chicken noodle soup. Hooray!

The Spam, however, isn't as good as I'd expected, so I toss the remainder aside for a raven or jay. As I crunch into my last cookie, a short-tail weasel pokes its head around the tent, scampers over to the Spam and begins to gobble it down.

"Well, hello there," I say.

The weasel eyes me, then indifferently crosses between me and the tent without as much as a sideward glance, and then disappears. Cute, round-eared, lithe and fearless for such a small creature, he's the stereotypical weasel. I've seen weasels twice before in the wild. Both ignored me, and one walked right across my feet.

As I dry my dishes, the whine of a mosquito finds my ears. That's no surprise, but I suddenly realize that it's the first bug I've heard since I landed. The wind is down, so perhaps the, moisture-absorbing dunes keep the bug numbers low. The mosquito wavers off, and as I return to my fire, a pack of distant wolves begin to howl.

Years ago, I played the clown while camped on the Thelon River. When wolves began to howl, I joined in, yowling back and forth with the wolves until they'd had their fill of my foolishness and went silent. Tonight, however, I'm not in the mood, perhaps because the howling reminds me of Sigurd Olson, the author and nature lover who helped establish Minnesota's Boundary Waters Canoe Area.

Olson, in one of his many books, had written that wolves rarely attacked people. One winter, however, while he was skiing back to his cabin beside a moonlit river, Sig became aware that several wolves had begun to follow him and, as you might expect, he began to hope that the wolves had read his book.

Armed only with a hunting knife, which he said he clutched "as if it were King Arthur's sword," he slowly continued toward his cabin until two large wolves stepped onto the trail and sat down facing him. Not knowing what to do, he stopped, not moving a muscle while he stared at the wolves. Finally, the larger of the wolves stood up, shook itself and disappeared into the woods, followed by the rest of the pack.

I doubt that Olson's wolves turned away out of fear. Instead, their behavior seems to have been prompted by inquisitiveness, then contemplation, and then perhaps by an impulse to make a grand gesture to a man they could have easily killed.

My fireside reading tonight will be Bill Bryson's, 500-page *A Short History of Nearly Everything,* which begins with the Big Bang and then leaps to the solar system. With my back to the fire for warmth and light, I begin to read, glancing up occasionally to admire a sunset awash in pastel purples and pinks. Bryson's writing is crisp and clean, but the flickering firelight and the fading sunset are tough on my eyes, so, knowing that the real thing can be found overhead, I decide to save Mr. Bryson for another evening. I douse the fire with a pot of water and stretch out onto my back.

As the steam and smoke dissipate and my night vision improves, the stars begin to shine. A gibbous moon peeks above the trees. The Milky Way appears, followed by the brightest of the 2,000 stars that the unaided eye can see at one time from anywhere on earth. I search for the Pleiades. Years ago, I could pick out its individual stars, but age has taken its toll, and the seven sisters that comprise it have become a Y-shaped blur. As the fainter stars begin to bloom, I begin to understand why a Chinese astronomer named Chuang Tzu declared near the end of his life, "My coffin will be heaven and earth; for the funeral ornaments of jade;

there will be the sun and the moon; for my pearls and jewels, I shall have the stars and constellations."

So how did we learn that the moon hung not close to the earth, as was once believed, but that it circled the earth at a distance of 250,000 miles? As far as we know, the first person to accomplish that feat was a Greek named Hipparchus, who, around 150 BCE used triangulation and got it dead on! Were I to repeat his method I'd ask a friend in Houston to check the angle of a given edge of the moon while I did the same in St. Paul. Knowing the distance between our locations, the rest is just geometry, which Hipparchus understood, thanks to another Greek named Euclid whose work we still teach today.

The Greeks, who had observed the Earth's shadow on the moon, knew by 300 BCE that Earth was a globe. They had also determined that the planet was much larger than the moon by timing the length of eclipses. The Church, however, denied the "roundness" of Earth for more than a thousand years, causing the great navigator, Ferdinand Magellan, to write, "The church says the earth is flat, but I know it is round, for I have seen its shadow on the moon, and I have more faith in a shadow than in the church."

In 1609, when Galileo got wind of the optical tubes being constructed in Holland, he quickly built several, each one better than the last, and as I lie on my back, I envision Galileo, mouth agape at discovering earlike handles on Saturn, Jupiter's multiple moons and a stunning multitude of stars in even the darkest regions of the sky. On observing that Venus exhibited moonlike phases, Galileo found proof that Venus orbited the sun, and not Earth. And when the stars' tiny pinpricks of light remained unchanged despite being magnified by his telescope, he realized that the stars must be terribly far away.

Galileo was not a humble man. As a scientist, physician

and inventor, the red-haired self-promoter had many talents, so it's not surprising that Galileo would trumpet the existence of Jupiter's satellites and the mountains he found on the moon, but in so doing, he ran afoul of the Church. He was ordered to appear before the Inquisition. Threatened with torture if he failed to recant, Galileo confessed to error and was sentenced to house arrest for the rest of his life. In 1980, *350 years after the fact,* the Church finally admitted that Galileo was right.

Two centuries after Galilco, Christian Huygens tried to estimate the distance to the stars by darkening more and more of a window until the remaining point of light from the sun approximated the intensity of Sirius as he recalled it. Some say that he used progressively smaller holes in a sheet of metal, but whatever the method, he settled on a tiny point that admitted about 1/28,000 of the sun's light, and reasoned that Sirius must therefore be about 28,000 times farther away than the sun—a distance of less than half a light-year. (A light year is the distance that light can travel in one year at 186,000 miles per second.) However, Sirius, despite being one of our closest stellar neighbors, is nine light-years away. Still, despite being limited by crude methods and lacking the knowledge that the brightness of stars is not determined by distance alone (they can vary from dim to intensely bright), Huygens did fairly well.

Proxima Centauri, the nearest star except for our sun, is about four light-years away. But what does that really mean? I think of it this way: the Concorde, which was our fastest commercial jet, could hit 1,500 miles per hour. Were we to set off for Proxima Centauri in the Concorde, we'd need a whopping big lunch and some anticlaustrophobia pills! Even at 1,500 mph, we'd be cooped up in the Concorde for seven years just to reach the sun, plus another 2 million years to arrive at Proxima Centauri. Were we to scoot along at 15,000 mph, like the probes we've sent to Jupiter, Venus and Mars, we'd need 200,000 years to make a one-way trip.

As the moon climbs higher, its radiance begins to smother the weaker stars, so with the aid of my binoculars, I begin to spy on the moon. I wonder if our powerful observatories could image any of the equipment that the astronauts left behind. I doubt it. If they could, we'd surely have seen the photos.

Morning. It's trying to rain, but the ceiling is good. If the weather holds, I should easily reach Fort Chipewyan, the oldest settlement in Alberta, or even Fort McMurray, a boom town that jumped from 10,000 to 60,000 in just a few decades when Canada began to mine the Athabasca Tar Sands, which are said to be the largest single oil deposit in the world.

Because of the rain, I delay breakfast, making do with a handful of dried fruit, some chocolate pudding and a vitamin pill for dessert. Finally, with my gear packed and cleaned of sand, which I hate to get in the plane, I fire up the Cub. Minutes later, I cross the mouth of the stunningly colorful William River and heads for Bustard Island (named for the crane-like bird) in heavy rain. Dead ahead is Fort Chipewyan, a Dene settlement founded in 1783 by Peter Pond, a hot-headed American who explored the route to Lake Athabasca, returning time and again in canoes brimming with trade goods, and with new maps that, as it turned out, were much too optimistic about the proximity of the Pacific Ocean.

Alexander Mackenzie, the head of the Northwest Company, realized that success would depend on expansion, so in 1789 he left Fort Chipewyan, which was known as the Athens of the West because of Mackenzie's 2,000-book library, and set off down the Slave River. Mackenzie, who relied on one of Pond's optimistic maps, hoped that the Slave would lead to the Pacific Ocean. For hundreds of miles, the Slave flowed north, then turned west, only to turn north again, becoming a 2,000-mile waterway that led not to the west, but north to the Arctic Ocean. Disillusioned, Mackenzie named the Natives' De Cho (Great) River the Disappointment River, though it bears his name today. Three years later, Mackenzie again left Fort Chipewyan, this time heading up the Peace River toward present-day Fort St. John™. On reaching the Pacific Ocean the following year, Alexander Mackenzie became the first person known to have spanned the North American continent.

By the beginning of the nineteenth century, beavers had become scarce in the Athabasca region, as were fox, otter and mink. To carry the men through the winter, the big lake was "mined" for fish every year, with an average of 50,000 whitefish, trout and pike being taken every year until fishing also began to decline. And then, a few decades later, London's upper crust became infatuated with silk. Silk hats became required, and beaver hats were out.

Despite the declining market for beaver pelts, trapping other fur bearers and the "mining" of the lakes continued with disastrous results. In 1880, not long after the HBC had swallowed the Northwest Company, Factor Roderick McFarlane worried about conditions at Fort Chipewyan and several other posts, writing, "owing to the scarcity of food animals, and the comparative failure of the fisheries, the Indians will suffer many privations between now and spring."

It's still pouring at Fort Chipewyan, so I pass it by. Why should I land just to get soaked while finding a place to eat?

Besides, it's only two hours to Fort McMurray, and the sky is brighter that way. Turning south, I begin to cross the world's largest inland delta, a land of waterlogged marshes fed by the convoluted channels of the Athabasca River. It's great country for beavers, muskrats, otters and mink, but the river's multiple loops remind me why I quit canoeing pretzel-like rivers that meander for thirty miles instead of flowing straight for ten.

Dipping low, I leave Wood Buffalo National Park, skimming up the Athabasca River. On these riverbanks, HBC men in harness once toiled, straining against the current to haul empty barges upstream. Vilhjalmur Stefansson, who rafted the Athabasca in the 1920s, noted "the smell of the tar which here and there trickled down the cut-banks of the river and which soiled our clothes whenever we went ashore." Farther downstream he came upon the remnants of a "government operation" that had (years before) struck a flow of natural gas. According to Stefansson, "someone lit the torch," and it was still burning.

Flying this low isn't safe, especially near populated areas, so I climb to 1,000 feet. To the east, south and west, 50,000 square miles of tar sands reach to the horizon. Covered by a thin blanket of muskeg, the sands contain from 1.7 to 2.5 trillion barrels of a heavy oil called bitumen, about one-fifth of which is recoverable with current techniques.

The seaplane base at Fort MacKay marks the end of the rain and the beginning of thousands of acres being mined by thirty-two companies, one of which is Syncrude, a consortium that began limited production in 1978, but has since added several multibillion-dollar expansion projects. A million barrels of oil are stripped from these sands every day, much of it destined for the United States, which relies on Canada for 18 percent of its oil.

An irregular gridwork of sprawling pits and angular

settling ponds march outward from either side of the river. Some would call it a moonscape, but it's no different from any open pit operation—you remove what's in the way to get at what you need. On the west side of the river, huge, red, 2,200-h.p., turbocharged excavators equipped with GPS displays and buckets that carve out fifty cubic yards per bite are dumping sand into grunge-yellow, $3.5-million Caterpillar trucks with 3,400-hp engines, six $20,000 tires and rear axles that weigh 37 tons. Moving back and forth from pit to plant at up to 40 mph, each truck delivers 300 tons of bitumen containing 200 barrels of oil to processing plants day after day. There, the sand is mixed with hot water to create a slurry that is pumped into settling vessels. The oil floats to the top, and the remainder goes back to mined-out areas, which are then covered with topsoil and replanted.

Bitumen in the deeper deposits is removed by injecting steam to make it easier to pump to the surface. The molasses-like bitumen from both processes is then pumped to a refinery, emerging as sweet crude oil—the good stuff that all nations desire. This seems pretty rosy, but there's a hidden price to the tar sands – and an implied warning: Heating the tar sands requires huge amounts natural gas, which increases costs. So why bother? Because world oil production has begun to decline, and with demand on the rise, even costly sources are becoming attractive. And the warning? We are taking the first steps toward scraping the bottom of the global oil barrel. Getting serious about alternate energy sources is long overdue.

At Fort McMurray, the north-flowing Athabasca is joined from the east by the Clearwater River, the voyageur route that linked the Mackenzie River system to Hudson Bay via the Churchill, Nelson and Hays Rivers. As the junction nears, I descend toward the seaplane base. A minute later, the Cub touches down on the Clearwater and turns into a long, appendix-like backwater. As I taxi into the backwater, I swing wide, bypassing the hidden sand bar that trapped me thirty years ago when I first came to Fort McMurray.

While the Cub is being fueled, I ask the dock hand to recommend a convenient hotel.

"The Podollan would be a handy," he says, pointing toward a tall building not far from the base.

"Thanks," I reply, "and what should I be sure to see before I leave town?"

He thinks for a moment, then says, "I guess I'd take in the Tar Sands tour and the Heritage Park on King Street."

"Okay, but if I have to pick one, which do you recommend?"

"Well," he says with a nod to the Cub, "You've probably seen more from your Cub than the tour can show you, so I guess I'd check out the Park."

At the Podollan Pub, I order a quarter-pound Californiaburger with onions, fries and a strawberry shake. The burger is delicious, but the pub is crowded with oil conventioneers, and it's much too loud for me. By the time I finish, I'm having doubts about spending a night in noisy surroundings, so I put off registering. Maybe I'll stay, but I'm already envisioning the hundreds of quiet lakes lying not far to the east.

A cabby in front of the Polladan puts down his copy of *Fort McMurray Today,* the local newspaper, and asks, "Where to?"

"Heritage Park."

As we head up Franklin Street, he asks, "Are you here for the convention?"

"No, I'm from the States—just flying around in a seaplane enjoying your country."

"Oh," he says, his eyebrows rising in the rear-view mirror. "So what do you think about Bush?"

"You mean our great 'decider,' King George? He should be impeached."

I watch him in the mirror. His eyes reveal that he's smiling, but he suddenly changes course.

"It sounds like your guys and my guys aren't hitting it off very well these days."

"Really? How's that?" I ask, thinking it's probably about Iraq, but I'm wrong.

"The paper here says that Washington keeps ignoring NAFTA and WTO rulings that favor Canada on a bunch of disputes, one of them being subsidies to U.S. corn growers that hurt our farmers. That's not going to help you guys get more oil from us, you know, especially with China buying more every year. Just yesterday I heard that China will be wanting half of all the oil we produce by 2010. The tar sands are already giving us a surplus of close to $6 billion a year—and that's just for Alberta. That's good news for us, but not for you, eh?

"Wow!"

Turning onto King Street, he stops at the entrance to Heritage Park, which houses a museum and an assortment of pioneer buildings, including the office/home of bush pilot Wop May and a display of bush pilot history. The other buildings, an old school plus equally old stores and churches, are standard fare, but I'm particularly taken by what the park calls its large "artifacts," the first being the dry-docked Radium Scout barge. Powered by two steam engines, the three-tiered barge served the Fort McMurray region until 1977 when it was moved to Heritage Park.

The second is an old Syncrude "bucketwheel," an odd-looking contraption on dozer tracks that supported a conveyor belt with scoops attached to it. The operator, who sat on a fire-trucklike ladder above it all, operated the rig when the first pit opened in 1959.

The third exhibit, a 1910 American Abell steam tractor,

brings memories of a similar tractor that my grandfather owned in 1935. I was three years old that summer, and when the huge, steel-wheeled machine came clanking into sight, I fled, bawling in terror, to my mother.

By the time I leave the exhibit, my mind is made up. I'll camp somewhere east of McMurray, trading people who shouldn't hoot through the night for owls that should. I'll miss a hot bath, but it's a small price to pay for a peaceful night in the bush. Besides, the lakes this far "south" should be warm enough for swimming—even for a pansy like me. Leaving now, however, creates a problem: it's too early to eat again, and I don't want to cook supper. I solve my dilemma with a detour to a nearby restaurant, where I buy a small double-cheese, beef and mushroom pizza. As I've said before, life is hard on the northern frontier!

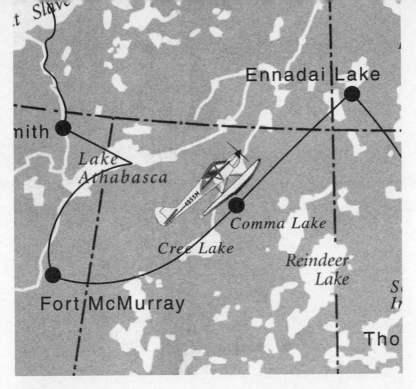

Chapter 10

Fort McMurray to Ennadai Lake, Nunavut

> *Science is not only compatible with spirituality; it is a profound source of spirituality. When we recognize our place in the immensity of light years and in the passage of the ages, when we grasp the intricacy, beauty and subtlety of life, then that soaring feeling, that sense of elation and humility combined, is purely spiritual.*
>
> —Carl Sagan

Hampered by fifty-six gallons of fuel in case I decide to fly to Hudson Bay without stopping for gas, the Cub struggles onto the step, and after a long take-off run claws its way into the air.

The Clearwater, though smaller than the broad Athabasca, is much more appealing. The Athabasca River is a broad, boring highway, but the Clearwater beckons like a tree-lined road, leading to surprises like Pinnacle Rocks and Whitemud Falls, where sulfur springs bubble down to the river. Above the Whitemud Falls, Mackenzie rhapsodized about the "extensive, romantic and ravishing" view, and wrote of voyageurs laboring in the valley below while the smoke from their fires rose like columns in the still evening air.

Following the Clearwater, the Cub flits past the northern end of the Methye Portage. Until the arrival of the *couriers du bois* (independent fur traders) and the Northwest Company's voyageurs, the northern Dene had been isolated from Europeans, but in 1778, the same Peter Pond who preceded Mackenzie finally crossed the Methye Portage, bringing trade goods, a new work ethic, a host of followers and, three years later, a deadly disease called smallpox. Almost 90 percent of the Dene died.

During winters that were said to require "blood like brandy, a body of brass and eyes of glass," Pond relied on a barely palatable-but-nutritious source of energy called pemmican, a greasy concoction of deer or buffalo meat, berries and bear fat. Three times during those travels, Pond shot to death those who had the nerve to dispute him, and three times escaped punishment, largely for lack of evidence.

Near Careen Lake, the Clearwater Valley abruptly changes direction, flowing down from the north and west. I love to follow rivers, but I'm heading for Cree Lake, an island-flecked blue sapphire that's rimmed with pristine beaches and hundreds of first-class campsites. Two hours pass as the Cub flies on, pushed by a sun that sends its shadow racing ahead, wavering across the treetops as if leading the way. The wind, which usually falters toward evening, begins to increase, nudging the Cub from side to side and making it rise and fall as if riding ocean swells. By the time I reach Cree Lake, the wind has streaked its face with white caps, foam and wind-whipped spray. I could camp on the sheltered shore, but if the wind changes during the night, I could become wind-bound by big waves on a lake that's sixteen miles wide and twice as long.

As the lowering sun pushes the Cub's shadow ever farther ahead, a small, comma-shaped lake with a narrow beach appears, so I yield to thoughts of pizza and a quiet bay where the wind can do me no harm. Better yet, small lakes are usually warmer than big lakes, and I'm due for a bath. The Cub descends, whisking over the shoreline pines, gliding over a broad field of tall, green reeds as its shadow returns to its maker and disappears in the ripples of "Comma Lake."

I build my evening fire well away from the Cub and set up my tent. When my fire's reduced to embers, I suspend a woven grate of green alder branches above the embers and add my foil-wrapped pizza. It's not as fast as a microwave, but it smells superb and tastes just great.

As I bite into the last piece, a gray jay ghosts down to perch atop my tent. I love gray jays, and I'm embarrassed to say that the first thing I ever shot was a trusting Canada jay. It was stupid, but sometimes kids do senseless things, and I instantly realized that I'd crossed some hidden line.

"So," I ask my guest, "do you like pizza?"

The jay, the bird that we call the "camp robber," tilts its trim, gray head.

I toss a chip of crust on the ground. The jay swoops down, picks up the crust and pauses as if to say thanks. He swallows it down, then waits for more.

The jay reminds me of an event that is said to have happened near the Minnesota-Ontario border just before the First World War, a time when many logging camps dotted the woods, one of which had a camp boss named Four-Bottle McGovern. Why Four-Bottle? Because it was Four-Bottle's custom to drink four pints of whisky per day—one in the morning, two in the afternoon and the last one at night.

One year Mc Govern came upon an Ojibwa party that included several young women, one of whom McGovern persuaded to over-winter at his camp.

They got along well for several winters, but when the girl took up with someone new, McGovern took offense and smashed her head with an ax. When the girl's relatives arrived in the spring, McGovern pleaded ignorance of her whereabouts, but a few months later, her body was found floating in a nearby lake. The Indians again questioned McGovern, who admitted the deed.

The outraged Natives pulled off his clothes and tied his arms and legs to trees, stretching him out like a hammock. They cut through the skin of his arms, chest, back and legs just enough so he'd bleed and left him hanging between the trees.

Canada jays and ravens have a wonderful sense of smell. Before long, the ravens and jays came swooping in and began to pick him apart. The story claims that they ate him alive, but it also says that Four-Bottle had so much whiskey in him that the jays got drunk, flying around in wobbly circles, running into trees and flopping on the forest floor until the booze wore off. And that, they say, is how gray jays came to be called whiskey jays, and also whiskey jacks.

The jay flies off with a piece of crust, but he's back in a minute. As he glides down to the beach, a movement in the water catches my eye. Something is swimming this way. It's too big for a muskrat, but it might be a beaver, the Cree's *amisk*. Beavers, however, are shy and not likely to approach an active campsite. It's a porcupine out for an evening swim—and why not? Their hollow quills support them well and perhaps, like me, he needs a bath.

One seventeenth century writer, who had seen the results of a porcupine encounter but not the event, wrote that the porcupine was "a very angry and dangerous creature, shooting a whole shower of quills." The porcupine's Latin name, *Erithizon dorsatum,* translates to "thorny pig," and though they can weigh up to eighteen pounds, this one is just a midsize porky.

Thanks to their 30,000 finely barbed quills, which they cannot throw, porcupines are safe from all but truly desperate or ignorant attackers, with two exceptions, humans and fishers. The latter bites the porcupine repeatedly in the face, which lacks quills, until it weakens, then flips it over and chews through its soft underbelly.

Porcupines love salt! They will attack sweaty boots and even car tires coated with road salt. Leave a sweat-soaked ax out overnight and it might be a hatchet come morning. As my visitor waddles ashore and shakes itself dry, I compose a Mowat-like poem.

The porcupine is slow and bristly,
and those who eat them say they're gristly,
but if you're a seeker of tasty thrills
you'd better not dine on horny pig quills.

As the porcupine wanders into the bush, I wonder why people accept the quill-throwing myth and so many other unlikely beliefs. Besides the quill throwing, there's the deadly quicksand myth in which the wet, gritty mineral relentlessly sucks desperate hikers down to their doom, even though they could easily "swim" to safety by lying down on their bellies. (The human body is much less dense than any slurry of water, sand or soil.) Some still argue that handling toads will cause warts while others believe that wood ticks leap onto passersby, despite the fact that they do not and cannot jump. One look at a tick's fragile legs provides the proof. They're nothing like grasshopper legs!

Heaping the fire with driftwood to speed my postswim warming, I strip off my clothes and head for the lake. The sun has set, leaving a pinking sky to light my way. With my float for a laundry table, I begin the old rub-a-dub while pine-scented, forest-cooled air flows out from the woods and onto the lake.

As I finish washing my shirt, tiny, prickling sensations begin to tickle my legs Bending over in the half-light of dusk, I discover a school of minnows nibbling away at a myriad of tiny air bubbles trapped in the hairs of my legs. That's weird, I say to myself, but it's not as odd as the ultrathin, yard-long, horsehair worms that swim like snakes in our fresh water lakes or the caddis fly larvae that crawl along the bottom, their sides and back covered with glued-on debris to disguise them from predators.

The minnows dart from gleaming bubble to bubble, gulping them down as if they're delicacies. They've discovered the ultimate diet food—lots of eating but zero calories. As they feast on nothing, I begin to feel guilty—like a sentient television set that regrets ensnaring minds with worthless fluff.

"Okay, minnies," I say to the throng, "fantasy time is over," and swim away, surging through invigorating, July-warmed water. I'm glad I passed up Cree Lake.

The Cub's wing struts become my laundry lines, and as I wring out my clothes, sending ripples far into the lake, I reflect on one of my favorite subjects—water.

What a marvelous thing is water. It covers 70 percent of the earth, distributing and moderating arctic cold and tropical heat. Even 15 percent of dust is water. We humans are 60 percent water; tomatoes are 95. Our blood chemistry is similar to that of the oceans from whence we evolved. Lose 2 percent of your water and you'll become thirsty, lose 5 percent and you'll soon go out of your mind, but a 12 percent drop is lethal.

Most liquids contract as they cool, as does water, but only water changes its mind and begins to expand when it reaches 39°F (4°C). Thus, as lakes and oceans cool, the coldest water lies on top of the rest, where it freezes, sheltering the water below from frigid winds that could freeze to the core all but the deepest of lakes.

Almost all chemicals are acids or bases, but water can be either. It's an almost perfect solvent. It can act as a catalyst, enabling chemical reactions like a cheering section that doesn't take part in the game. Water carries nutrients through all living matter and removes metabolic waste. It has the highest surface tension of all room temperature liquids except mercury, which is why it can support a magnetized needle to make a primitive compass. Despite its surface tension, water exhibits capillarity, which lets it invade its surroundings and even flow uphill. Water transmits sound five times faster than air, which is why, when you hit two rocks together while you're underwater, you hear a clink, not a clunk.

Water is essential to life, but if you make it from H1 instead of H2, you get heavy water, which looks the same but behaves quite badly. Seeds will not germinate in heavy water. If you drink it, you die.

Thanks to the Gulf Stream, which carries more heat north in one hour than all of the warmth produced by coal in a year, tropical plants can flourish in southern Ireland. Early American ship captains who understood the Gulf Stream (thanks largely to Benjamin Franklin) knew why sailing from America to Britain took two weeks less than the return trip, but British didn't, so they often sailed against the Stream, which put them at a disadvantage.

Contrary to popular belief, water is slightly compressible. Were it not, the oceans would rise enough to submerge 10 million square miles of lowlands that include Florida, the Netherlands and a big chunk of India. Most North Americans have an abundance of water, but much of the world does not. 97 percent of the world's fresh water is locked away in ice, leaving us just 3 percent, most of which comes from wells with falling water levels caused by a world population that has quadrupled in the last 100 years.

When I bend beneath the water to rinse the soap from my hair, the baptism scene from *Oh Brother, Where Art Thou* fills my mind. The Coen brothers' movie treated the subject lightly, but baptism has ancient roots, arising first from Confucian custom, but also from the Hindu ritual of bathing in the Ganges, and from the rituals of Egyptians who revered the Nile.

Among the first of the gods were the water gods. The Babylonians believed that water came from deep in the earth, delivered by Enki, the god of springs and rivers. The Incans worshipped Wiracocha, who arose from the water to create the sun, the moon and the stars. The Apache and Blackfoot believed that nothing moved until the Old Man floated past on a raft and commanded the world into existence. Some North American tribes envisioned a muskrat that dove to the bottom of an eternal ocean and returned with a clump of mud, but for others, a deep-diving loon surfaced with a beak full of clay. Tahitians also created an aquatic myth, believing that their islands had been lifted up from the ocean floor by powerful gods. And in two Moses-like beliefs, Sargon, the founder of Babylon, is rescued from the reeds by Akki, the water carrier, and Karna, the subject of an Indian story, is found floating on the Ganges, each to be later abandoned, Noah-like, to a flood[TN].

In North America, an adaptation of the water source is popular—the belief that humans were created from mud, a mixture of the biblical dust and water. The ancient Chinese, however, believed that a lonely goddess fashioned the first humans from yellow mud, just as the Greeks proclaimed that Prometheus used mud to make the first man, whom Athena breathed into life. Oddly enough, the process of evolution also depends on water, relying in part on evidence that life first arose in the oceans billions of years ago, and then evolved during the multi-billion generations that followed.

With paintings, photographs and fountains we honor water. Claude Debussy, who understood that water could batter or soothe, gave musical voice to the wave, the spray and the mist in a work that he named *La Mer*.

The black flies have gone to bed, leaving only a few mosquitoes, so I towel off beside the fire and add a touch of repellant. Turning to Bryson's *Short History,* I begin where I stopped last night, this time with better lighting from my oversize fire. Bryson, like me, is a fan of slime molds, the fungi that can be as beautiful as the yellow, gumdroplike growths I once found clinging to the bark of a box elder tree, or as repulsive as miniature cow pies. According to Bryson, there are thousands of different slime molds, and "when times are good, they exist as one-celled individuals, much like amoebas. But when conditions grow tough, they crawl to a central gathering place and become, almost miraculously, a slug."

In time, the slug reorganizes itself into a tiny plant-like structure with a bulbous fruiting body filled with spores at the top. When the time is right, the bulb explodes, scattering thousands of spores to the wind to begin their lives as independent, single-celled organisms, each one capable of someday uniting with millions of its kin to form another ambulatory slug. How neat this is. Oh sure, a bedtime tale about slime mold slugs won't appeal to some, but it's just the thing for fact-junkies like me.

An hour passes. My eyelids sag. The book that I held while reading about Walbachia, "the most rampantly infectious organism on earth"—but not to humans—has slipped from my hands. Like a child who has fallen asleep while sitting up, I'm on the verge of toppling over. Blinking myself awake, I brush the sand from Mr. Bryson. My fire is in embers, and the northern lights have begun to parade. Guided by their light, I head for my tent, thinking with each step how fortunate I am to be camped in surroundings that millions would love to share.

As I settle into my sleeping bag, I make plans for tomorrow. If the weather behaves, I'll head northeast toward Kasba and Ennadai Lakes or east across Reindeer Lake to Southern Indian Lake and Thompson or perhaps southeast to the Pas and Lake Winnipeg. I could ask Eeenie, Minee and Moe again, but I'll leave it up to the wind. Tomorrow, I'll follow any westerly wind, but if it blows from the northeast, east or southeast, I'll fly whatever course will keep it off of my nose

I had pitched my tent amidst a grove of jack pines to keep the sun from flooding the tent with light, but at 6:00 I'm awakened by the uneven plop!—PLOP!—PLOP! of something hitting the tent. As the plopping continues, I crawl from the tent. A squirrel is harvesting pinecones, which fall to the tent below. If it weren't so funny, I'd shoo him away, but it's a lovely, clear sky morning, and a little company will further brighten the day.

The squirrel, perhaps attracted by the scent of frying pancakes and bacon, scoots part way down the nearest tree. From his perch on an out-of-reach branch, he watches me, chirring while he tries to decide if I'm a bad guy or just an irritation. When I toss a pancake to the base of his pine, he climbs down the opposite side with one cautious eye protruding beyond the trunk. The rest of his body remains hidden while the eye skids down the tree.

He's afraid, but the pancake smells sooo good. After a few false starts and as many retreats, he finally stops at the edge of the pancake, lifts the edge to his mouth and begins to eat. Then, deciding to make it a carry-out, he lifts one edge of the pancake with his mouth and, instead of dragging it backwards to the trees, he tries to run forward with the edge between his teeth. The supple flapjack bends backward, leaving what was the far side beneath his advancing feet—and the squirrel goes end over end. He picks himself up, and then looks at me like someone who's just committed a faux pas and hopes he wasn't seen. Returning to the pancake, he repeats the performance, ending up flat on his back again. The more I laugh, the more indignant he seems.

"Listen, dummy," I say, "you can't push a flapjack, but if you go around to the other side, you could pull it."

The squirrel, who isn't about to listen to some ignorant tourist, performs yet another flip, leaving me howling, which sends him chattering up his tree.

Now truly offended, he refuses to return, so I impale the flapjack on a stick, raise it over my head and drape it over a branch.

"There," I say, "you'd better get busy or the jays will eat it for you."

The smoke from my campfire rises like a marble column, but when it climbs above the pines it trails off to the northeast as I'd hoped it might, so I'll head northeast today.

Spreading out my charts, I match the upper margin of the Wollaston chart to the lower edge of the Rankin Inlet chart, then draw a line from "Comma" Lake to Hatchet Lake and on to Nunavut's Ennadai Lake. I then draw a second line from Ennadai southeast to Thompson. My pocket tape says that it's 300 miles to Ennadai Lake plus about 400 more to Thompson. With no wind, I'll need thirty-six gallons of gas, but I still have forty-four, and there are several fueling sites to the south of Ennadai Lake.

When the Cub climbs above the trees, I scan the horizons. It's clear to the north, but the hills to the south are mantled in clouds.

This is pleated country. All of the rivers, hills and the eskers follow a pattern carved by glaciers that grooved the land from northeast to the southwest, making navigation a breeze—just follow Cushing Creek northeast to Hatchet Lake and then head for Kasba and Ennadai Lakes.

Northern Saskatchewan houses the mineral-rich Athabasca Basin, where uranium once was king. Uranium, however, fell from favor when the rush to build nuclear bombs and power plants diminished, only to return amidst controversy in 1989 when a huge spill at the Rabbit Lake mine caused Natives to demand that the government acknowledge their treaty rights over natural resources and take steps to protect the environment.

Uranium has long been used to color glass and ceramics, but not until the twentieth century did we realize that uranium could deliver huge amounts of energy through a process called nuclear fission. Spurred by increasing demand for uranium, new mines at Key Lake, Rabbit Lake and at Cliff Lake are showing great promise, but the best is McArthur River, which sits atop the world's largest high-grade uranium deposit, estimated to contain more than 400 million pounds of uranium oxide. As a consequence, uranium might well become Saskatchewan's equivalent to the Athabasca tar sands.

Hatchet Lake passes below. There, Cameco, the big dog in the uranium business, is developing a mine that is expected to yield uranium ore 100 times richer than average ores from elsewhere around the world.

In the late sixties, Wes and I camped for one night on the north shore of Hatchet Lake. The following morning, we were surprised to see a boat motor by, so we waved it ashore. Out stepped George Fleming, the owner of the newly established Hatchet Lake Lodge, which, unknown to us, was less than a mile away. Over breakfast at the lodge, George told how he'd emigrated from Scotland in the fifties, and then managed a Saskatchewan HBC store on the upper Churchill River until he realized that working for the Bay would never fulfill his dreams.

As he was about to leave for New Zealand, George met a man enamored with Hatchet Lake, and the two decided to build Hatchet Lake Lodge, which opened in 1964, later adding a 6,000-foot runway. Today, George Fleming's Hatchet Lake Lodge wins high praise from professional fisherman from all around the world.

Hatchet Lake, like its much larger neighbor, Wollaston Lake, lies south of the tree line, but as the hours pass and Kasba Lake begins to fill the horizon, the trees begin to thin. Unlike Wollaston, Cree and Reindeer Lakes, which are littered with islands, Kasba is almost island-free. Forty-five miles long and fifteen wide, it's the last major lake before Ennadia Lake, one of the ancestral homes of the Ihalmiut that Farley Mowat wrote of in *The Desperate People* and in *People of the Deer*.

When I began to head north in the sixties, I was intrigued by the 90,000-square-mile region between Great Slave Lake and Hudson Bay called the "Zone of Inaccessibility." After Churchill, my next stop was the weather station at Ennadai Lake, which lay well within that zone. There, I was pleased to find the barrel of fuel I'd paid Chuipka Airways to deliver and a crew that was starved for company.

All that has changed. The zone is gone from the charts. The weather station has been abandoned. Many Native communities now have airstrips, as do an increasing number of resorts and outpost camps like those at Nueltin, Henik,

Kasba, Snowbird and Dubawnt Lakes, one of the latest being a new resort near the south end of Ennadai Lake.

Resting beside a twenty-mile esker that parallels the lake's western shore, Ennadai Lake Lodge and its runway are easy to spot. And as I begin a long descent toward some of the sub-Arctic's finest tundra polygons, which lie eighty miles beyond the lodge, I try to remember the name of the man I met at the lodge in 2002.

I'd left Lynn Lake earlier that morning, angling northwest to Reindeer Lake, then north to Kasba and Ennadai Lakes when I noticed a new runway and a resort on the lake's southwestern shore. Because it was just past noon and I can smell food from as high as 10,000 feet, I throttled back and landed to see what might be cooking. I was greeted by several guests, one of whom had just caught a huge northern, and by one of the guides, who told me that I'd just missed lunch.

The lodge, which opened in 2001, sits high on a rise with an excellent view of the lake. When I asked the guide if they'd used winter cat trains to bring in building supplies, he said, "No. It's just too far. We plowed a runway out on the ice and flew it in on DC-3s."

Turning toward the lengthy building with a large central dining room, I said, "That's a lot of material. How many trips did it take?"

"I wasn't here for some of them, so I really don't know, but I was here when one flight crashed, and I'll never forget it."

"Really," I exclaim, "and how did that happened?"

"They'd already flown in one or two loads that day, but on this one, the plane landed too far down the runway. The pilot added power to go around, but when he pulled up the nose to climb, it went up so far that the plane quit flying and crashed. Both pilots died."

"And the cause?"

"Well, they were carrying crates and about two tons of

2 x 4s, so we think that the load might have shifted toward the tail when they tried to go around. If it did, it's no wonder they crashed."

The guide and his guests were about to go lake trout fishing, so I thanked them for waiting and headed up to the lodge where the cook delayed closing while I wolfed down a plate of beef stew.

The esker that forms the runway ducks beneath a bay to emerge on the opposite shore, where it wavers north toward the polygons that my father and I walked among in 1968, drawn there by the words "tundra polygons," printed on our chart. Neither of us knew what they were, but because we had to refuel at the nearby Ennadai weather station anyway, we decided to have a look. As we approached the area, the source of the name became apparent, for the face of the tundra looked like the end of a huge honeycomb, with some of the "cells" being thirty feet across.

We hadn't planned to stop, but the extent and the regularity of the hexagonlike patterns demanded a closer look. We later learned that the Ennadia polygons were frost-sorted polygons, the type that form when repeated freezing and thawing slowly moves particles outward, forming a square-to-hexagonal rim, the other type being formed by ice-wedges that create raised borders.

Some say that a smooth landing is mostly luck, two in a row is all luck and three in a row is a lie, but despite their skepticism, my landing at Ennadai Lake is a "greaser" for the fourth time in a row. After beaching the Cub, I walk across the boldly patterned ground. Here, I photographed my father with his ancient Argus as he stood in the center of one of the most perfect hexagons. I subsequently sent that photo and others of Thelon River caribou and musk oxen to the National Geographic Society in the hope that they'd send a photographer to capture Canada's northern landforms and wildlife, but they must have missed my point. Their response, without mentioning my suggestion, merely informed me that my photos didn't meet their standards. They were right, but that wasn't my purpose.

As I step from polygon to polygon, crossing rims that rise like mini-walls against their neighbors, I remember standing with my father on adjacent "squares," looking like two chessmen on a giant chessboard. Since I wrote *True North,* both of my parents have died. Both were still sharp enough to be able to read the first draft, but by the time the book had been published, my mother barely knew me, and when I placed the book in my father's hands, he looked at it without comprehension. It could have been a brick.

Now, I'm the senior male on the family tree, and as I stand within my private polygon, a feeling of loneliness washes over me. The abandoned weather station that I had planned to visit one final time still calls from a dozen miles to the north, but my mood has changed. Returning to the Cub, I check the course line to Southern Indian Lake and on to Thompson. It's a 400-mile hop, but I loaded up with fuel at McMurray, so I still have plenty to spare.

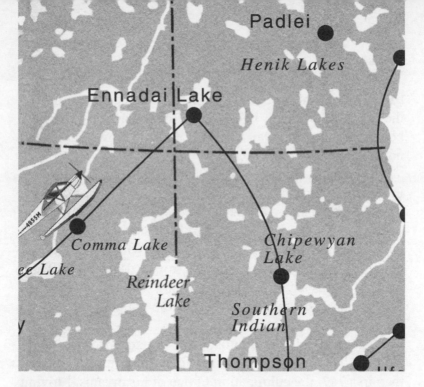

Padlei

Henik Lakes

Ennadai Lake

Comma Lake

e Lake

Chipewyan Lake

Reindeer Lake

Southern Indian

Thompson

Chapter 11

Ennadai Lake to Chipewyan Lake, Manitoba

> *Flying is hypnotic, and all pilots are willing vic-*
> *tims to the spell. Their world is like a magic island*
> *in which the factors of life and death assume their*
> *proper values.*
>
> —ERNEST K. GANN

The wind that brought me to Ennadai Lake becomes a hindrance when I leave the lake behind. Knowing that winds usually shift in a clockwise direction with altitude, I climb to 7,500 feet, and, sure enough, when I check my groundspeed, the wind is on my tail and I'm doing 92 mph, about four more than I'd be making if I'd stayed down low.

For more than an hour, 100-mile-long Nueltin Lake, which staples treeless Nunavut to the spruce-moose forests of Manitoba, slowly passes by, guiding me back from the barrens to a land ribbed with long and lofty eskers, one of the most prominent being the Robertson esker, which begins in Nunavut near Nueltin Lake and flows across the northwestern Manitoba.

Another hour passes, and when Big Sand Lake comes into view I begin to wonder what I'd do if I were granted a big pile of wishes—a pile so large that I could afford to fritter a few away. I think I'd start by resurrecting Leonardo da Vinci, the fifteenth-century scientist who predicted that humans would fly, the genius who saw birds not as fluff and feathers but as an "instrument working within mathematical law, which instrument it is within the capacity of man to reproduce with all its movements."

After a visit to the Smithsonian Air and Space Museum, I'd take the perceptive da Vinci for a ride in my Cub, and then in a 747, the culmination of one of his dreams. Moving on, I'd bring Isaac Newton to a "equal and opposite" shuttle launch at Cape Canaveral, and drive Galileo and William Hershel, the builders of telescopes, to the top of Mauna Kea, where a dozen magnificent telescopes derived from their work gather astonishing images from the fringes of space. I'd escort Darwin™ through Colorado's Dinosaur National Monument and visit a modern museum filled with hundreds of fossils ranging from primitive life forms to complete dinosaurs, and I'd show Alfred Wegner™ data from satellite photos, GPS readings and sea floor spreading, all of which prove that his widely scorned theory of continental drift was right on the money!

As I wonder whom else to invite, my head begins to droop. I jerk upright, alarmed that I'd begun to fall asleep. Lindbergh fell briefly asleep and entered a spiraling dive while crossing the Atlantic, but I'm no Lindbergh, and once is enough, so I look for a place to land. Directly ahead lies a long, multi-bayed body of water called Chipewyan Lake.

It's a fitting choice because here, the land of the Chipewyans meets the land of the Cree.

The lake's many bays offer a choice of narrow beaches, but the brush leaves little room for a tent. Finally, at the lake's southern end, I spot a bay that ends in a wide, ramplike slab of shelf-rock with an adjacent campsite that will do just fine. I land well out in the lake, and as the Cub slows to idle, I twist around to reach my fishing rod and begin to troll toward shore.

Even rumbling along at idle, the Cub's too fast for the lure, so I turn off one of its two magnetos. The engine slows and my flickering lure descends. A minute passes without action, and then another. Then, as I switch to the other magneto to avoid fouling the unused plugs, I feel a twitch. I tell myself it's just the bottom or a weed, but a hard tug follows, accompanied by a flurry of jerks—and I'm sure I've caught a walleye.

I let the idling Cub ground itself on the ramp-like granite while I crank in line. Climbing out, I net a beautiful gold and black walleye pike, the grand prize for many lovers of freshwater fish. Minutes later, I'm standing in the water beside my fish-cleaning table, the top of one of my floats. I slide my knife along its spines, handling it with care, for the spines in a walleye's dorsal fin can easily (and painfully) puncture flesh.

With a pound of firm, white, boneless fillets sizzling in butter, coffee boiling in one pot and dried peas in another, my eyes wander past the Cub to a forest bathed in the amber shades of evening. How many times have I camped in a beautiful place like this on my travels across the North? I try to count them, but by the time I pass twenty, I realize that I've probably forgotten more than those I recall.

When supper's done, I drape the remains of the walleye across a jack pine branch. At the water's edge, I pick a

handful of scouring rushes that some call horsetails—
primitive plants that contain silica crystals, and as a Canada
jay swoops down to peck at the walleye, I clean my dishes
the old-fashioned way with a handful of scouring rushes.
It's slow, but they finally shine.

The jay reminds me of the terrible end of Four-Bottle
McGovern, and as I think about the story, I remember an
alternative explanation of how Canada jays came to be
called whiskey jacks. The Cree, knowing that the friendly
jay often came calling for food, had named them *wiska-
zhon-shish,* which is variously translated as "the little one
that works at the fire" or "he who comes to the fire."
Trappers dropped the ending "shish" to arrive at whiskey
john, which soon became whiskey jack.

With great food, good company and a beautiful
campsite glowing in the soft light of a waning sun, I ask
myself, what more could one want? Besides the usual "jug
of wine and thou," I can think of just one addition: were the
shoreline graced with a scattering of lofty white or Norway
pines among the smaller jack pines, the scene would be
complete.

I select a level spot for my tent, search the ground for
the knobs that change into golf balls beneath my sleeping
bag in the middle of the night, and begin to set up my tent,
a job that I will dislike until someone invents an inflatable
tent or one that responds to the touch of a remote.

As I shorten a tent-stay with a sheepshank knot, my
grandfather leaps to mind. There was a man who knew his
knots. My grandfather began his adult life as a sailor, and
not just as an ordinary sailor, but as a young man who sailed
away from his Vestnes, Norway, home, not to return for
years. On four-masted clipper ships, he repeatedly sailed
around the world, gathering stories that enthralled me.

He described the 1890 wharves of San Francisco and
the bars where sailors were given drugged whiskey, then

"shanghaied" off to ships that needed crews. He told how sailors lubricated clocks with kerosene so they'd run fast and sell better on the Hong Kong wharves. In 1900, he turned his back on the sea and immigrated to a farm in northern Minnesota, where, always the sailor, he built a fourteen-foot sailboat out of hand-sawn ash when he could finally spare the time. My father inherited the heavy-but seaworthy boat, and then it became mine until time and the weather took it away. Now, all that remains of my grandfather's boat is the rudder that hangs on my workshop wall.

I like to believe that my grandfather's years on the sea still live on in me, for I love to watch the ocean. I enjoy the fecund scent of tepid tidal basins, and I love to stand beside large bodies of water when storms blacken their faces, raising waves rise to ominous heights.

I toss my foam mattress and sleeping bag into my tent and stiffly crawl inside. As I close my eyes to begin my nap, I total up the day. I've flown at least 600 miles, and right now, that's more than enough.

A rifle shot awakens me. Jerking upright, I look through the netting. Concentric circles of wavelets are spreading outward across the lake. Well, I say to myself, a squirrel woke me up this morning, so why not a beaver now?

I've slept for three hours, and now I'm hungry, so out come the camp stove, a package of beef stroganoff and my assortment of cans. I'm hoping for mixed fruit, but get onion soup instead. Still hoping to find mixed fruit, and ready to pour it into a depression in the rock for the critters if it's just more soup, I open another can. It's mixed fruit with lots of cherries. Hooray, I say to myself, this is first-class living!

When my dishes are done and my evening fire is well underway, I walk along the shoreline toward a long narrow point that curves into the lake. Thinking to save a few steps,

I stroll across the point, crunching reindeer lichens beneath my feet. As I reach the opposite side, a large mound about twenty yards from shore comes into view—a beaver house—the animal's refuge from predators and its winter home.

During, the seventeenth and eighteenth centuries, when tales of strange creatures from across the sea fascinated the Old World, facts were scarce, and the few that were available were often embellished or sometimes even ignored. Englishmen who took the term "beaver lodge" too literally wrote books like *The Beauties of Nature and Art,* which portrayed beavers with heads like bull terriers. Walking around like men, they carried planks on their shoulders that they joined together to make round-topped buildings that were divided into cubical apartments.

Another tale claimed that male beavers, having learned that their castor glands were prized by humans, would, upon seeing a hunter, "castrate" themselves with a single bite, thus preserving their lives by leaving the glands behind. If a castrated beaver was mistakenly pursued, the animal was said to hoist its rear skyward "to show that he lacked the sought-after parts," and would therefore be left alone.

Despite these fanciful tales, it's a fact that a beaver's anal scent glands produce a substance called castoreum, which has been used in perfumes, in chewing gum (oh, yuck) and as a cure for headaches because, as it turns out, castoreum contains salicylic acid, the active ingredient in aspirin.

A scattering of aspen stumps parallels the shore. All bear parallel gouges left by beaver teeth, and as I return to camp, I spot a beaver gnawing on a six-inch thick aspen just across the bay. For three minutes, long, inch-wide strips of aspen fall to the ground until the tree crashes down.

It's time to take my second (and undoubtedly futile) sample in search of diamonds, so I dig out my strainer, shovel and pot. I feel a little ridiculous, but, what the heck, several companies are already prospecting in Manitoba, so why not me?

To avoid disturbing the beaver, I cross over the point and wade out into the bay, which is rimmed with water smartweed, the lovely, pink-blooming weed that settlers once used to treat "ailments" of their posteriors. The remedy was effective, but it had a remarkable sting, which brought it the name arse-smart, later sanitized to "smartweed." The pink blossoms attract me, and, knowing that the light is fading, I hustle back to the tent for my camera, then squat down in the water, eye-to-eye with the blossoms and take several photographs.

The water is warm and soothing, so I hardly notice it as I begin to dig. Here, unlike at Q lake, there's no sand to fall into the hole, but there are roots to contend with plus an occasional stone and mud that releases bubbles that smell like methane and rotten eggs. When I'm two feet down and pretty well splattered with muck, the texture changes, so I take my sample, run it through the sieve, return to camp and clean myself off in the clear water at the base of my shelf-rock "beach."

I decide to sort through my samples now instead of taking them home. What would I say to the customs agents if they ask, "What's in the bags?" Do I want to say "diamond ore samples?" No way!

After adding an eighth of an inch of water to the bottom of my frying pan, I add a few teaspoons of my Q Lake sample and swirl it around to spread the "ore" into a thin layer. With the aid of my flashlight and magnifying glass, I begin to search for tiny red or purple crystals of pyrope and for emerald green chrome diopside, the telltale signs of diamonds. By the time I'm half way through the Q Lake sample, I'm convinced that I'll see nothing but sand, but I persevere. I've carried the stuff this far, so why not check it all.

The Q Lake sample fails to show color, so I dump it out

and start on the beaver bay sludge, which yields some color, but nothing like the garnet pyropes that I seek or the malachite green of chrome diopside. Oh well, I say to myself, I probably couldn't handle being rich anyway.

The forest beside my campsite rises above a carpet of lush cloudberries (think raspberries on steroids), bunchberries, fireweed, Labrador tea and a scattering of orange mushrooms. Beneath the trees, fiddlehead ferns taper gracefully upward as they curve toward a delicate tip. I'm tempted to go for a walk, but the sun has set. It's too dim for walking, so I retrieve my fishing rod and lures from the Cub, wade knee-deep into the lake and, just for fun, cast my teaspoon lure far beyond the Cub.

Three casts bring no takers, but on the fourth retrieve I let the lure settle a little longer, and something gently takes the hook. It could be another walleye or, now that I'm farther south, even a small-mouth bass, but when I reel it in I find not a walleye, but a clam that clamped down on my line when it passed between its shells, then bumped along the bottom, convincing me that I'd caught a fish.

I throw the clam back and cast again, and again, and again. As I'm about to quit, a two-pound northern nails my lure. "Lucky you," I say as I release it. "I've already eaten, so you won't have to stay for supper.

In northern pike or muskellunge country it's not unusual to have one of these big-mouth predators make a run at a fish as you reel it in. On one occasion, a northern hung onto a walleye I'd caught so tightly that I managed to net them both. Boaters who trail a hand in the water on an idyllic summer day have had their fingers bitten by northerns, which are also known as jackfish, tundra shark, snake and poor-man's salmon.

Northerns, being lunge-feeders, not only strike anything that moves, they will chase it right onto the shore. In *Reaching North,* Jamie Bastedo wrote, "A determined pike once leapt clear onto a rocky shore in pursuit of my wife's red and yellow socks—while her feet were still in them." A Russian fisherman, pleased to have caught a large northern, decided to kiss it on the mouth. The pike, doing what comes naturally, clamped down on the man's nose so firmly that even after it was beheaded, it could not be released and had to be freed by a surgeon. One northern Alberta fisherman boated a fifty-five-pound pike that might well have set a record, but then failed to take the necessary steps to have it recorded. His error left standing a Canadian record set by an Athabasca Lake northern that weighed all of forty-two pounds.

As I contemplate the northerns, another tree comes crashing down, followed by silence so pure that I can hear the rasping of beaver teeth as it attacks yet another aspen on the opposite side of my bay. In the distance a loon calls and another answers. Others join in, filling the silence with the crazy laughing, yodeling and mournful calls given only to loons. The moon has yet to rise and the stars have begun to appear, shining like lonely sentinels adrift in a blackened sky I search the sky for northern lights, but none appear. Perhaps, like me, they're tired tonight and they've already gone to bed.

I've always been a dreamer. Most of my dreams make sense when I'm sleeping, but they're absurd when I open my eyes. Tonight, however, my dreams include a recurrent-but-sensible dream of a warm August night in the sixties when I went to visit the stars.

I was sitting alone on my front porch steps beneath a fading primrose sky, when I heard my Beechcraft call, so I drove out of town to the darkened field, and as the airport beacon endlessly painted the hangar white, then green, then white, then green, I pushed open its heavy doors. Flipping on the hangar lights, I climbed into my Bonanza, settled into its comfortable seat, and relaxed while savoring its singular scents, its solidity and its latent speed. Prompted by a voice that urges, let's fly, let's fly, I rolled out 5114 Charlie, performed a leisurely preflight and started the smooth-running engine.

Accelerating quickly, the lightly loaded Beech climbed into the tranquil sky. With nowhere special to go, I spiraled upward while the streetlights dimmed and the horizons expanded, set aglow with glimmering yard lights.

On reaching 12,000 feet, I throttled back and trimmed for level flight. With my hands in my lap, I ruddered the Beech through gentle figure-eight turns, twisting beneath the Milky Way as the city glow beneath me spun first this way, then that. Radiating outward from the airport like the glittering spokes of a Ferris wheel, highways shining with the dots and dashes of headlights became flickering strips of visual Morse code. To the north, small explosions of light rode the spoke that led to Slayton and Marshall; to the west sparkled Sioux Falls, South Dakota, to the south—Sioux City, Iowa. Heading east, a string of slow-moving vehicles crawled like luminous procession caterpillars toward airport beacons at Jackson and Fairmont, but the brightest spoke led northeast to Windom and the valley town of Mankato, then on to the sunrise-like radiance of Minneapolis and St. Paul.

As a full moon glinted upward from lakes and ponds, the earth seemed to mirror the stars, flickering with hundreds of "campfires"—the yard lights of farms below.

When lightning began to dance across the western sky, I turned on my radio. A line of Dakota thunderstorms was about to maul Brookings, but with three hours to burn 'til the storms arrived, I flew on through silky air while rain poured down on the distant farms, and my strobes winked back at the white-hot rivets that bonded the patchwork sky.

Jerked alert by a sudden *CRACK,* I reached for my flashlight, and discovered the shattered body of a June bug pasted upon my windshield. What a shame. Was this humble creature carried aloft by the distant storms, and then swept along by the jet stream just to fall through my prop, or was he a high-flier like me, propelled by his genes to reach for the moon on the final flight of his life?

The thunderstorms, set aglow by their own internal strobes, drew closer, and the once-smooth air became restless, rolling like ocean swells raised by a distant storm. Throttled back, the Beech began a long descent, arcing down through swanlike turns as I spiraled back to Earth. Gear down, mixture rich, flaps to twenty, prop set for high rpm. Pillowed in undulating, cool night air, I turned on base, then settled onto final. The approach lights flashed past as the nose-high Beech descended, its gear reaching for the ground like the feet of a landing goose as we entered the tunnel of light.

I parked the Beech in the hangar. Leaving the doors open wide, I cut the hangar lights and felt my way to the cockpit. Settling into the Bonanza's commodious seat, I closed my eyes. While the tick of the cooling engine faded, I slipped into the arms of night.

When the marmalade shades of morning probed my east-facing eyes, I yawn myself awake. The Bonanza, its engine cold and silent, seemed not to have moved an inch I wondered—was my orbiting flight nothing more than a hangar-bound dream, a fantasy flight while the stars shown bright? And then it began to rain.

Perhaps other people have many recurring dreams, but this is the only dream that returns to me again and again, and though my other dreams are black and white, in this dream, my white, red and black-striped Bonanza always gleams in vivid color.

I reach for my flashlight to check the time, but it's dead, so I rummage around in my packsack for spares. By the time I find and insert them, I'm wide awake, so I decide to check on the Cub. When I switch on the flashlight and light leaps from my hand as if by magic, I think of a Russian Jew named Conrad Hubert who immigrated to the U.S. in 1890 to escape persecution by the orthodox Catholic majority.

A few years later, a friend showed Conrad an electrically lit flowerpot that he'd just invented. Young Conrad, however, envisioned more than well-lit flowers, and quickly converted the flowerpot light into a portable flashlight that could brighten the darkest corner. Conrad died in 1928, leaving an estate worth $8 million, about $2 billion today, all of it generated by the firm that he founded, the Ever-Ready Company.

The Cub is just as I'd left it, but I'm wide-awake and the night is warm. The sky overhead is still untouched by the aurora, so I lie down on my back to watch for shooting star. Two weeks from now the Perseid meteor showers will be in full bloom, but tonight, the earth is only beginning to enter the trail of comet dust that will bring on the mid-August show.

A minute later, one of the thousands of meteors that plunge into our atmosphere every minute, escaping notice by day but lighting tiny flares at night, streaks briefly across the sky. Like a short-lived spark or the career of a young starlet, it flashes brightly before it dies. About 300 tons of rock falls onto the earth every day in particles as tiny as dust motes or as large as the chunk that crashed through the house of a Georgia woman, leaving a huge bruise on her thigh. Some, like the hundred-foot meteor that created the Winslow, Arizona. crater, are large enough to affect the weather. That's big, but it's insignificant compared to the meteor that struck the Gulf of Mexico some 65 million years ago, causing a horrendous climate change that doomed the dinosaurs and hundreds, perhaps thousands, of other species as well.

It's unlikely that the earth will be struck by a major comet, meteor or asteroid in the near future, but because any major strike would be an unparalleled disaster, astronomers have begun to watch for deep space objects with trajectories that might do us harm. If that seems silly, consider the effects of the fragments of comet Shoemaker-Levy that slammed into Jupiter in 1994. Despite its great mass, the damage to the planet was astonishing. Were a similar comet to strike the earth with even a glancing blow, it is highly probable that only the simplest life forms—perhaps bacteria—would survive.

Shooting stars, comets and exploding stars have long been associated with the birth and deaths of gods and kings, and they've also been favored by theologians who let imagination rule.

In 1578 a Lutheran bishop declared that comets were made of "the thick smoke of human sins...that gradually grew into comets." One hundred years later, a theologian named Christopher Ness called comets "signs from heaven" that signify drought and portend war. Well, drought happens somewhere almost every year, and our eagerness to follow warlike leaders still stacks the odds in their favor.

Science, fortunately, has gradually replaced superstition,

but it's been a long and difficult fight. When Halley's comet arrived in 1910, an Oklahoma sheriff was forced to intercept religious fanatics who were determined to sacrifice a virgin to appease the comet, but when it returned in 1982, the comet found no fanatics and no frightened virgins. In their place were space probes designed to analyze the comet's nature and the size of its nucleus, which they reported was about four miles wide and ten miles long.

Then, amidst progress, came disaster. On March 26, 1997, the worst mass suicide on U.S. soil occurred when thirty-nine devout members of the Heaven's Gate church committed suicide, believing that they needed to shed their earthly "containers" before they could board a space ship trailing behind the Hale-Bopp comet. The youngest was twenty-six, the oldest, seventy-two. What a shame.

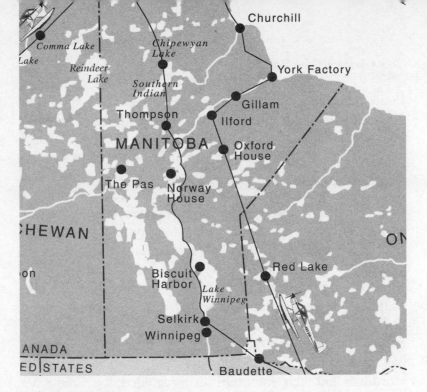

Chapter 12

Chipewyan Lake to Lake Winnipeg, Manitoba

> *I have seen maybe a thousand northern lakes,*
> *and they all look alike in many ways, but there*
> *was something different about that little lake that*
> *held me hard. I sat there perhaps half an hour,*
> *like a man under a spell, just looking it over.*
>
> — JOHN J. ROWLANDS, FROM CACHE LAKE COUNTRY

It's just ninety minutes to Thompson, a nickel-mining town that, like Churchill and others, calls itself "the Hub of the North." However, because of oversleeping, a leisurely breakfast and an aerial tour of the once-pristine, 100-mile long Southern Indian Lake, which has become a muddy disaster, I won't reach Thompson 'til noon.

The Churchill River, which begins in western Saskatchewan near the lake named for the notorious Peter

Pond, has coursed through Southern Indian Lake and on to
Churchill for thousands of years, providing the Cree who
have lived on its shores some of the best fishing in the world
and a healthy resort economy. But in 1974, the river's outlet
from Southern Indian Lake was greatly restricted to divert
much of the Churchill's flow to electricity-generating dams
that span the Nelson River. The project's been good for
owners of power-hungry factories and homes, but it's been
a disaster for the Cree who lived along the shores of
Southern Indian Lake. Thirty years after the lake was
flooded, erosion continues to gnaw at the shorelines despite
Manitoba Hydro's predictions that erosion would end in
five years. Every year, an area as large as Winnipeg washes
away. Mercury once locked in permafrost and vegetation
has invaded fish, fowl and humans. With their resorts made
worthless and their communities threatened, the Cree have
been compelled to move, abandoning the lake forever
because of the silt, the forest debris and the contaminants it
now contains.

   As I leave the lake behind, I wonder if the destruction of
Southern Indian Lake was another one of the many
"unintended consequences" that so often result from poor
planning or inadequate data, or if it happened because the
need for more power simply trumped a search for
alternatives. Regardless of the reasons, it's a fact thousands
of Canadian and northern U.S. businesses and homes,
including mine, rely on power generated by the Nelson
River dams—and from the penalty paid by the displaced
Cree. Hmmm.

Pat Chartier, the Thompson seaplane base operator, is reluctant to let strangers taxi up to his pier—and with good reason: There's an invisible eddy the runs *upstream* on his side of the Burntwood River. The eddy can and has caused a disaster when "newbies" taxied toward an aircraft tied to the pier, expecting the current to cancel their forward motion, but suddenly learned that it's running the opposite way.

It's just a short walk to Riverview Restaurant, where I ease my hunger with a big cheeseburger, onion rings, fries and a delicious strawberry shake, gobbling them down at one of the outdoor tables while swatting the biggest horse flies I've ever see. Locals call them bull-nose flies, and their bite is like poking your finger into an electric outlet.

From Thompson south, fuel will be plentiful, so I stow my empty gas bags in a float compartment and taxi away from the pier. With the wing tanks full, I'll have more than enough to reach the border.

As I climb away from Thompson, I pass the Muskeg Express, which is about to begin its overnight run to Churchill. My course will take me south over Sipiwesk, Cross and Playgreen Lakes to big Lake Winnipeg, the source of the Nelson River, and as I cross the string bogs to the southeast of Norway House, I spot an small cabin on the tip of a crescent-shaped lake. Well obscured by trees, it's seclusion, and the fact that it's almost invisible reminds me of another remote cabin that I chanced upon in the eighties.

The lake I'd selected for the night would have been too small for a Cessna 180, but it was a "piece of cake," for my Cub. A narrow stream meandered away from the lake, connecting it to a small river that led to a larger waterway. The lake's small size and seclusion guaranteed a peaceful night, so I landed, set up my tent, caught a fish for supper, and after cleaning the dishes, sat down beside my fire with my back to the woods and began to enjoy the view.

As the sunset faded, I heard a twig snap, and when I

turned toward the sound I almost leaped out of my skin. Standing at the edge of the firelight about ten yards away was a stocky man with a rifle cradled in his arms.

"Jeez," I exclaimed as I scrambled to my feet while trying to collect my wits, "You almost scared the life out of me!"

"Sorry," he said. "I've been trying to decide if I should say hello or stay out of sight. You're the first person that's ever stopped here, and I've been using this lake for years."

Puzzled, I told him, "I can't see how I missed seeing your cabin or your boat when I circled to land. If I'd seen them, I wouldn't have stopped."

"That's because I built my shack away from the shore and I pull my canoe into the woods where it's hard to see. I came out here to get away from pe… well, you know, and I want to keep it that way."

"Sorry," I said, "I didn't mean to bother you."

Well," he said, "I tell you what. Why don't you bring your sleeping bag and stay in my shack tonight. A bear's been prowling around, so you might as well play it safe. By the way, I'm John."

"Thanks. I'm George," I said as we shook hands. "I don't worry much about black bears, but I'd like to see your place."

As we walked the narrow, almost invisible trail to his cabin, John pointed to claw marks on several trailside trees.

"This one is feeling frisky," he said.

John's cabin was located in a tight grove of jack pines beside an elevated food cache and an empty 8 x 8-foot frame.

"Now I know why I didn't see your cabin," I said, "but what's the frame for?"

"It's for stretching moose or caribou hides."

Built of jack pine logs and chinked with strips of fiberglass insulation, John's 16 x 16-foot cabin had a small kitchen opposite the entrance, a bed on one side and a long, wide bench on the other. I set my foam mattress and sleeping bag on the bench and examined the cabin while John began to make coffee.

A wood burner with a metal chimney that extended through the roof was centered in the room, but what caught my attention was a wall almost covered with books.

"Wow," I said, "this reminds me of Mackenzie's "Little Athens" at Fort Chipewyan! Have you read all these books?"

"So you know about Mackenzie, do you?" he asked, then continued. "Yes, I've read every one but that bunch over there," pointing to a box of a dozen or so books at one end of his pine-slab kitchen counter "I'll have those read by fall."

"I'm a big reader, too," I said, then added, "Mind if I look around?

"Not a bit."

On the shelves, which, like the table and chairs were also made from pine slabs, I found *Les Miserables, Candide, Trinity, The Cruel Sea,* Ludwig's *Napoleon, Cache Lake Country, The Discoverers, The English Patient, Fate is the Hunter,* an unexpurgated *Gulliver's Travels,* a second edition of *The Wizard of Oz,* Seldes' *The Great Quotations* plus books by Dickens, Cervantes, Kipling, Voltaire, Poe, Turow, Asimov and Michener—an eclectic mix if ever there was one.

"You know," said John, "at first I thought you might be having engine trouble, so I walked over. When I saw that you didn't, I watched you a while, and then decided to say hello."

As the evening progressed, John began to talk about his past.

"I first saw this country from an airplane in the seventies, and canoed it a few years later. I'd gotten lucky in the market plus I sold a start up company for enough so I'd never need to work again. The year before I built this cabin, my wife died in a car crash, so with no kids and nothing to hold me back, I picked this little lake because it was a long way from the bustle I'd come to hate. I figured if I got lonesome, I could always go back."

"So how old were you when you built the cabin?"

He paused, "I built it in 1980, so I'd have been about thirty-six. At first I came in late June and left in August, but now I come as soon as the ice is out and stay until the bay begins to freeze. It's a three-day paddle to where they fly in my supplies, and I've got a little outboard for when the wind is strong. It's worth it to me to make the trip because that way, not even the pilot knows where I live, and because I'm at the end of this long creek, no one comes this way.

"I don't think I could hack it," I said. "I can stand myself for maybe three days, but then I get antsy. Don't you ever get lonely?"

"Not really. I read and go fishing and hunting." Pointing to an easel in a corner, he said, "I'm teaching myself to paint and I have a decent telescope for when the nights are clear. Someday, I'd like to have a solar-powered computer—and there's always wood to cut for the cool days of spring and fall."

"So what about winter? Have you ever stayed over?"

"I tried it once, but I didn't like it. The days were too short and I got bothered by all the tracks leading to the cabin. Anyone flying by would instantly know that someone was living here, and that would be the end of my privacy."

He turned toward me, and after a pause asked, "What about you? What brings you to a place like this?"

I told him how I'd always read about the North, how I spent a part of my summers exploring different parts of northern Canada and Alaska. As I described my past, I wondered if he was just being polite, but when I stopped back in later years, he had remembered every detail.

After a game of chess, which he won, we called it a night. As I was about to fall asleep, he said, "By the way, if you hear things in the night or if something runs across your sleeping bag, it's just a mouse, so shoo it away. There might not be any tonight, but when it gets cold, I can't keep them out. I'd trap them, but I kinda like the little buggers."

When we walked out the door in the morning, we heard a loud huff as a mother bear and two cubs went running behind the cabin. Looking around the corner, we spotted the cubs high in a tree while the mother patrolled below. Fortunately, I'd brought my camera, so, using the ladder from John's cache, I climbed onto the roof of his cabin to get a shot of the cubs. Then, because we didn't want to get mama riled, we headed straight for the lake and walked the shoreline back to the Cub.

At the end of that visit, I gave John a sack of cookies and a few cans of soda and wished him luck. As we shook hands, John said, "I'm glad you stopped. If you want to come back next year, it's okay with me."

We exchanged a yearly letter, and I returned for a visit in 1988, the year that he was limping about, having nicked his leg with an ax. I stopped again in 1996 and again in 2003.

On my last visit, when he learned that I'd written two books, which I gave him, and had begun a third, he became truly enthusiastic, talking well into the night about books he had enjoyed, ending up with two that, despite their other good qualities, had given offense.

"Look at this," he said, instantly retrieving two widely spaced books from his shelves as if he'd used them every day. "These are high-quality books, but both of them have a major error that should have been caught."

The first was the *Rivers and Lakes* volume of the "Planet Earth" series by Time Life™. John, seated on his bed, read aloud the offending text: "Rain that falls on much of the state of Montana, 800 miles to the west, drains into Lake Superior."

He looked at me to be sure that I had caught the error,

which I had, and then began his indictment. "Imagine that!" he said. "From Montana all the way to Lake Superior! Last I heard, much of Montana, all of South Dakota and most of North Dakota drain into the Missouri River, and most of northern Minnesota drains into the Mississippi, but these people, who are supposed to be experts, would have us believe that the Lake Superior watershed extends 800 miles to the west instead of just sixty—and I know it's sixty because I checked. Hadn't they heard of Lewis and Clark and the Missouri River? And what about Minnesota being the source of the Mississippi, the Father of the Waters?" What the hell were they thinking?

"Now look at this one," he said, handing me Peter Newman's *Company of Adventurers*. "I've read every one of Newman's books, and I like them, but in this one he begins by telling about two guys in northern Saskatchewan who spot something metallic hanging high in a spruce tree. On climbing the tree, they find a copper frying pan with HBC stamped on its handle, so they conclude that the pan had been hung on a sapling and then forgotten, rising higher every year as the tree grew taller.

I knew where he was going, so I smiled as he continued his harangue. "It's a great story, but unless Saskatchewan has miraculous trees, it's wrong. Trees, as I'm sure you know, gain height by adding to the tip of the previous growth like a builder places block onto block. Anything hung five feet from the ground would stay there year after year. It amazes me that that this competent author and his editors would let this pass. Maybe they should get out of the office and look at some trees."

I wanted to defend the authors, but I knew that John was right. Experience has taught me that minor errors, like my inexplicably writing "east" instead of "west' in the first edition of *True North,* can be very hard to detect.

In 2004, when I wrote to John, who was then in his sixties,

he was slow to respond, finally writing that his solitary life had begun to lose its shine. I wrote again in 2005, hoping to see him once more. When I received no response, I wrote to the store where he purchased his yearly supplies and learned that John had moved to Australia, perhaps permanently.

The Cub picks up Lake Winnipeg near an oval, sand-rimmed lake separated from the big lake by an esker bristling with tall Norway pines. The tops of the pines bear odd dots of white, so I descend in a wide circle. As the Cub approaches the pines, the white spots become bald eagles launched into flight. What a fantastic campsite this would be! Sheltered from, but adjacent to, the big lake, I could fish either shore and pitch my tent with nesting eagles. Unfortunately, it's too early to stop. Maybe next year, I tell myself, as I mark another big S (for sand beach) on my chart.

An hour passes as I cruise above the waves, pulling up to cross the wooded points of the lake's escalloped shoreline, then descending again on the opposite side. And as Poplar River comes into sight, I remember a flight that began well enough on a cold November morning a few years ago, but ended in tragedy just a few minutes later.

It was ten in the morning when a commercial pilot and two passengers took off from the Poplar River airport, bound for the town of Fairford, just a one-hour flight away. Hurried aloft by its powerful engine, the Cherokee began to charge across the thirty-five miles of Lake Winnipeg that separate Poplar River from the tip of Reindeer Island. Despite an outside air temperature of 34°F and scattered clouds at 6,000 feet, the pilot and his passengers rode in comfort as the settlement fell behind.

Suddenly, a mist of oil began to streak the windshield,

soon followed by a flood. A glance at the oil pressure gauge confirmed the obvious—zero oil pressure—almost certainly a broken oil line or a blown propeller seal. Calling MAYDAY, the pilot reported engine failure, gave his location, and said he'd try to reach Reindeer Island. Though rocky and wooded, a crash landing there would be infinitely better than ditching in the three-foot waves of a close-to-freezing lake.

By the time the pilot radioed, "Descending through twenty-three hundred feet...don't know if I can make Reindeer Island...might have to put her in the water," two RCMP Twin Otters that had been operating nearby were heading for Reindeer Island.

Shortly after the second transmission, the Cherokee's ELT (emergency locator transmitter) began to operate, but soon stopped, probably due to the aircraft sinking. Despite a thorough two-day search of the area, no signs of the aircraft or its occupants were found.

I wonder if there was anything they could have done that might have saved their lives. Life jackets would have bought them a few minutes, and that's if the ditching went well, but if they'd flown south instead toward Berens River to cross the lake where it's half as wide, the engine would have failed while they were still over land, and there, they might have survived. Finally, if they had flown their original course just 2,000 feet higher (if the ceiling allowed), they'd have been able to glide three to four additional miles, perhaps enough to reach the island.

A few miles south of Poplar River, near a place called Marchand Point, I notice a small shack on a rise near the shore. I'd planned to camp farther south, perhaps on Tamarack Island, but the shack tugs at me, so I circle back. If it isn't locked, I won't have to mess with the tent. Weathered gray, the shack leans away from the prevailing westerly winds as if dreading the next big blow. I imagine a trapper huddled in the rickety shack while a howling blizzard sends a dusting of snow whistling through the cracks.

Spotting a narrow beach not far from the shack where the water's sufficiently deep, I throttle back and land. The beach is littered with clamshells, perhaps left behind by otters. If so, I hope they return. As my sons used to say, "Wouldn't that be neat?"

Thirty yards of glacier-grooved bedrock lead to my private abode. On opening the door, I discover that the hinges are so loose that it not only opens outward, it opens halfway inward as well. The eight by eight-foot shack lacks windows, but the open door and the cracks between its vertical boards admit an abundance of light. One wall bears a faded 1986 calendar promoting a Winnipeg bank. Except for a rickety table that's speckled with fish scales, there's not a stick of furniture and only one cooking utensil—a frying pan that's nailed to the wall—through the center of the pan!

The place isn't spotless, but it's good enough. Back at the Cub, I set a soda in the lake to cool, then carry my portable radio, camp stove, foam mattress, sleeping bag and sack of snacks to the shack and begin to explore the palace grounds.

My shack sits precariously on four, stump-like chunks of firewood. I'm amazed it hasn't blown down, but perhaps it has, only to be propped up again and again. Peering underneath, I find one good oar and the business end of its broken mate, a snarl of rotting fishnets and the battered cowling of a 5-hp Martin outboard—a motor from the 1950s that I haven't thought of for years.

A faded green, flat-bottom boat with the hand-lettered word *Marie* on its bow lies inverted behind the shack in a bed of purple lupines. Its stern has fallen away from the hull, and its canvas covering lies in shreds. Envisioning *Marie* plowing slowly across Lake Winnipeg with a load of fisherman, I decide that she's not just an empty hull, she's a vessel loaded with memories.

The sound of running water meets my ears. Pushing through a stand of alder, I find a narrow stream cascading down a staircase of platterlike stones. The rocks, sculpted by water and time into smooth, free-flowing forms, are decorated with delicate traceries of pink quartz.

Where the stream nears the lake, it tumbles down a four-foot cascade, spreading quivering bubbles across a yard-wide pool. The bubbles, propelled by a tangent current, circle the pool, coalescing into larger, multilobed spheres until they burst or are carried away to the lake. Standing spread-legged over the rafted bubbles like a small Colossus of Rhodes, I bend low for a closer look at the quivering, lens-like bubbles, each one reflecting my image back to me. It occurs to me that the bubbles would provide the ultimate self-portrait, so I take several photos as the bubbles pass between my legs. Later, as I watch the bubbles drift into Lake Winnipeg, I'm tempted to cast a line beyond them, but I'm done with fishing. Except for entertaining my grandchildren, I probably won't wet a line again this year.

Returning to the shack, I come upon a rusting stovepipe that brings to mind a tale of a Yukon prospector named Charlie who yielded to curiosity and broke the code of the bush.

Chilled to the bone by a blizzard, weak from hunger, and knowing that he couldn't go much farther, Charlie was about to surrender when he spotted a dim yellow light during a lull in the storm. Stumbling toward it, he was thrilled to see that the light was coming from a window— and a window meant warmth and food. When he pounded on the door it was opened by a grizzled trapper much like himself who quickly took Charlie in. For five days the storm raged on, and for five days, the trapper played the perfect host while Charlie, who had traveled the bush and knew that questions were sometimes unwelcome, took care to mind his own business.

The moss-chinked, log shack was unremarkable except for one detail—the trapper's wood burner was hung quite close to the roof, an awkward arrangement that required the trapper to stand on a chair to feed the fire within.

Every day, the prospector's eyes furtively sought out the stove, searching for an explanation. When the storm finally blew itself out, and Charlie prepared to leave, he apologetically burst out, "Dang it friend, I'm sorry to ask you this, and I hope you don't mind, but it's driving me crazy. I just have to ask why you put that stove up near the ceiling instead of down on the floor."

The trapper smiled. "Well, Charlie," he said, "I guess that's a fair question. I put 'er up there 'cause I've only got one length of stovepipe."

Back at the shack, which, despite the stovepipe, doesn't have a stove, I begin to tidy up, first sweeping the floor with a handful of balsam branches, which make a fragrant broom. With my floor "clean," I spread out my foam mattress and sleeping bag, prop the table in a corner and set my camp stove on it.

There's no room for an evening fire between the shack and the beach, but a nearby rocky point will do, so I gather some driftwood and begin to prepare my sunset fire. When I walk farther down the beach for more wood, I discover a game trail leading down to the lake. I follow it inland for a few hundred yards, passing white cedars that have been neatly trimmed of greenery within eight feet of the ground by foraging deer and a scattering of white spruce, the loftier cousins of the often ragged looking black spruce that range from northern Alaska and the Northwest Territories to the northern tier of states.

Black spruce can grow almost everywhere—even in bogs. Every year, their acidic needles fall to the forest floor making it hostile to acid-intolerant plants. Low-lying branches eventually contact growing beds of moss and send down banyan-like roots. From each root, new stems arise. Given time, as many as fifty satellite trees can surround the parent tree.

At the edge of a small clearing, a scattering of orange and yellow hawkweed, bright, white daisies and dandelion blossoms remind me that that I've flown a long way south. I bend over to pick a daisy, then jerk back. A fawn lies curled up just beyond the flowers on a bed of fiddlehead ferns, its tan coat flecked with white flashes as if placed by an artist's brush. The fawn lies motionless. Its eyes remain closed. Except for the slight movement of its chest, it could easily be dead.

I stand quietly, scanning the forest for its parent. Seeing nothing, and thinking that I shouldn't touch the fawn, I head back to the lake. When I return with my camera, the fawn is gone.

It's suppertime, and I'm hungry for steak. While imagining a T-bone steak smothered with onions and mushrooms, I consider my options, then and settle on freeze dried stroganoff, dried apricots, cookies and coffee. Later, as I pack my stove and dishes away, I come upon a few slices of questionable bacon that I'd forgotten about, so I toss them outside for the critters and head for my waiting fire.

The rocks, still warm from the afternoon sun, are firm but relaxing. As the sun dips below the horizon, random thoughts begin to troll through my mind. I see myself and my two sons, age eight and ten, at our diningroom table, each of us drawing imaginative lakes with bays, beaches, cabins, rivers, beaver houses and reefs wherever we want them—an exercise that encouraged imagination. I remember the mixture of sadness and pride that I felt when first one, and then the other drove off to college. The sadness soon left, but the pride has remained, with both of them leading responsible lives.

A veery rolls out its lovely call, which surprises me because I've never heard one this far north. I search for the right adjective to describe its melody. Is it spiraling? Circular? Metallic? Attenuated? It's all of these and more.

The sky turns crimson as my fire burns down to embers. A firefly goes winking by, perhaps attracted by the sparks, and as I turn to follow its flight, I discover that that the bushes behind me are filled with blinking lights.

When my grandchildren were small, we trapped fireflies in plastic jars. The kids were afraid at first, perhaps because the code-like flashes of the lightning bugs looked hot, but before long they were running around, trying to collect enough of the quarter-inch beetles to be able to read by their yellow-green light. I wonder if they remember that evening, but I doubt it. It's a memory I treasure, but for them, it was probably just one of many briefly captivating events in their vibrantly young and wide-eyed lives.

When I look up at the stars, I remember driving to the top of Hawaii's 14,000-foot Mauna Kea with my wife and our youngest son, passing a hefty, four-wheel-drive snowblower along the way. Working with Mauna Kea's many telescopes, astronomers have discovered several large stars that are whipping around the center of our Milky Way galaxy at the incredible speed of 1,860 miles per second! I try to imagine whirling a sun-sized stone on an incredibly long string—the string in this case being gravity from an immensely powerful black hole that Einstein had called dark stars. This black hole has not only captured our galaxy's suns, it is reeling in the string, drawing them ever closer. With every sun that eventually goes whirling into the hole, the power of the black hole grows. Eventually, even our sun, though it lies far from the galaxy's center will also be at risk. I wonder what happens to all that mass, all that energy, and I wonder if the brilliant quasars that brighten our skies might be the other side of black holes that are sucking in stars from a neighboring universe. Why not?

I envision a traveler from another galaxy who enters our spiral galaxy and then our circular solar system. He lands on our revolving Earth, where he learns that all matter consists of tiny particles that have electrons spinning about them like minor galaxies. Will he begin to wonder if this sort of structure endlessly repeats itself like an Escher drawing or like the oriental view that Earth rides the back of a giant tortoise that rides another tortoise that rides yet another, leading to the old joke that "it's turtles all the way." Or might the system be circular like a snake attempting to swallow its tail so that one day he finds himself back in the galaxy he originally left? Is it also astronomically true that what goes around comes around?

Those who cling to smug theologies of "just one earth designed just for us" scoff at the idea that intelligent life could exist beyond Earth, but I disagree. Imagine billions of galaxies, each with billions of suns and millions of planets, many of which would host conditions suitable for life. (In 1995, astronomers Michael Mayer and Didier Quelos detected the first known planet orbiting a star other than our sun. Since then, other astronomers have added dozens.) Now grant each of those planets billions of years for life to evolve, and it becomes not just possible but probable that our supposedly intelligent species is far from alone.

Carl Sagan, the author of *Cosmos* and *Contact,* agreed, as have many others, one of the first being Metrodorus, who, in 400 BCE, wrote, "To consider our earth the only populated world in infinite space is as absurd as to assert that in an entire field sown with millet, only a single grain will grow."[TN]

The moon, tinged bronze by the smoke of distant fires, finally rises above the trees, reminding me that it's bedtime, but I stay. I think of the cold, silvery moons of Baker Lake and Bathhurst Inlet, and I wonder if it was a smoky moon like this that tempted Aristarchus to calculate its size and distance more than 2,000 years ago, which he did to within 10 percent of what we know today to be true. How many of us could do the same, using observation and logic alone?

When I'm still awake at two o'clock, I dig into my packsack for one of my rarely used sleeping pills. Aided by my pharmacological wonder, sleep comes quickly, restoring my body and mind to keep me from going round the bend. All day long, we mute our less than admirable impulses, but sleep, without the warden of consciousness at work to make us toe the line, lets us go a little nutty when no one else will know.

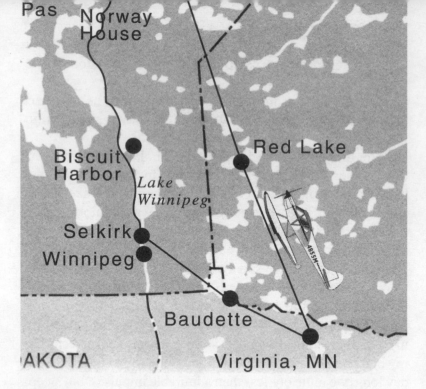

Pas
Norway House
Biscuit Harbor
Lake Winnipeg
Red Lake
Selkirk
Winnipeg
Baudette
AKOTA
Virginia, MN

Chapter 13

Lake Winnipeg to Lake Vermilion

> *No pessimist ever discovered the secrets of the stars, or sailed to an uncharted island, or opened a new heaven to the human spirit.*
>
> —HELEN KELLER

The morning sunrise spreads across Lake Winnipeg, setting it all aglow. Beside the trail to the Cub, a dragonfly clings to a wild pink rose, its wings bejeweled with tiny drops of dew. Unable to fly, it waits for the sun to remove its burden.

While thinking about the dragonfly, I climb into the Cub and then feel a little foolish because for the first time in years, I've forgotten to prop it to life. As I climb out, I remember a similar incident from my less than glorious past. After releasing my Lake amphibian from its tie-down chains, no amount of power would make it move. Puzzled, and almost convinced that my brakes had somehow locked, I shut down the engine, walked around the plane and found the tail still chained to the ramp.

While the engine warms, I draw a line on my chart from my campsite to Biscuit Harbor, a seaplane base/resort on the western side of the lake. My chart and all of our atlases are based on the work of a sixteenth-century Dutchman named Gerard Mercator who, despite being swept up by the Inquisition on charges of heresy, luckily survived.

Mercator, who wanted to find a way to convert cumbersome globes to convenient, two-dimensional maps, faced two problems: first, the old theology-based maps that made Jerusalem the center of the world—the maps that the churches favored—were useless to navigators and, second, because the earth is a sphere, it is impossible to accurately display east-west distances to the north and south of the equator on a two-dimensional map.

To envision the problem, we might paint the features of the earth on a tennis ball, slice it in half from pole to pole and then attempt to flatten one of the halves into a two dimensional map. Something has to give. Mercator solved the problem by keeping the lines of longitude, the north-south lines, parallel instead of having them converge as they approach the poles. North-south distances on such a map remain accurate, and if the area covered by the map is not too great, the east-west distances are exaggerated so slightly that only surveyors would care. However, when the area portrayed is large, the distortion becomes huge. A Mercator map of the globe, which spreads the poles across the top and bottom of the map, distorts east-west distances so severely that Greenland looks bigger than Africa, though it's only one-sixth as large.

It's just an hour to Biscuit Harbor, so I delay breakfast and take to the air, and as the *Tundra Cub II* draws close to the Harbor, I think of the first *Tundra Cub,* which I sold to buy a faster, roomier four-place Cessna. The Cub then passed through two owners before it was purchased by Tom Ahlers, a great guy from Missouri who, after reading *True North,* called one evening to ask if I'd take a trip with him. By that time, I'd sold my Cessna and had purchased another Cub, so when summer arrived we headed off to Churchill.

Gregarious Tom hit it off with everyone. He loved Churchill and Gillam and had a ball at York Factory. Mosquitoes didn't bother Tom, who was too busy having fun. When we stopped for the night at Ilford's Gold Trail hotel, he insisted on giving the Cree constable a ride in the Cub despite the fact that his passenger's sumo wrestler-like girth put the Cub well over gross. Nevertheless, away they went, struggling onto the step and into the air. Back and forth they flew. When they returned, out crawled a happy constable who'd just had the ride of his life.

The next day brought us to Biscuit Harbour, where, because the resort was new, the owner gave us the Jacuzzi-equipped honeymoon suite at a bargain rate in the hope that we'd "spread the word." The following day, Tom and I flew side by side for a couple of hours until Tom peeled off to the east to attend Red Lake's Norseman festival, while I turned south for home.

A year or so later, the phone rang. The caller was sobbing. It took a while, but I finally realized that the caller was Tom's beloved Mary. When she finally gained control, I heard what I'd feared.

"Tom is dead," she sobbed.

"Oh, Mary," I said, then inadequately added, "I'm sooo sorry! What happened?"

Between sobs and tears and pauses for breath, she explained.

"He was working on a tractor...where we're building our home... He pushed on a tree with the bucket...and...a branch broke off...hit him...he died."

The funeral was well attended, for the couple had hundreds of friends. Tom's death came as a blow to me. Three years earlier, I'd lost Wes Miller, my flying friend for decades, to cancer. Wes and I had flown in the Yukon and Northwest Territories, gathering many of the tales that appeared in *True North,* and we'd flown together in Belize and Australia. At the time that he died, we lived in distant cities. On hearing from a mutual friend that Wes wouldn't last much longer, I called him at the hospital at a time when I knew he'd be alone. We talked about getting lost while flying to Ayers Rock, and of climbing the great stone pyramids of Guatemala's Tikal—Wes with his daughter, Marcia, and me with my son, Chris. We remembered fireside cribbage games on fog-bound Kelly Lake and landing in the South Nahanni River just above 300-foot high Virginia Falls.[TN]

Wes, who knew that I was about to leave on another trip in the same Cub that he had once owned, finally said, "I'd better go now. When you get to Lake Athabasca, look in the back seat. Maybe I'll be sitting there, wedged between the gas bags."

I managed to say, "Okay, Wes," and hung up. Two days later, he died.

Wes was older than I, but vigorous Tom was at least ten years younger, and it's not supposed to happen that way. Now, this time with no warning, another of my flying friends was gone. Damn.

When Tom and I arrived at Biscuit Harbor, we were pleased to see a woman mechanic working on the engine of a de Havilland Beaver—an occupation traditionally held by men— and as I taxi inside the breakwater and hike up to the restaurant,

I wonder if she's still here. The first person I encounter is the manager. It's been years, so I'm not surprised that he doesn't remember me, but he remembers Tom and the *Tundra Cub*. And the lady mechanic? She moved away years ago.

Breakfast, for me, is the most important meal of the day. I sometimes skimp on it when I'm camping and I'm eager to get going, but when I find a restaurant, I live it up, so I order a ham and cheese omelet, pancakes, a side of hash browns and a double order of bacon. My Dad ate whatever he liked and lived to ninety-three, so why not me?

A woman at a nearby table is having a one-sided "discussion" with her husband, who is trying to appear interested, about a sixteenth-century French "visionary" named Nostradamus. Referring to a pocket book, she tells him that Nostradamus predicted Hitler, the atom bomb and 9-11, all of which is total baloney because nothing in his *Les Propheties* even comes close. The "Hitler" she refers to has nothing to do with Adolph. Her error derives from a Nostradamus poem that mentions "Histler," which is a portion of the Danube River.

I want to tell her this and a lot more, but I don't think she'd take it well, so when I finish eating, I stop briefly beside their table and after a generic greeting, say, "I heard you talking about Nostradamus, who is one of my favorite subjects. If you have Internet access, you should check him out on the net. There's lots of information there."

She gives her husband a "See—I told you so" look and thanks me. I hope they check out the internet. If they do, they'll discover that Nostradamus made a pile of vague-but-poetic predictions that can be applied to almost any event by people who want to believe but don't bother to read his often distorted and misquoted work.

Had I the time, and she, the interest, I'd explain how real predictions work, using the example of a mid-nineteenth-century, astronomer named John Michell, who predicted the existence of black holes, the massive stellar objects with gravitational fields so intense that not even light can escape. Unlike Nostradamus, who made scads of vague predictions, and is often judged "right" by his fans who ignore his failures, Michell made just one closely worded prediction based on science and reason—and hit it bang on the head.

While the dock-hand tops the tanks, I take a seat on the bench near a man dressed top to bottom in Levi-blue who was returning from Thompson but had to land at Biscuit Harbor when his engine misbehaved.

"Are you in mining," I ask.

"No," he says, "I'm an ichthyologist."

Concerned that I might not know what he means, he adds, "I study fish. I've been working out of Thompson and around Southern Indian Lake."

When he learns that I'm from Minnesota, he asks what I've heard about diverting excess water from North Dakota's Devil's Lake into the Red River, which flows north along the Minnesota-North Dakota border into Manitoba and Lake Winnipeg.

"We're concerned about two things: the high sulfate levels in Devil's Lake water and the likelihood that the diversion could introduce new predators into Lake Winnipeg, which already has problems.

"New predators in the food chain," he continues, "can really make trouble. A few years ago, someone introduced northerns into several California lakes, and the fish population fell so fast that the DNR had to mount an expensive campaign to eliminate them."

"The Devil's Lake thing is news to me," I say, "but I know what you mean about northerns I call them 'fresh water barracudas.' So—do you just work in Canada or do you go to other countries as well?"

"Two years ago," he replies, "I was near the headwaters of the Amazon for a while and then on the Orinoco— a truly amazing river! Four thousand species live in its waters, and most of them are fish."

"So," I ask, "how would a piranha stack up against a northern?"

"Frankly," he says, "piranhas are overrated. Sure, piranhas have a mouthful of amazing teeth, and they'll bite if you mess with them, but I've seen kids jumping and swimming in piranha waters and none of them got scratched. I'd put my money on the northern!"

"Me, too," I say, although my wager would be based on regional pride. Go northerns!

When he hears that I've been to Belize, he says, "Let me give you a little advice. If you ever get down where I was, and you decide to swim in the rivers, don't urinate while you're in the water. That's safe enough in most of the world, but the rivers there harbor tiny worm-like fish that live on blood. They hone in on the ammonia emitted by the gills of other fish, then attach themselves like lampreys and live on the fish's blood.

"The thing is," he continues, "to them, ammonia is just ammonia, and they're just as willing to swim into the urethra of a urinating human. Once inside, they attack whatever is handy. Man or woman—it makes no difference. Only surgery gets them out."

"Oh, man," I say. "I'll surely remember that!"

As I'm about to leave, he asks where I'm heading.

"I'll probably stop at Selkirk because I've never been there, and then I'll head for home."

"Really," he says, "I grew up near Selkirk, but we moved away when I was sixteen. If you have a chance, try to find someone to tell you how Selkirk got its name. Maybe Bob Polinuk, he runs the seaplane base, can help you. The way I remember it, some rich "Brit" named Selkirk went bust while trying to fill the place with immigrants. It's a pretty good story."

The town of Selkirk and the Selkirk Air seaplane base owe

their existence to the Red River, which begins between Minnesota and North Dakota. For more than 200 years, fur traders and settlers moved up the Red from Lake Winnipeg to the fertile prairies that join the United States and Canada. Some moved even farther west to a tiny outpost on the banks of the North Saskatchewan River that we now call Edmonton.

When I get to Selkirk, Bob Polinuk is flying a charter, so I ask the clerk how the town got its name, but he hasn't a clue. As I settle my bill, he says, "You might try Tony Peltier. He's big on history—always talking about the old days. Bores me to death."

When Tony answers the phone, I plead my case. It's almost noon, so I offer to buy him lunch if he'll pick me up. Ten minutes later, Tony arrives in an old Mercury Meteor, which he apologizes for, saying that his wife has the good car, and we're off to Grrumpy's, stopping on the way at the Marine Museum, which is home to the SS *Keenora,* a 158-foot steam boat built in 1897 that served on Lake of the Woods, the Red River and Lake Winnipeg until it was adopted by the museum about thirty years ago.

At nearby Grrumpy's, Tony begins to fill me in while we wait for our fish (walleye) and chips (French fries).

"First off," he says, "I'll give you the short version, because the whole story would take all day. And second, most people think that Selkirk was English, but he wasn't. He was a Scottish Lord. His proper name was Thomas Douglas, the fifth Earl of Selkirk, and the Earl was enormously rich. But what matters is that this guy actually cared about his tenants, unlike the other Lords and Earls who didn't give a damn.

"In 1811 Selkirk bought 160,000 square miles of what is now part of northern Minnesota and southern Manitoba from the Hudson's Bay Company and began to ship over hundreds of starving Irish and Scottish peasants so they could build a new life along the Red River. It was a great idea, but the whole thing eventually fell apart."

"So how did that happen?"

"Well," says Tony, "first we have to back up a little. It's true that Selkirk wanted to help his tenants, but he also hoped to profit from the recovery of undervalued HBC stock, which had dropped from 250 to 50 pounds sterling, so he bought controlling interest in the company, which is how he managed to get his hands on a chunk of land that was even bigger than Britain!

"For payment, Selkirk agreed to supply the HBC with 200 servants every year for ten years—their wages to be paid by the HBC, which Selkirk controlled.

"The first immigrants arrived at York Factory in September, 1812, which was too late to head inland, so they spent a miserable winter at York Factory. They finally reached Selkirk the following summer, but like your Pilgrims, they'd have died without the aid of the Natives."

As I try to eat and scribble notes at the same time, Tony plunges on.

"Things went well for a while, but then Selkirk made a big mistake. He tried to micro-manage everything like some Old World feudal lord. But this was the New World, and people didn't want to be treated like serfs.

"Selkirk decreed that the competing Northwest Company must leave his lands. No Northwester would be allowed to cut timber, and any timber they'd already cut would be seized. He ordered all Northwest buildings destroyed. Finally, he declared that no one could take food or game from his lands without permission, which outraged the Metis, that's half-breeds, you know, because they'd been doing that for decades. In 1815, open warfare between Selkirk and the Metis and the Northwesters broke out.

"Selkirk asked for help from Ottawa, but was refused, so he rushed two hundred soldiers west from Montreal, retook the territory that had been occupied by the Metis and Northwesters, and had the Northwesters shipped to Toronto for trial.

"Now," says Tony, "the story gets sort of weird. In fact, if it wasn't so serious, it'd be funny. When the Northwesters got to Toronto, they were released on bail, and the judge ordered Selkirk arrested. This really ticked off Selkirk, who was back at Red River, so when the constable arrived Selkirk slapped him in jail, having respect only for English law—not Canadian law.

"Hold on a minute, Tony," I beg, flipping from one page of my notebook to the next. "I need to catch up." How, I wonder, can anyone talk so fast and eat at the same time?

He gives me fifteen seconds, then shifts back into high.

"In 1817, a Royal Proclamation ordered the NWC and the HBC into court, where they were 'advised' to merge. A few years later, they did just that and Selkirk, who was forced to sell his land, lost his fortune. After paying a minor fine, he moved to France, where he died around 1820, the same year that Mackenzie, his arch rival, also died."

"So," I say, "the settlers must have appreciated his good intentions or they wouldn't have kept his name?"

"That's right," he says, "and in 1882 when the town was incorporated, the name 'Selkirk' became official."

At the seaplane base I file a flight plan to Baudette with an Adcus request (Advise Customs) and offer Tony a ride in the Cub.

"Thanks," he says, "but I'm scared to death of those things. I've had three car crashes, but at least they happened on the ground."

"Okay, Tony," I say, "I understand."

I'm tempted to point out that "on the ground" is where airplanes crash, too, but I doubt that he'd change his mind.

I fire up the Cub, wave to Tony and take off into a

gusting southwest wind. It's 150 miles to Baudette, and every mile covers part of the bottom of ancient glacial Lake Agassiz, the huge lake that once covered much of Manitoba, North Dakota and northern Minnesota. Fed by the waters of melting, mile-thick glaciers, the lake's outflow, the great River Warren, dug the deep, broad valley that now houses the much smaller Minnesota River.

Normally, I'd fly straight to Baudette, but today I'll angle east for a look at West Hawk Lake, one of the many meteor craters that march northwest across Canada from West Hawk Lake to Reindeer Lake's Deep Bay and nearby Gow, then on to Carswell and Pilot Lake Craters on opposite sides of Lake Athabasca. Most are filled with water, but some, like Carswell, are dry. Some show potential for uranium, as at Carswell, where it's already being mined.

West Hawk Lake, however, being rimmed with homes, looks no different than many southern lakes. Except for its circular shape, nothing about it says "crater." The high, steep shorelines that define Ungava's New Quebec Crater are absent, and there's no central island like the one that graces Gow Lake.

The Trans-Canada Highway finally falls behind, followed by aptly named Shoal Lake and fifty miles of Lake of the Woods, the Voyageurs' *Lac du Bois*. At the lake's southeast corner, the Rainy River flows into the lake near Sable Island—and "sable" in French, means "sand."

When my sons were three and five, we stayed at a nearby resort and picnicked on Sable Island. There, you can wade out 100 feet before the water covers your knees, making it a perfect spot for children to learn to swim or practice their penmanship by scrawling their names on the island's broad "boardwalks" of sand. My youngest did just that, and I treasure my photo of three-year-old Lars sitting proudly beside his name—everything right except the S, which he'd made like a Z.

Baudette appears as I punch in 122.8 on my radio to call Tom Nelson, the airport manager. Minutes later, the Cub settles onto the broad Rainy River and pulls up to a pier where a U.S. Customs agent is waiting, clipboard in hand. The questions are similar to those at Canadian Customs, but the mood is less friendly—a change that began soon after 9-11.

Beyond Baudette, the horizon fills with eighty miles of forest and bog. Paradoxically, in this part of the Land of 10,000 Lakes, there are no lakes. Only their ghosts remain, living on as spruce and balsam-rimmed bogs, the result of eutrophication, the long process that slowly ages lakes by adding yearly loads of wind-blown leaves and needles, the detritus of the forest. With every century, the depth of a lake decreases. The ring of open water minutely narrows. In time, the lake becomes a pond, its ripples restricted by expanding beds of white and yellow water lilies, followed by swaying bull rushes and shore-hugging sweet gale.

Winter arrives, and as the volume of oxygen-laden water beneath the ice decreases with every century, fish begin to die—walleyes, perch and pickerel first, followed by rough fish like suckers and bullheads. Minnows and crayfish perish, then frogs and clams. In time, the lake succumbs to vegetation, and the great blue heron no longer comes to call. The last speck of open water disappears, replaced by a spongy, floating bog you can walk across with snowshoes.

When Lake Vermilion appears, I prepare to violate basic flying rule number one, which warns pilots to avoid flying "near the edge of the air, which can be recognized by the appearance of ground, buildings, the sea, trees and interstellar space." The rule is correct, but I can't avoid the edge forever, so I throttle back and land while avoiding a scattering of boats that get faster every year.

The cove where I park the Cub is just a short walk from my cabin, where I'll leave my camping gear. A sun-spotted trail wanders up through a forest littered with over-ripe blueberries, perky, green club moss and last fall's russet pine needles—a mixture of life and decay. I pause at the base of a lightning-scarred, hundred-foot pine that was ten feet tall when I was a child. Its windward roots have been pulled from the earth by a brief-but-powerful storm that was strong enough to tilt the pine but too weak to finish it off.

When I step across the brook that I played beside as a boy, I think of Heraclites, the Greek who observed, "It is not possible to step into the same river twice." "Everything changes," said Heraclites, including people like me.

I've had a billion breaths on this planet, which makes me seventy-four. Almost every spring, I've paused beside this brook while mallards courted in a nearby bay. A few months later, I've watched leaves of orange, red and brown go floating past, their fluttering come to an end, their usefulness seemingly gone. In the Lake of the Sunset Glow, the leaves decay. Some of their atoms drift down the Vermilion, Rainy, Winnipeg and Nelson Rivers to the oceans where life began.

As my brook goes bubbling by, I wonder if I'll ever fish the Reversing Falls of Wager Bay, return to Marble Island or hike Baffin Island's Pangnirtung Pass. I hope so, but a year from now, will the body be willing when the mind says go? James Knight returned to the Arctic at the age of seventy-nine, so why not me—so why not me?

Tennyson would have urged me on despite my mounting years. "Tis not too late to seek a newer world," wrote Tennyson, but he also tied people like me to hurrying brooks like mine:

And once again I curve and flow
To join the brimming river
For men may come and men may go
But I go on forever.

Epilogue

A few months later, I sold the *Tundra Cub II* and began to consider a faster replacement. Winter intervened, and when spring arrived, I was still undecided. In early May, when I'd begun to wonder if I'd have wings by the time that summer arrived, the phone rang early one morning.

"Mr. Erickson, please," said a pleasant female voice with a French accent.

"Speaking," I replied.

"Mr. Erickson," she continued, "you are the author of *True North?* Yes?"

"That's right," I said.

"My name is Catherine Tobenas, and I'm hoping you'll join our International Air Rally as a reporter this summer. Our flight of twenty-five aircraft will leave Oshkosh at the end of AirVenture, fly north through Quebec and cross the Hudson Straits to Baffin Island and Frobisher Bay, which we now call Iqualuit. The rally, which will include aircraft from South Africa, Switzerland, the United States and Canada, will end at the Hotel Manoir Richelieu on the St. Lawrence River. We'll be pleased to pay your expenses if you'll write an article about the rally for the aviation magazines."

I couldn't believe my ears! For forty summers, I'd been flying the North on my own nickel, and now, on the first summer that I lacked an aircraft, I was being offered a free trip to one of the few places I'd yet to see.

Two months later, I was on my way to Baffin Island, visiting Cree and Inuit villages scattered along the way. For a "low and slow" seaplane pilot like me, it was a joy to briefly co-pilot a Pilatus P-12 at 300 mph and 27,000 feet, to join other pilots in their Huskies, Cessnas and Pipers— and to photograph Hudson Strait icebergs from a Cirrus, the aircraft made at the tip of Lake Superior where *Back to the Barrens* began.

The rally went well. I'm booked for the Maritimes in 2007 and maybe Alaska in 2008. My search for that special airplane continues. Perhaps I'll never find it, but oh, what a ride it's been!

Bibliography

Whoever writes a book, plunders a library.

—ANON

Alexander, Bryan & Cherry. 1988. *The Eskimos*. New York: Crescent Books.

Atwood, Margaret. 1995. *Strange Things: The Malevolent North in Canadian Literature*. New York: Oxford University Press.

Aydon, Cyril. 2005. *A Book of Scientific Curiosities*. New York: Carroll and Graf.

Ballantyne, Robert. 1848. *Hudson's Bay*. New York: T. Nelson.

Beattie & Geiger. 1993. *Dead Silence: The Greatest Mystery in Arctic Discovery*. New York: Viking.

Beals, C.F. 1968. *Science, History and Hudson Bay*. Ottawa: Queen's Printer.

Bronowski, Jacob. 1973. *The Ascent of Man*. New York: Little, Brown & Company.

Bruemmer, Fred. 1974. *The Arctic*. New York: Quadrangle.

———. 1972. *Encounters with Arctic Animals*. New York: Amer. Heritage.

Bryson, Bill. 2003. *A Short History of Nearly Everything*. New York: Broadway Books.

Burke, James. 1978. *Connections*. Boston: Little, Brown & Company.

Berton, Pierre. 1988. *The Arctic Grail*. Toronto: McClelland & Stewart.

Calef, George. 1995. *Caribou and the Barren-Lands*. Toronto: Firefly Books.

Davis, Richard & Guravich, Dan. 1982. *Lords of the Arctic*. New York: Macmillan.

Dyson, John. 1979. *The Hot Arctic*. Boston: Little, Brown & Company.

Erickson, George. 2003. *Time Traveling with Science and the Saints*. Buffalo, NY: Prometheus Books.

————. 1999. *True_North: Exploring the Great Wilderness by Bush Plane*. Toronto: Thomas Allen Publishers; New York: Globe Pequot (2003).

Ferris, Timothy. 1988. *Coming of Age in the Milky Way*. New York: Morrow.

Freuchen, Peter. 1961. *Book of the Eskimos*. New York: World Publishing.

Gann, Ernest K. 1944. *Flying Circus*. New York: Viking Press.

Grinnell, George. 1996. *A Death on the Barrens*. Toronto: Northern Books.

Hall, Sam. 1988. *The Fourth World*. New York: Random House.

Hart, Matthew. 2002. *Diamond*. New York: Penguin Books.

Hauf, Tim. *Little Trees, Big Sky*. Canada.

Heacox, Kim. *Bush Pilots of Alaska*. Portland: Graphic Arts Center Publishing.

Hearne, Samuel. 1802. *Journey from Prince of Wales Fort in Hudson's Bay to the Northern Ocean in the Years 1769–1772*. Philadelphia: Joseph and Jane Crukshank.

Herter's Professional Guide's Manual.

Hing, Robert. 1992. *Tracking Mackenzie to the Sea*. Manassas: Anchor Watch Press.

Hummel, Monte. 1984. *Arctic Wildlife*. Toronto: Key Porter.

Innis, Harold. 1962. *The Fur Trade in Canada*. New Haven: Yale University Press.

Kurelek, William. 1978. *The Last of the Arctic*. Toronto: Pagurian Press.

Laut, Agnes C. 1908. *Conquest of the Great Northwest*. New York: Outing Publishing.

Leslie, Edward. 1988. *Desperate Journeys, Desperate Shores*. Boston: Houghton Mifflin.

Lopez, Barry. 1987. *Arctic Dreams*. New York: Bantam.

Lyall, Ernie. 1979. *An Arctic Man*. Edmonton: Hurtig Publishers.

MacDonald, Malcolm. 1943. *Down North*. New York: Oxford University Press.

Matheson, Shirlee. 1994. *Flying the Frontiers*. Saskatoon: Fifth House Publishers.

Matthiesen, Peter. *The End of The World*.

McPhee, John. 1976. *Coming into the Country*. New York: Farrar, Straus & Giroux.

Mirsky, Jeannette. 1934. *To the North*. New York: Viking.

Morrison, Philip and Phyllis. 1987. *The Ring of Truth*. New York: Random House.

Mowat, Farley. 1963. *Never Cry Wolf*. Boston: Little, Brown & Company.

————. 1962. *Canada North*. Boston: Little, Brown & Company.

————. 1959. *The Desperate People*. Boston: Little, Brown & Company.

————. 1952. *People of the Deer*. Boston: Little, Brown & Company.

————. 2000. *Walking on the Land*. Toronto: Key Porter Books.

Murie, Olaus. 1973. *Journeys to the Far North*. Palo Alto: America West Pub. Co.

Newman, Peter. 1988. *Company of Adventurers*. New York: Penguin.

———. 1995. *Empire of the Bay*. Toronto: Viking Canada.

Olesen, Dave. 1994. *North of Reliance*. Minocqua, WI: NorthWord Press.

Price, Ray. 1970. *The Howling Arctic*. Toronto: P. Martin.

Raffan, James, ed. 1986. *Wild Waters*. Toronto: Key Porter Books.

Raymo, Chet. 1991. *The Virgin and the Mousetrap*. New York: Viking.

Redfern, Ron. 1983. *The Making of a Continent*. New York: Random House.

Rytchetnik, Joe. 1995. *Alaska's Sky Follies*. Anchorage: Epicenter Press.

Sagan, Carl. 1995. *The Demon-Haunted World*. New York: Random House.

———. 1997. *Billions and Billions*. New York: Random House.

Seldes, George. 1960. *The Great Quotations*. Secaucus: Lyle Stuart.

Steele, Peter. 2003. *The Man Who Mapped the Arctic*. Vancouver: Raincoast Books.

Stefansson, Vilhjalmur. 1922. *My Life with the Eskimo*. New York: Macmillan.

———. 1921. *The Friendly Arctic*. New York: Macmillan.

Tryck, Keith. 1980. *Yukon Passage*. New York: Quadrangle.

Turner, Dick. 1980. *Wings of the North*. Surrey: Hancock House.

Weiner, Jonathan. 1986. *Planet Earth*. New York: Bantam.

White, Andrew. 1896. *A History of the Warfare of Science with Theology*. Gloucester: Peter Smith Publishers.

Walker, Barbara G. 1983. *The Woman's Encyclopedia of Myths and Secrets*. New York: Harper & Row.

Young, Steven. 1989. *To the Arctic*. New York: John Wiley & Sons.

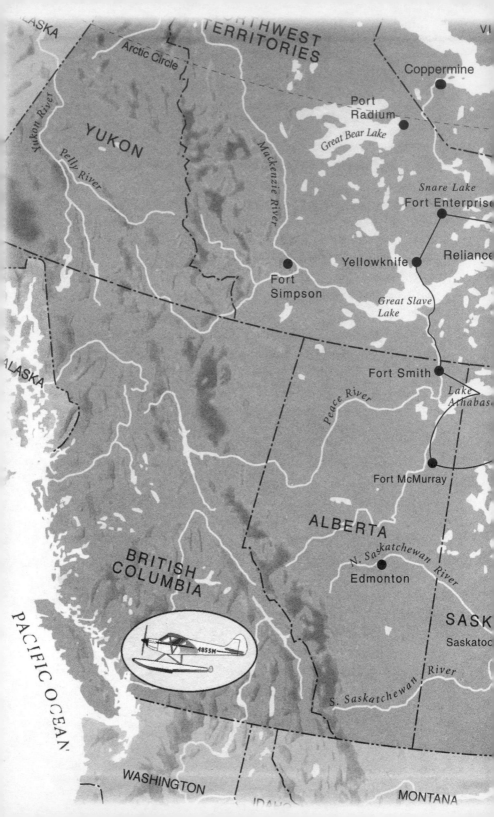

Index

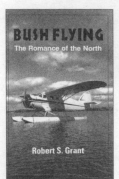

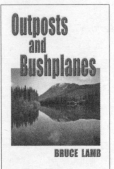
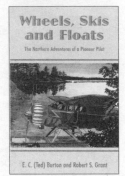